WHITE LIKE ME

Reflections on Race from a Privileged Son
THE REMIX: REVISED AND UPDATED EDITION

TIM WISE

SOFT SKULL PRESS
AN IMPRINT OF COUNTERPOINT

Cover design by Faceout Studio
Interior design by Maria E. Torres, Neuwirth & Associates, Inc.

Soft Skull Press
An Imprint of COUNTERPOINT
2560 Ninth Street, Suite 318
Berkeley, CA 94710

www.softskull.com
www.counterpointpress.com

Distributed by Publishers Group West
Printed in the United States of America
The Library of Congress has cataloged the first edition as follows:
Wise, Tim J.
White like me: reflections on race from a privileged son / by Tim Wise.
p. cm.
ISBN 978-1-59376-425-8

1. Racism—United States, 2. United States—Race relations. 3. Wise Tim J.
4. Whites—United States—Social conditions. I. Title.
E185.615.W565 2005
305.8'00973—dc22
2005001052

12 11 10

CONTENTS

INTRODUCTION

TO THE THIRD EDITION

IT IS DIFFICULT for me to believe that nearly seven years have passed since I began writing this book's first edition. But as I examine the calendar on my desk and look across the room at my daughters—now nearly eight and ten—I find it impossible to deny how long it's been, and how much has happened between then and now.

When I first thought of writing *White Like Me*, I never anticipated that it would strike the chord it seems to have struck with so many, that it would be taught in hundreds of colleges, even high schools, or that it would be read by so many who would then let me know how the work had affected and even changed them.

In one case, I was informed that my words had helped save a marriage. I felt pretty good about that until a few months later, at which point I was told by someone else that my book had helped hasten her divorce. I apologized for any role I may have played in the dissolution of her relationship, but was told not to worry, that it had been for the best, and that it had taken my book for her and her now ex-husband to realize that their differences, rooted in racial identity and their experiences around racism, were too vast to bridge. Okay then, *I guess you're welcome*, was all I could think to say. Not very creative, but it was the best I could come up with at the time.

Yet, even as *White Like Me* has made such an impact, like any book on a topic as fluid as race, it runs the risk of becoming dated. The contours of the racial dialogue in the United States are constantly changing, so in order to stay relevant, this volume needed yet another updating, especially given the election of Barack Obama as president in November

2008. Considering how quickly folks rushed to pronounce the United States "post-racial" in the wake of Obama's victory—after all, how can we have a race problem, and how can there be white privilege if a man of color can be elected president?—I knew almost as soon as he had won that I would need to revisit the main theses of this book yet again. In the meantime I have written two other books challenging the post-racial thesis (*Between Barack and a Hard Place* and *Colorblind*), but given the shelf-life of *White Like Me*, addressing some of the same issues within these pages seems equally important.

Though on the surface the election of a man of color to the highest office in the land might suggest the demise of racism as a persistent social force—and the subsequent death of white privilege—in truth, it says nothing of the kind. Just as the election of women as heads of state in Pakistan, India, Israel, or Great Britain (among others) hardly signaled the eradication of sexism in those places, so too the election of a black man in the United States hardly speaks to the issue of racism facing 85 million people of color here. Individual success and accomplishment says little about larger institutional truth.

Additionally, and as I explained in *Between Barack and a Hard Place*, many who voted for Barack Obama in 2008 were persons who, by their own admission to pollsters, continue to adhere to racist stereotypes about black Americans. The fact that they were able to carve out an exception to their prejudices by viewing Obama as differing from an otherwise negative black norm may indicate that they are free from the all-consuming bigotry that was normative in generations past, but it hardly suggests a racial ecumenism that extends to people of color generally. If support for Obama was, in part, due to his seeming "different" from other black men, we could even say that racism, albeit of a 2.0 variety, was instrumental in *helping* him attract support from white voters.

Finally, let us recall that Barack Obama downplayed issues of race within his campaign, rarely if ever spoke to concerns about racial inequity, and went out of his way to distance himself from his former pastor, Rev. Jeremiah Wright, so as to curry favor with white voters who found Wright's condemnations of U.S. foreign policy and our history of racism troubling. Such truths suggest that in some ways, Obama's victory was *evidence* of white privilege, rather than a refutation of it. To the extent he has had to remain relatively silent about race matters lest his political star be dimmed by a volcanic eruption of white backlash, his success, given what was required to attain it, stands as the ultimate confirmation of ongoing white political power.

Since the election of Barack Obama, evidence of white privilege has been even more ubiquitous than before. With the emergence of the Tea Party movement, the nation has been treated to images of thousands of mostly white, ultra-conservative activists surrounding lawmakers and screaming at them to vote against health care reform legislation, carrying guns to rallies just to show they can, or spouting off about the potential need for secession or even revolution. Needless to say, if black or Latino activists (or Arab American or Muslim activists angered by racial and religious profiling, post-9/11) were to surround lawmakers and scream at them like petulant children, one can only imagine how it would be perceived by the public. They would be seen as insurrectionaries, as terrorists, as thugs; but when older whites do it, they are viewed as patriots exercising their First Amendment rights. If people of color showed up to rallies armed, or were calling for revolution, it doesn't take much imagination to know how differently they would be viewed, compared to whites engaged in the same activities.

In the first two editions I chose to forego simple chronology in telling this story. My thinking at the time was that it was best to break the book down by themes, rather than to proceed linearly. In part this was because I generally prefer thematic discussions to those driven by a slavish devotion to a particular timeline; further, it was because I wanted the points herein to be crystal clear. I wanted to leave no doubt as to what I was saying, and it seemed as though telling stories under thematic headings would better accomplish that goal than to simply tell the stories and hope they would speak for themselves. As much as this method seemed to work at the time, I have recently come to question the approach. Reading back over the book this many years later, I found myself wincing at the seemingly forced nature of it all. Yes, the theme-driven narrative made things easy, both for me as a writer and for those reading the work. But something about it fails to satisfy; its mixture of the narrative, memoir voice on the one hand, and the analytical, polemic voice on the other, meant that in the end neither voice was as strong or clear as it could have been.

Mostly, what I realized as I read back over the volume was that in some ways I hadn't stayed true to the purpose of the book, or the initial impetus for it. I had written *White Like Me* thanks to an admonition from people of color I knew in New Orleans to "take inventory" of my life, to get clear on why I cared so much about racism, to understand my own motivation for challenging it. Until I did this, they insisted, my work would be unfocused, my contributions minimal, my willingness to stay in the struggle transitory at best. Get clear on *your* motivation, they told me, beyond the politics and the ideological stuff that's in your head. Figure out what it is about your *heart* and even soul that compels you.

So I began to explore that question and had spent nearly twelve years on it before sitting down to write this book the first time. By then, the answer was as clear as the sound of our youngest girl, a year old at the time, crying in the night over the baby monitor in her room. When I had sat down and begun to take inventory, it had become impossible to miss how race had been implicated year in and year out, all throughout the course of my existence. Hardly any aspect of my life, from where I had lived to my education to my employment history to my friendships, had been free from the taint of racial inequity, from racism, from whiteness. My racial identity had shaped me from the womb forward. I had not been in control of my own narrative. It wasn't just race that was a social construct. *So was I.*

And as much as we all like to believe we're special (and God knows, white men are encouraged in this conceit well enough), I simply failed to accept that this story was mine alone. Although others will have experienced whiteness differently to various extents, I felt certain there were aspects of my past that dovetailed with those of others, and that if we could begin to excavate some of that, perhaps we could break the seemingly intractable impasse between white folks and folks of color; perhaps we could move the dialogue forward by coming to see ourselves in the center of the problem, rather than seeing racism as some abstract sociological concept about which the black and brown must worry, but about which whites shouldn't lose much sleep. Only by coming to realize how thoroughly racialized our white lives are can we begin to see the problem as ours, and begin to take action to help solve it. By remaining oblivious to our racialization we remain oblivious to the injustice that stems from it, and we remain paralyzed when it comes to responding to it in a constructive manner.

This time, I've opted to tell these stories—many from the previous volumes and several that had been left out—more or less chronologically, in an attempt to highlight the way that race flows throughout a life from the beginning. All the themes discussed in the first two editions will still find exploration here, but they will do so within a narrative that is much more of a story than a mere collection of relatively disjointed reflections. I don't know if this will be a better or worse approach than the last two. But I know that, for now, it is the way I must tell the story. It is the voice in which I need to speak. Life is lived chronologically, after all. So perhaps its recounting should be chronological too.

Thank you, all who have made the book a success thus far, and all those who are reading it now for the first time. If you are among the latter, you are reading a much better book than your predecessors did. I hope you'll find that it was worth the wait.

Nashville, March 2011

PREFACE

"WHAT HAPPENED TO YOU?"

IT'S A QUESTION no one likes to hear, seeing as how it typically signifies an assumption on the part of the questioner that something is terribly wrong, something that defies logic and begs for an explanation.

It's the kind of query one might get from former classmates on the occasion of one's twenty-year high school reunion: "Dear God, what the hell happened to you?" As a general rule, people don't ask this question of those whom they consider to have dramatically improved themselves physically, emotionally, or professionally. Instead, it is more often asked of those considered to be seriously damaged, as if the only possible answer to the question would be, "Well, I was dropped on my head as a baby," to which the questioner would then reply, "Aha, *I see.*"

So whenever I'm asked this, I naturally recoil for a moment, assuming that those inquiring about the matter likely want to know *what happened* to me, only so that they may, having obtained the answer, carefully avoid at whatever cost having it (whatever *it* may be) happen to them. In my case, however, the cynicism with which I greet the question usually turns out to be unwarranted. Most of the persons who ask me "what happened" seem to be asking less for reasons of passing judgment than for reasons of genuine confusion.

As a white man, born and reared in a society that has always bestowed upon me advantages that it has generally withheld from people of color, I am not expected to think the way I do. I am not supposed to speak against and agitate in opposition to racism and institutionalized white supremacy. Indeed, for people of color, it is often shocking to see white people even *thinking* about race, let alone challenging racism. After all, we don't have to spend much time contemplating the subject if we'd rather not, and white folks have made something of a pastime out of ignoring racism, or at least refusing to call it out as a major social problem to be remedied.

But for me, ignoring race and racism has never been an option. Even when it would have been easier to turn away, there were too many forces and circumstances pulling me back, compelling me to look at the matter square in the face—in *my* face. Although white Americans often think we've had few first-hand experiences with race, because most of us are so isolated from people of color in our day-to-day lives, the reality is that this isolation *is* our experience with race. We are all experiencing race, because from the beginning of our lives we have been living in a racialized society, in which the color of our skin means something socially, even while it remains largely a matter of biological and genetic irrelevance. Race may be a scientific fiction—and given the almost complete genetic overlap between persons of the various so-called races, it appears to be just that—but it is a social fact that none of us can escape no matter how much or how little we may speak of it. Just as there were no actual witches in Salem in 1692, and yet anti-witch persecution was frighteningly real, so too race can be a falsehood, even as racism continues to destroy lives and, on the flipside, to advantage those who are rarely its targets.

A few words about terminology: When I speak of "whites" or "white folks," I am referring to those persons, typically of European descent, who by virtue of skin color or perhaps national origin and culture are able to be perceived as "white," as members of the dominant racial group in the Western world. I do not consider the white race to be a real thing, biologically, as modern science pretty well establishes that there are no truly distinct races, genetically speaking, within the human species. But the white race certainly has meaning in social terms, and it is in that sense that I use the concept here.

As it turns out, this last point is more important than you might think. Almost immediately upon publication, this book's first edition came under fire from various white supremacists and neo-Nazis, who launched a fairly concerted effort to discredit it, and me as the author. They sought to do this by jamming the review boards at Amazon.com

with harsh critiques, none of which discussed the content—in all likeli-
hood none of them had read the book—but which amounted to ad
hominem attacks against me as a Jew. As several explained, being Jewish
disqualifies me from being white, or writing about my experiences as a
white person, since Jews are, to their way of thinking, a distinct race of
evildoers that seeks to eradicate Aryan stock from the face of the earth.

Of course, on the one hand (and ignoring for a second the Hitlerian
undertones), it is absurd to think that uniquely "Jewish genes" render Jews separate from "real" whites, despite our common and recent
European ancestry. And it's even more ridiculous to think that such
genes from one-fourth of one's family, as with mine, can cancel out the
three-quarters Anglo-Celtic contribution made by the rest of my ancestors. But in truth, the argument is irrelevant, given how I am using the
concept of whiteness here. Even if there were something biologically
distinct about Jews, this would hardly alter the fact that most Jews, especially in the United States, are sufficiently light-skinned and assimilated
so as to be fully functional as whites in the eyes of authority. This wasn't
always the case, but it is now. American Jews are, by and large, able to
reap the benefits of whiteness and white racial privilege, vis-à-vis people
of color, in spite of our Jewishness, whether viewed in racial or cultural
terms. My "claiming to be white," as one detractor put it, was not an
attempt on my part to join the cool kids. I wasn't trying to fool anyone.

Whiteness is more about how you're likely to be viewed and treated in a white supremacist society than it is about what you are, in any
meaningful sense. This is why even some very light-skinned folks of
color have been able to access white privilege over the years by passing
as white or being misperceived as white. Whiteness is, however much
clichéd the saying may be, largely a social construct. This is a book
about that construct and how it plays out in the larger culture. It is not
a scientific treatise, and thus it is quite impervious to whatever science
may or may not have to say about race, now or in the future.

As for the concept of privilege, here too, clarification is in order. I
am not claiming, nor do I believe, that all whites are wealthy and powerful. We live not only in a racialized society, but also in a class system, a patriarchal system, and one of straight supremacy, able-bodied
supremacy, and Christian hegemony. These other forms of privilege,

and the oppression experienced by those who can't access them, mediate but never fully eradicate something like white privilege. So I realize that wealthy whites are more powerful than poor ones, white men more powerful than white women, able-bodied whites more powerful than those with disabilities, and straight and cisgendered whites (the latter being a term for those who are not transgendered) more powerful than gay, lesbian, bisexual, or transgendered whites.

But despite the fact that white privilege plays out differently for different people, depending on these other identities, the fact remains that whiteness matters and carries great advantage. So, for example, although whites are often poor, their poverty does not alter the fact that relative to poor and working-class persons of color, they typically have a leg up. In fact, studies suggest that working-class whites are typically better off in terms of assets and net worth than even middle-class blacks with far higher incomes, due to past familial advantages. No one privilege system trumps all others every time, but no matter the ways in which individual whites may face obstacles on the basis of non-racial factors, our race continues to elevate us over similarly situated persons of color.

The notion of privilege is a relative concept as well as an absolute one, a point that is often misunderstood. This is why I can refer to myself as a "privileged son," despite coming from a dysfunctional family that was not even close to wealthy. Relative to persons of color, whites receive certain head starts and advantages, none of which are canceled out because of factors like class, gender, or sexual orientation. Likewise, heterosexuals receive privileges relative to LGBT folks, none of which are canceled out by the poverty that many straight people experience. So too, rich folks have certain privileges on the basis of wealth, none of which vanish like mist just because some of those wealthy persons are disabled. While few of us are located only in privileged groups, and even fewer are located only in marginalized or oppressed groups—we are all occasionally privileged and occasionally targets—the fact remains that our status as occasional targets does not relieve the obligation to address the ways in which we receive unjust advantages at the expense of others. As my friend and colleague Jacqui Wade puts it, "We all have a couple of nickels in the quarter." This book is about my nickels. They are not the only ones, but they are the only ones over which I can take ownership.

There would be nothing wrong with someone writing a book like this and dealing only with male privilege, straight privilege, class privilege, Christian privilege, or able-bodied privilege. Likewise, those in other countries could write about privilege and oppression systems there: Japanese privilege vis-à-vis ethnic Koreans and the Buraku caste in Japan, upper-caste privilege in India and the oppression of the Dalits there, or Jewish privilege in Israel and the institutionalized mistreatment of the Palestinians. Those would all be illuminating. But this book is about white privilege in the United States, because it is real and must be confronted. It is not more important than the other types of privilege, but it is important enough to merit its own examination.

Once again, I would like to thank my loving, supportive, and patient wife, Kristy, for all she has brought to my life. Also, I have to thank our two wonderful daughters, Ashton and Rachel. I hope that in my desire for a better world for all, I haven't neglected the world that is closest to home and to my heart. In that regard, I will try to do better.

I also need to thank a number of other people, including my parents, LuCinda and Michael Wise, and my friends, most notably Albert Jones, my best friend for roughly thirty-five years, for all of your support and wisdom, and for serving as a sounding board for my politics all these years. And finally, thanks to everyone who has inspired, supported, and influenced my work as a writer, activist, and aspiring anti-racist ally. These include, in no particular order: Bob Zellner, Dorothy Zellner, Anne Braden, Lance Hill, Larry Powell, Ron King, Ron Chisom, Barbara Major, David Billings, Diana Dunn, Marjorie Freeman, Sharon Martinas, Chris Crass, James Bernard, Francie Kendall, Michael Eric Dyson, Derrick Bell, Kevin Powell, "Coach" Jimmy Coit Jackson, Angela Davis, Ray Winbush, Molly Secours, Betita Martinez, Felicia Gustin, Jean Caiani, Lauren Parker-Kucera, Catherine Wong, Eddie Moore Jr., Victor Lewis, Michael Benitez, Hugh Vasquez, Joe Feagin, Ted Quandt, Kimberle Crenshaw, Peggy McIntosh, Jesse Villalobos, Judy Watts, Donna Johnigan, Olayeela Daste, Haunani Kay-Trask, Justin Podur, Brian Awehali, Richard Davis, Mab Segrest, Horace Seldon, Paul Marcus, Robert Jensen, Randall Robinson, Paul Kivel, Rose Jackson, Caroline Blackwell, Rev. Johnny Youngblood, and the entire St. Paul Community Baptist Church family in Brooklyn.

BORN
TO BELONGING

"People who imagine that history flatters them (as it does, indeed, since they wrote it) are impaled on their history like a butterfly on a pin and become incapable of seeing or changing themselves, or the world. This is the place in which it seems to me, most white Americans find themselves. Impaled. They are dimly, or vividly, aware that the history they have fed themselves is mainly a lie, but they do not know how to release themselves from it, and they suffer enormously from the resulting personal incoherence."

—JAMES BALDWIN,
"THE WHITE MAN'S GUILT" *Ebony*, August 1965

IT IS NOTHING if not difficult to know where to begin when you first sit down to trace the story of your life. Does your life begin on the day you came into this world, or does it begin before that, with the lives of your family members, without whom you would never have existed?

For me, there is only one way to answer the question. My story has to begin before the day I entered the world, October 4, 1968, for I did not emerge onto a blank slate of neutral circumstance. My life was already a canvas upon which older paint had begun to dry, long before I arrived. My parents were already who they were, with their particular life experiences, and I was to inherit those, whether I liked it or not.

When we first draw breath outside the womb, we inhale tiny particles of all that came before, both literally and figuratively. We are never merely individuals; we are never alone; we are always in the company of others, of the past, of history. We become part of that history just as surely as it becomes part of us. There is no escaping it; there are merely different levels of coping. It is how we bear the past that matters, and in many ways it is all that differentiates us.

I was born amidst great turmoil, none of which had been of my own making, but which I could hardly have escaped in any event. My mother had carried me throughout all of the great upheavals of that tumultuous year, 1968—perhaps one of the most explosive and monumental years in twentieth century America. She had carried me through the assassinations of Martin Luther King Jr. and Robert Kennedy, through the decision by President Johnson not to seek re-election in the midst of the unfolding murderous quagmire in Southeast Asia, and through the upheaval in the streets of Chicago during that year's Democratic Party convention. I think that any child born in 1968 must, almost by definition, be especially affected by the history that surrounded him or her upon arrival—there was too much energy floating around not to have left a mark.

Once born, I inherited my family and all that came with it. I also inherited my nation and all that came with that; and I inherited my "race" and all that came with *that* too. In all three cases, the inheritance was far from inconsequential. Indeed, all three inheritances were connected, intertwined in ways that are all too clear today. To be the child of Michael Julius Wise and LuCinda Anne (McLean) Wise meant something; to be born in the richest and most powerful nation on earth meant something; and to be white, especially in the United States, most assuredly meant something—a lot of things, truth be told. What those inheritances meant, and still mean, is the subject of this inquiry, especially the last of these: What does it mean to be white in a nation created for the benefit of people like you?

We don't often ask this question, mostly because we don't have to. Being a member of the majority, the dominant group, allows one to ignore how race shapes one's life. For those of us called white, whiteness simply is. Whiteness becomes, for us, the unspoken, uninterrogated norm, taken for granted, much as water can be taken for granted by a fish.

In high school, whites are sometimes asked to think about race, but rarely about whiteness. In my case, we read John Howard Griffin's classic book, *Black Like Me*, in which the author recounts his experiences in the Jim Crow South in 1959 after taking a drug that turned his skin brown and allowed him to experience apartheid for a few months from the other side of the color line. It was a good book, especially for its time. Yet upon re-reading it ten years ago, one statement made by the author, right at the beginning, stuck in my craw. As Griffin put it:

> How else except by becoming a Negro could a white man hope to learn the truth . . . The best way to find out if we had second-class citizens, and what their plight was, would be to become one of them.

Though I hadn't seen the trouble with the statement at sixteen when I had read *Black Like Me* during the summer before my junior year, now as an adult, and as someone who had been thinking about racism and white privilege for several years, it left me cold. There were two obvious problems with Griffin's formulation: first, whites could have learned the truth by listening to real black people—not just white guys pretending to be black until the drugs wore off; and second, we could learn the truth by looking clearly at our own experiences as whites.

Although whiteness may mean different things in different places and at different times, one thing I feel confident saying is that to be white in the United States, regardless of regional origin, economic status, sex, gender identity, religious affiliation, or sexual orientation, is to have certain common experiences based upon race. These experiences have to do with advantage, privilege (relative to people of color), and belonging. We are, unlike people of color, born to belonging, and have rarely had to prove ourselves deserving of our presence here. At the very least, our right to be here hasn't really been questioned for a long time.

While some might insist that whites have a wide range of experiences, and so it isn't fair to make generalizations about whites as a group, this is a dodge, and not a particularly artful one. Of course we're all different, sort of like snowflakes. None of us have led exactly the same life. But irrespective of one's particular history, all whites born before, say, 1964 were placed above all persons of color when it came to the economic, social, and political hierarchies that were to form in the United States, without exception. This formal system of racial preference was codified from the 1600s until at least the mid-to-late '60s, when the nation passed civil rights legislation, at least theoretically establishing equality in employment, voting, and housing opportunity.

Prior to that time we didn't even pretend to be a nation based on equality. Or rather we did pretend, but not very well; at least not to the point where the rest of the world believed it, or to the point where people of color in this country ever did. Most white folks believed it, but that's simply more proof of our privileged status. Our ancestors had the luxury of believing those things that black and brown folks could never take as givens: all that stuff about life, liberty, and the pursuit of happiness. Several decades later, whites still believe it, while people of color have little reason to so uncritically join the celebration, knowing as they do that there is still a vast gulf between who we say we are as a nation and people, and who we really are.

Even white folks born after the passage of civil rights laws inherit the legacy of that long history into which their forbears were born; after all, the accumulated advantages that developed in a system of racism are not buried in a hole with the passage of each generation. They continue into the present. Inertia is not just a property of the physical universe.

In other words, there is enough commonality about the white experience to allow us to make some general statements about whiteness and never be too far from the mark. Returning to the snowflake analogy, although as with snowflakes, no two white people are exactly alike, few snowflakes have radically different experiences from those of the average snowflake. Likewise, we know a snowflake when we see one, and in that recognition we intuit, almost always correctly, something about its life experience. So too with white folks.

* * *

AT FIRST GLANCE, mine would not appear to have been a life of privilege. Far from affluent, my father was an on-again, off-again, stand-up comedian and actor, and my mother has worked for most of my life in marketing research.

My parents were young when they had me. My father was a few months shy of twenty-two and my mother had just turned twenty-one when I was conceived, as legend has it in a Bossier City, Louisiana, hotel. Interestingly, my parents had opted to crash there during one of my father's stand-up tours, because having first tried to get a room in next-door Shreveport, they witnessed the night manager at a hotel there deny a room to a black traveler. Incensed, they opted to take their business elsewhere. Little could they have known that said business would involve setting in motion the process by which I would come into the world. In other words, I was conceived, appropriately, during an act of antiracist protest.

My parents had dated off and on since eighth grade, ever since my father knocked over a stack of books that my mom had neatly piled up in the middle school library. My mom, having little time for foolishness, had glared at him, her flaming red hair and single upraised eyebrow suggesting that he had best pick them up, and then perhaps plan on marrying and starting a family. The relationship had been rocky though. My mom's folks never took well to my dad, in part because of the large cultural gap between the two families. The Wises were Jews, a bit too cosmopolitan and, well, *Jewish*, for the liking of the McLeans. This is not to say that my mom's parents were anti-Semitic in any real sense. They weren't. But as with their views on race, the McLeans were just provincial enough to make the thought of an interfaith relationship difficult to swallow.

So too, they also worried (and in this they couldn't have been more on the mark), that my father simply wasn't a very suitable suitor for their little girl. Besides being Jewish, the problem was *him*. Had he been an aspiring doctor or lawyer, the McLeans might well have adored him. But a man whose dreams were of performing in comedy clubs? Or acting? Oh no, that would never do. And his father, though a businessman, owned *liquor stores*, and according to rumor, he might know and even be friends with mobsters. After all, weren't all booze-peddlers mafia-connected, or in some way disreputable, like Joe Kennedy?

In 1964, right before my parents were to begin their senior year of high school in Nashville, my mom's folks moved the family to West Virginia, at least in part because West Virginia was far from Mike Wise. After graduation, my mom went to a two-year women's college in Virginia, while my dad went West and obtained entrance to the prestigious acting program at Pasadena Playhouse. But within two years they were back together, my dad having given up on California when he realized that being discovered took time and more effort than he was prepared to put in. They married in May 1967, and spent the better part of the next year traveling around the country while my dad did comedy, finally ending up in that Bossier City Howard Johnson's, where their bodies and the origins of my story would collide. My mom pregnant, it was time to move home and begin a family, and so they did.

All throughout my childhood, my parents' income would have fallen somewhere in the range of what is politely considered working class, even though their jobs were not traditional working-class jobs. Had it not been for the financial help of my grandparents, it is likely that we would have been forced to rely on food stamps at various points along the way; most certainly we would have qualified for them in several of my years as a child. For a while my father had pretty consistent work, doing comedy or dinner theatre, but the pay was rotten. By the time I was in second grade, his employment was becoming more spotty, forcing my mom into the paid workforce to help support the family.

I spent the first eighteen years of my life in a perfectly acceptable but inadequately maintained 850-square-foot apartment with dubious plumbing, a leaky air conditioner, certainly no dishwasher or washing machine, and floor-boards near the sliding glass door in my bedroom that were perpetually rotting, allowing roly-polies or slugs to occasionally find their way inside. The walls stand out in my mind as well: thin enough to hear every fight my parents ever had and to cave in easily under the weight of my father's fists, whenever the mood struck him to ventilate the plaster, as happened with some regularity. But even before the busted-up walls or leaky faucets at the Royal Arms Apartments, there had already been quite a bit of family water under the proverbial bridge. Examining the source of that stream provides substantial insight into the workings of privilege, and the ways in which even whites who lived in modest surroundings, as I did, had been born to belonging nonetheless.

Even if you don't directly inherit material advantages from your family, there is something empowering about the ability to trace your lineage back hundreds of years, as so many whites but so few persons of color can. In 1977, my third grade teacher encouraged us to trace our family trees, inspired by the miniseries "Roots," and apparently unaware of how injurious it might be for black students to make the effort, only to run head first into the crime of slavery and its role in their family background. The exercise provided, for the whites at least, a sense of pride, even *rootedness*; not so much for the African American students.

Genealogy itself is something of a privilege, coming far more easily to those of us for whom enslavement, conquest, and dispossession of our land has not been our lot. Genealogy offers a sense of belonging and connectedness to others with firm, identifiable pasts—pasts that directly trace the rise and fall of empires, and which correspond to the events we learned about in history classes, so focused were they on the narratives of European peoples. Even when we personally have no desire to affiliate with those in our past about whom we learn, simply knowing whence you came has the effect of linking you in some great chain of mutuality. It is enabling, if far from ennobling. It offers a sense of psychological comfort, a sense that you belong in this story known as the history of the world. It is to make real the famous words, "This land is *my* land."

When I sat down a few years ago to examine my various family histories, I have to admit to a sense of excitement as I peeled back layer upon layer, generation after generation. It was like a game, the object of which was to see how far back you could go before hitting a dead end. Thanks to the hard work of the fine folks at Ancestry.com, on several branches of my family tree, I had no trouble going back hundreds, even *thousands* of years. In large measure this was because those branches extended through to royal lineage, where records were kept meticulously, so as to make sure everyone knew to whom the spoils of advantage were owed in each new generation.

Understand, my claim to royal lineage here means nothing. After all, since the number of one's grandparents doubles in each generation, by the time you trace your lineage back even five hundred years (assuming generations of roughly twenty-five years each), you will have had as many as one million grandparents at some remove. Even with pedigree collapse—the term for the inevitable overlap that comes when cousins marry cousins, as happened with all families if you go back far enough—the number of persons to whom you'd be connected by the time you got back a thousand years would still be several million. That said, I can hardly deny that as I discovered those linkages, even though they were often quite remote—and despite the fact that the persons to whom I discovered a connection were often despicable characters who stole land, subjugated the masses, and slaughtered others in the name of nationalism or God—there was still something about the process that made me feel more real, more alive, and even more purposeful. To explore the passing of time as it relates to world history and the history of your own people, however removed from you they may be, is like putting together a puzzle, several pieces of which had previously been missing; it's a gift that really can't be overstated. And for those prepared to look at the less romantic side of it all, genealogy also makes it possible to uncover and then examine one's inherited advantages.

Going back a few generations on my mother's side, for instance, we have the Carter family, traceable to John Carter, born in 1450 in Kempston, Bedfordshire, England. It would be his great-great-great-grandson, William, who would bring his family to the Virginia Colony in the early 1630s, just a few of twenty-thousand or so Puritans who came to America between 1629 and 1642, prior to the shutting down of emigration by King Charles I at the outset of the English Civil War.

The Carters would move inland after their arrival, able to take advantage in years to come of one of the New World's first affirmative action programs, known as the "headright" system, under which male heads of household willing to cross the Atlantic and come to Virginia were given fifty acres of land that had previously belonged to one of at least fourteen indigenous nations whose members had lived there.

Although the racial fault lines between those of European and African descent hadn't been that deep in the earliest years of the Virginia Colony—race-based slavery wasn't in place yet, and among indentured servants there were typically more Europeans than Africans—all that would begin to change in the middle of the seventeenth century. Beginning in the 1640s, the colony began assigning blacks to permanent enslavement; then in the 1660s, they declared that all children born of enslaved mothers would be slaves, in perpetuity, themselves. That same decade, Virginia announced that no longer would Africans converted to Christianity be immune to enslavement or servitude. Then, in the wake

of Bacon's Rebellion in 1676, during which European and African labor-
ers joined forces to overthrow the government of Governor Berkeley,
elites began to pass a flurry of laws intended to limit black freedom,
elevate whites, and divide and conquer any emerging cross-racial alli-
ances between the two groups.

In 1682, the colony codified in law that all whites, no matter their
condition of temporary servitude, were to be seen as separate and
apart from African slaves, and that they would enjoy certain rights and
privileges off limits to the latter, including due process in disputes with
their masters, and the right to redress if those masters abused them.
Furthermore, once released from indenture, white servants would be
able to claim up to fifty acres of land with which to begin their new lives.
Ultimately, indentured servitude would be abolished in the early eighteenth century, replaced by a dramatic upsurge in chattel slavery. Blacks,
along with "mulattoes, Indians, and criminals," would be banned from
holding public or ecclesiastical office after 1705, and the killing of a
rebellious slave would no longer be deemed murder; rather, according
to Virginia law, the event would be treated "as if such accident had never
happened."

The Carters, as with many of the Deanes (another branch of my
mother's family), lived in Virginia through all of this period when
whiteness was being legally enshrined as a privileged space for the first
time. And they were there in 1800, too—like my fourth great grandfather, William M. Carter—when a planned rebellion by Thomas
Prosser's slave, Gabriel, in Henrico County, was foiled thanks to other
slaves exposing the plot. As a result, Gabriel was hanged, all free blacks
in the state were forced to leave, or else face re-enslavement, and all education or training of slaves was made illegal. Paranoia over the Gabriel
conspiracy, combined with the near-hysterical reaction to the Haitian
revolution under way at that point, which would expel the French from
the island just a few years later, led to new racist crackdowns and the
extension of still more advantages and privileges to whites like those in
my family.

Then there were the Neelys, the family of my maternal great-grand-
mother, who can be traced to Edward Neely, born in Scotland in 1745,
who came to America shortly before the birth of his son, also named

Edward, in 1770. The Neelys would move from New York's Hudson Valley to Kentucky, where Jason Neely, my third great-grandfather, was born in 1805. The land on which they would settle, though it had been the site of no permanent indigenous community by that time, had been hunting land used in common by the Shawnee and Cherokee. Although the Iroquois had signed away all rights to the land that would become Kentucky in the Treaty of Fort Stanwix in 1768, the Shawnee had been no party to the treaty, and rejected its terms; not that their rejection would matter much, as ultimately the area came under the control of whites, and began to produce substantial profits for farmers like Jason Neely. By 1860, three years after the Supreme Court in its *Dred Scott* decision announced that blacks could never be citizens, even if free, and "had no rights which the white man was bound to respect," Jason had accumulated eleven slaves, ranging in age from forty down to two—a number that was quite significant by local and even regional standards for the "Upper South."

And then we have the two primary, parental branches of my family: the McLeans and the Wises.

The McLeans trace their lineage to around 1250, and at one point were among the most prosperous Highland clans in Scotland, but having allied themselves with Charles Edward Stuart (claimant to the thrones of England, Ireland, and Scotland), they lost everything when Stuart (known as Bonnie Prince Charlie) was defeated at the Battle of Culloden in 1746. The McLeans, as with many of the Highlanders, supported the attempt to restore the Stuart family to the thrones from which it had been deposed in 1688. Once the royalists were defeated and the Bonnie Prince was forced to sneak out of Scotland dressed as an Irish maid, the writing began to appear on the wall for the McLeans and many of the Highland Scots who had supported him.

With that, family patriarch Ephraim McLean (my fifth great-grandfather) set out for America, settling in Philadelphia before moving South in 1759. Once there, Ephraim would be granted over twelve thousand acres of land in North Carolina and Tennessee that had previously belonged to Catawba and Cherokee Indians, and which had been worked by persons of African descent for over a century, without the right of the latter to own so much as their names. Although the family

TIM WISE 11

version of the story is that Ephraim received these grants deservedly, as payment for his service in the Revolutionary War, there is something more than a bit unsatisfying about this narrative. While Ephraim served with distinction—he was wounded during the Battle of King's Mountain, recognized as among the war's most pivotal campaigns—it is also true that at least 5,000 blacks served the American Revolution, and virtually none of them, no matter the distinction with which they served, received land grants. Indeed, four out of five blacks who served failed to receive even their freedom from enslavement as a reward.

Ephraim's ability to fight for the revolution was itself, in large part, because of white privilege. Although the Continental Congress authorized the use of blacks in the army beginning in 1777, no southern militia with the exception of that in Maryland allowed them to serve. Congress, cowed by the political strength of slave owners, as well as threats by leaders in South Carolina to leave the war if slaves were armed and allowed to fight, refused to press the issue. As such, most blacks would be kept from service, and denied the post-war land grants for which they would otherwise have been eligible.

In the early 1780s, Ephraim became one of the founding residents of Nashville, and served as a trustee and treasurer for the first college west of the Cumberland Mountains, Davidson Academy. On the board with him were several prominent residents of the area including a young Andrew Jackson, in whose ranks Ephraim's grandson would later serve during the 1814 Battle of New Orleans, and alongside whom his great-nephew, John, would serve during the massacre of Creek Indians at Horseshoe Bend.

Ephraim's son, Samuel (my fourth great-grandfather), was a substantial landowner, having inherited property from his dad. Although the records are unclear as to whether or not Ephraim had owned slaves, Samuel most certainly did, owning at least a half-dozen by the time of his death in 1850.

It has always fascinated me how families like mine have sought to address the owning of other human beings. Because it is impossible to ignore the subject altogether, those descended from slave owners opt instead to rationalize or smooth over the unpleasantness, so as to maintain the convenient fictions about our families to which we have so often become tethered. And so, in the McLean family history, compiled by a cousin of mine several years ago, slave-ownership is discussed in terms that strive mightily to normalize the activity and thereby prevent the reader from feeling even a momentary discomfort with this detour in an otherwise straightforward narrative of upright moral behavior. So we learn, for example, that Samuel McLean, my fourth great-grand-father, "owned much land and slaves, and was a man of considerable means." This is stated with neither an inordinate amount of pride nor regret, but merely in the matter-of-fact style befitting those who are trying to be honest without confronting the implications of their honesty. Say it quickly, say it simply, and move on to something more appetizing: sort of like acknowledging the passing of gas in a crowded room, but failing to admit that you were the author.

A few pages later, the reader is then treated to a reproduction of Samuel McLean's will, which reads, among other things:

> I give and bequeath unto my loving wife, Elizabeth, my Negro woman, named Dicey, to dispose of at her death as she may think proper, all my household and kitchen furniture, wagons, horses, cattle, hogs, sheep, and stock of every kind, except as may be necessary to defray the expense of the first item above.

In other words, Elizabeth should sell whatever must be sold in order to hold on to the slave woman, for how would she possibly survive without her? But there is more:

> I also give the use and possession of, during her natural life, my two Negroes, Jerry and Silvey. To my daughter Sarah Amanda her choice of horses and two cows and calves, and if she marry in the lifetime of my wife she is to enjoy and receive an equal share of the property from the tillage, rent and use of the aforesaid 106 acres of land and Negroes Jerry and Silvey, that she may be the more certain of a more comfortable existence.

Furthermore, if Sarah were to marry before the death of her mother, she and her husband were to remain on the property with Elizabeth so as to continue to benefit "from the land and Negroes." However, if mom were to die before the wedding of Sarah, then the daughter was instructed to sell either the land or the slaves and split the proceeds among her siblings. Either way, Dicey, Jerry, and Silvey would remain commodities to be sure. Choosing freedom for them was never an option, for in that case, the McLeans might have to learn to do things for themselves: they might have to wash their own clothes, grow their own food, nurse their own wounds, make their own beds, suckle their own babies, and chop their own wood, all of which would make them less "certain of a more comfortable existence," so it was out of the question.

To his son, Samuel D. McLean, Sam Senior bequeathed "a Negro boy named Sim," who would then be handed down, not unlike an armoire, to his son John, my third great-grandfather. Then, according to family legend (and in what can only be considered the Margaret Mitchell version of the McLean's history), Sim went happily off to the Civil War with his master. What's more, we even have dialogue for this convenient plot twist, as Sim exclaims (and I'm sure this is a direct quote, transcribed faithfully at the time), "I've taken care of Mr. John all his life and I'm not going to let him go off to war without me." Cue the harmonica. For his loyalty, we learn that "Sim got a little farm to retire on because the McLeans knew he would not get a pension of any kind." No indeed, as property rarely receives the benefit of its very own 401(k) plan.

To his daughters, Sam McLean gave the slave woman Jenny and her child, and the slave woman Manerva and her child, and in both cases "any further increase," which is an interesting and chillingly dehumanizing way to refer to future children. But we are to think nothing of this subterfuge in the case of the children of Manerva or Jenny. We are to keep telling ourselves that they are not people, and we are to keep repeating this mantra, no matter how much they *look* like people. Pay no attention to such small and trivial details.

Though many would excuse the barbarity of enslavement by suggesting that such an institution must be judged by the standards of its own time, rather than today, I make no such allowance, and find it obscene when others do so. It is simply not true that "everyone back then felt that way," or supported slavery as an institution. Those who were enslaved were under no illusion that their condition was just. As such, and assuming that the slave owner had the capacity for rational and moral thought on par with his property, there is no excuse for whites, any whites, not to have understood this basic truth as well. Furthermore, even if we were only to consider the views of whites to be important—a fundamentally racist position but one we may indulge for the sake of argument—the fact would remain that even many whites opposed slavery, and not only on practical but also on moral grounds.

Among those who gave the lie to the notion of white unanimity—which notion has served to minimize the culpability of slave owners—we find Angelina and Sarah Grimké, John Fee, Ellsberry Ambrose, John Brown (and his entire family), and literally thousands more whose names are lost to history. Indeed, if we look hard enough we find at least one such person in my own family, Elizabeth Angel, whose opposition to the institution of slavery led her to convince her own family to free their chattel and to oppose enslavement at every turn. Though Elizabeth's connection to the McLeans—her daughter was the wife of my great-great grandfather, John Lilburn McLean—and her opposition to an institution in which they were implicated might seem worthy of some exploration, in the official family history it is missing altogether. Rather than hold Elizabeth up as a role model for her bravery (which would have had the effect of condemning the rest of the family by comparison), the cousin who compiled the McLean biography passed over such details in favor of some random and meaningless commentary about the loveliness of her haberdashery, or some such thing.

But no excuses, no time-bound rationalizations, and no paeans to our ancestors' kind and generous natures or how they "loved their slaves as though they were family" can make it right. Our unwillingness to hold our people and ourselves to a higher moral standard—a standard in place at least since the time of Moses, for it was he to whom God supposedly gave those commandments including the two about stealing and killing—brings shame to us today. It compounds the crime by constituting a new one: the crime of innocence claimed, against all visible evidence to the contrary.

In truth, even those family members who didn't own other human beings had been implicated in the nation's historic crimes. This was true, indeed, for most any southern family in the eighteenth and nineteenth centuries. State authorities made sure of that, by passing laws that enlisted the lower-income and middling whites in the service of white supremacy. In 1753, Tennessee passed its Patrol Act, which required whites to search slave quarters four times each year for guns or other contraband. By the turn of the century, and at which time large parts of my own family had made the trek to the state, these searches had been made into monthly affairs. By 1806, most all white men were serving on regular slave patrols for which they were paid a dollar per shift, and five dollars as a bonus for each runaway slave they managed to catch.

Throughout the period of my family's settling in middle Tennessee, laws required that all whites check the passes of blacks they encountered to make sure they weren't runaway slaves. Any white refusing to go along faced severe punishment. With no record of such racial apostasy having made it into our family lore—and surely such an example of brazen defiance would have been hard to keep quiet had it occurred—it seems safe to say that the McLeans, the Deanes, the Neelys, and the Carters all went along, regardless of their direct financial stake in the maintenance of the chattel system.

Likewise, although whites were members of nearly thirty antislavery societies in Tennessee by 1827, there is nothing to suggest that any of my family belonged to one. Nor is there anything to indicate that my kin objected to the uprooting of the Cherokee in the 1830s, even though many whites in the eastern part of the state did. And when Tennessee's free blacks were stripped of the right to vote in 1834, or when the first Jim Crow laws were passed, also in Tennessee, in 1881, there is nothing in our family history that would portend an objection of any kind. In reading over family documents, handed-down stories and tales of all sorts, it is nothing if not jarring to note that race is almost completely absent from their discussions, which is to say that for so many, white supremacy was so taken for granted as to be hardly worth a fleeting moment of consideration, let alone the raising of one's voice in objection. You can read their accounts of the time, and never know that you were reading about families in the United States, a society of institutionalized racial terror, where there were lynchings of black men taking place weekly, where the bodies of these men would be not merely hanged from trees but also mutilated, burned with blowtorches, the ears and fingers lopped off to be sold as souvenirs.

That was the way this country was when my family (and many of yours) were coming up. And most white folks did nothing to stop it. They knew exactly what was going on—lynchings were advertised openly in newspapers much like the county fair—and yet the white voices raised in opposition to such orgiastic violence were so weak as to be barely audible. We knew, but we remained silent, collaborating until the end.

In marked contrast to this tale, in which European immigrants came to the new country and were immediately welcomed into the emerging club of whiteness, we have the story of the Wises (not our original name), whose patriarchal figure, Jacob, came to the United States from Russia to escape the Czar's oppression of Jews. Theirs was similar to the immigrant stories of so many other American Jews from Eastern Europe. You've heard the drill: they came here with nothing but eighteen cents and a ball of lint in their pockets, they saved and saved, worked and worked, and eventually climbed the ladder of success, achieving the American dream within a generation or two.

Whether or not it had been as bleak as all that, it certainly hadn't been easy. Jacob's arrival in 1907 was not actually his first time to make it to the United States. He had entered New York once before, in 1901, but had had the misfortune of cruising into the harbor only ten days or so after an American of Eastern European descent, Leon Czolgosz, had made the fatal decision to assassinate President William McKinley. McKinley had lingered for a week after the shooting, and died just a few days before the arrival of my great-grandfather's boat. As the saying goes, timing is everything—a lesson Jacob would learn, sitting in steerage and coming to realize that he had been literally just a few days too late. So back he went, along with the rest of his shipmates, turned away in the shadow of Lady Liberty by a wave of jingoistic panic, anti-immigrant nativism, hysteria born of bigotry, and a well nurtured, carefully cultivated skill at scapegoating those who differed from the Anglo-Saxon norm. That Czolgosz claimed to be an anarchist, and thus his shooting of McKinley came to be seen as a political act, and not merely the lashing out of a madman, sealed Jacob's fate for sure. To the authorities, all

Eastern Europeans were to be viewed for a time as anarchists, as criminals, and later as communists. Czolgosz was to be executed, and tens of thousands of Eastern Europeans and other "undesirable" ethnics would be viciously oppressed in the following years.

The mind of a twenty-first-century American is scarcely equipped to contemplate just how long the trip back to Russia must have been, not merely in terms of hours and days, but as measured by the beating of one's heart, the slow and subtle escape of all optimism from one's tightened lungs. How painful it must have been, how *omnicidal* for Jacob, meaning the evisceration of everything he was, of everything that mattered to him—the extermination of hope. Though not of the same depth, nor coupled with the same fear as that which characterized the journey of Africans in the hulls of slave ships (after all, he was still a free man, and his journey, however aborted, had been voluntary), there must have been points where the magnitude of his despair was intense enough to make the distinction feel as though it were one without much meaning.

So he returned to Minsk, in modern-day Belarus, for another six years, it taking that long for him to save up enough money to make the journey again. When he finally came back, family in tow, it would be for keeps. His desire for America was that strong, borne of the belief that in the new world things would be different, that he would be able to make something of himself and give his family a better life. The Wise family continued to grow after his arrival, including, in 1919, the birth of Leon Wise, whose name was later shortened to Leo—my grandfather.

Jacob was the very definition of a hard worker. The stereotype of immigrants putting in eighteen hours a day is one that, although it did not begin with him in mind, surely was to be kept alive by him and others like him. There is little doubt that he toiled and sacrificed, and in the end there was a great payoff indeed: his children did well, with my grandfather graduating from a prestigious university, Vanderbilt, in 1942. What's more, the family business would grow into something of a fixture in the Nashville community that the Wise family would come to call home.

But lest we get carried away, perhaps it would be worth remembering a few things about Jacob Wise and his family. None of these things take away from the work ethic that was a defining feature of his character, but they do suggest that a work ethic is rarely enough on its own to make the difference. After all, by the time he arrived in America there had been millions of black folks with work ethics at least as good as his, and by the time he passed at the age of ninety-three, there would have been millions of peoples of color who had lived and toiled in this land, every bit as long as he had. Yet with few exceptions, they could not say that within a mere decade they had become successful shop owners, or that one of their sons had gone on to graduate from one of the nation's finest colleges. Even as a religious minority in the buckle of the Bible belt, Jacob was able to find opportunity off-limits to anyone of color. He may have been a Jew, but his skin was the right shade, and he was from Europe, so all suspicions and religious and cultural biases aside, he had only to wait and keep his nose clean a while, and then eventually he and his family would become white. Assimilation was not merely a national project; for Jacob Wise, and for millions of other Jews, Italians, and Irish, it was an implicitly racial one as well.

Even before assimilation, Jacob had been able to gain access to opportunities that were off limits to African Americans. His very arrival in the United States—as tortuous and circuitous as was the route that he had been forced to take in order to achieve it—was made possible by immigration policies that at that moment (and for most of our nation's history) have favored those from Europe over those from anywhere else. The Naturalization Act of 1790, which was the very first law passed by the U.S. Congress after the ratification of the Constitution, made clear that all free white persons (and only free white persons) were to be considered citizens, and that this naturalization would be obtained, for most all whites, virtually as soon as we arrived. Yet, during the period of both of Jacob's journeys—the one that had been cut short and the one that had finally delivered him to his new home—there had been draconian limits, for example, on Asian immigration. These restrictions would remain in place until 1965, the year his grandson, my father, would graduate from high school. If that's not white privilege—if that's not affirmative action of a most profound and lasting kind—then neither concept has much meaning any longer; and if that isn't relevant to my own racialization, since it is the history into which I was born, then the notion of inheritance has lost all meaning as well.

And there is more of interest here too, as regards the Wise's role in the nation's racial drama. Though whites who came to America after the abolition of slavery can rightly claim they had played no part in the evil that was that particular institution, it is simply wrong to suggest that they are not implicated in the broader system of racial oppression that has long marked the nation. In addition to the receipt of privileges, which stem from the racial classification into which they were able, over time, to matriculate, there are occasionally even more active ways in which whites, such as the Wises, participated in the marginalization of black and brown peoples.

It was only a few years ago, during a workshop that I was attending (not as a facilitator but rather as a participant), that I really came to appreciate this fact. During the session, we had all been discussing our family histories, and at one point I mentioned, almost as an afterthought, that my comfort in and around communities of color likely stemmed from the fact that my paternal grandfather had owned and operated a business in the heart of Nashville's black community for many years—an establishment I had visited dozens of times, from when I had been only a small child until I was a teenager.

Prepared to move on to another subject and wrap up my time to share, I was interrupted by a black man, older than myself, whose ears and eyes had quite visibly perked up when I had mentioned my grandfather and his business in North Nashville.

"I'm originally from North Nashville," he noted. "What kind of business did he have?"

"A liquor store," I responded. "My family owned liquor stores all over town and my grandfather's was on Jefferson Street."

"Your grandfather was Leo Wise?" he replied, appearing to have known him well.

"Yes, yes he was," I answered, still not certain where all this was headed.

"He was a good man," the stranger shot back, "a very good man. But let me ask you something: Have you ever thought about what it means that such a good man was, more or less, a drug dealer in the ghetto?"

Time stood still for a second as I sought to recover from what felt like a serious punch to the gut. I could feel myself getting defensive, and the look in my eyes no doubt betrayed my hurt and even anger at the question. After all, this was not how I had viewed my grandfather—as a drug dealer. He had been a businessman, I thought to myself. But even as I fumbled around for a reply, for a way to defend my grandfather's honor and good name, I began to realize that the man's statement had not been a condemnation of Leo Wise's humanity. It was not a curse upon the memory of the man to whom I had lovingly referred as Paw Paw all of my life. Anyway, he was right.

The fact is, my grandfather, who had spent several of his formative years living with his family on Jefferson Street, indeed made his living owning and operating a liquor store in the black community. Though the drug he sold was a legal one, it was a drug nonetheless, and to deny that fact or ignore its implications—that my grandfather put food on his family's table (and mine quite often) thanks to the addictions, or at least bad habits, of some of the city's most marginalized black folks—is to shirk the responsibility that we all have to actually *own* our collaboration. His collaboration hadn't made him a bad person, mind you, just as the black drug dealer in the same community is not necessarily a bad person. It simply meant that he had been complex, like all of us.

The discussion led to the discovery and articulation of some difficult truths, which demonstrated how messy the business of racism can be, and how easy it is to both fight the monster, and yet still, on occasion, collaborate with it. On the one hand, my grandfather trafficked in a substance that could indeed bring death—a slow, often agonizing death that could destroy families long before it claimed the physical health or life of its abuser. On the other hand, he, unlike most white business owners who operate in the inner-city, left a lot of money behind in the community, refusing to simply abscond with it all to the white suburban home he had purchased in 1957, and in which he would live until his death.

Even the man who had raised the issue of my grandfather's career as a legal drug dealer was quick to point out the other side: how he had seen and heard of Leo paying people's light bills and phone bills, hundreds of times, paying folks' rent hundreds more; how he paid to get people's cars fixed, or brought families food when they didn't have any;

how he paid people under the table for hauling boxes away, moving liquor around, or delivering it somewhere, even when he could have done it himself or gotten another store employee to do it. The man in the workshop remembered how my grandfather would slip twenty dollar bills to people for no reason at all, just because he could. By all accounts, he noted, Leo had continued to feel an obligation and a love for the people of the Jefferson Street corridor, even after he had moved away. But what he had likely never noticed, and what I had never seen until that day, was that he and his commercial activity were among the forces that kept people trapped, too. Not the same way as institutional racism perhaps, but trapped nonetheless.

He had not been a bad person, but he had been more complicated than I had ever imagined. He had been a man who could count among his closest friends several black folks, a man who had supported in every respect the civil rights movement, a man whose proximity to the black community had probably done much for me, in terms of making me comfortable in nonwhite settings. But at the same time, he had been a man whose wealth—what there was of it—had been accumulated on the backs, or at least the livers of black people. Neither his personal friendships nor his political commitments had changed any of that.

That structural dynamic had provided him privilege, and it had been my own privilege that had rendered me, for so long, unable to see it.

* * *

LOOKING BACKWARDS IN time then, it becomes possible to see whiteness playing out all along the history of my family, dating back hundreds of years. The ability to come to America in the first place, the ability to procure land once here, and the ability to own other human beings while knowing that you would never be owned yourself, all depended on European ancestry.

Nonetheless, one might deny that this legacy has anything to do with those of us in the modern day. Unless we have been the direct inheritors of that land and property, then of what use has that privilege been to us? For persons like myself, growing up not on farmland passed down by my family, but rather, in a modest apartment, what did this past have to do with me? And what does your family's past have to do with you?

In my case, race and privilege were every bit as implicated in the time and place of my birth as they had been for my forbears. I was born in a nation that had only recently thrown off the formal trappings of legal apartheid. I was born in a city that had, just eight years earlier, been the scene of some of the most pitched desegregation battles in the South, replete with sit-ins, boycotts, marches, and the predictable white backlash to all three. Nashville, long known as a city too polite and erudite for the kinds of overt violence that marked the deep South of Alabama or Mississippi, nonetheless had seen its share of ugliness when it came to race.

When future Congressman John Lewis, Bernard Lafayette, Diane Nash, James Bevel, and others led the downtown sit-ins against segregated lunch counters in February 1960 (two weeks after the Greensboro, North Carolina, Woolworth's was similarly targeted by students from North Carolina A&T), the modern youth-led component of the civil rights struggle was officially born, much to the chagrin of local thugs who attacked the protesters daily. Someone had apparently forgotten to tell them, as they put out cigarettes on the necks of these brave students, that Nashville was different.

Of course, why would they think it was? Violence had marked resistance to the civil rights struggle in Nashville, as it had elsewhere. In 1957, racists placed a bomb in the basement of one of the city's soon-to-be integrated schools, and a year later did the same at the Jewish Community Center because of the role Dan May—a local Jewish leader and head of the school board—had played in supporting a gradual (and actually quite weak) desegregation plan. Although the bombers in those instances galvanized opposition to outright terrorist tactics, ongoing resistance to integration delayed any truly meaningful movement in that direction until 1971, when busing was finally ordered at the high-school level. It would be 1974, the year I began first grade, before busing would filter down to the elementary level. This means that the class of 1986, *my* graduating class, was the first that had been truly desegregated throughout its entire educational experience; this, more than thirty years after the Supreme Court had ruled that segregation was illegal, and that southern schools must desegregate "with all deliberate speed." There had been nothing deliberate or speedy about it.

But when it comes to understanding the centrality of race and racism in the society of my birth, perhaps this is the most important point of all: I was born just a few hours and half a state away from Memphis, where six months earlier, to the day, Dr. King had been murdered. My mom, thirteen weeks pregnant at the time, had been working that evening (not early morning, as mistakenly claimed by Bono in the famous U2 song), when King stepped onto the balcony outside room 306 of the Lorraine Motel, only to be felled a few seconds later by an assassin's bullet. Upon hearing the news, the managers of the department store where she was employed decided to close up shop. Fear that black folks might come over to Green Hills, the mostly white and relatively affluent area where the Cain-Sloan store was located, so as to take out vicarious revenge on whitey (or at least whitey's shoe department), had sent them into a panic. No doubt this fear was intensified by the fact that the downtown branch of the store had been the first target for sit-ins in the city, back in December 1959, when students had attempted to desegregate the store's lunch counters.

A minor riot had occurred in Nashville the year before the King assassination, sparked by the overreaction of the Nashville police to a visit by activist Stokely Carmichael (Kwame Ture), from the Student Non-Violent Coordinating Committee, who would soon become "Honorary Prime Minister" of the Black Panther Party. Although the violence had been limited to a small part of the mostly black North Nashville community around Fisk University—and even then had been unrelated to Carmichael's speeches in town, contrary to the claims of then-Mayor Beverly Briley and the local media—by the time King was killed, white folks were on high alert for the first signs of trouble.

That I experienced my mother's bodily reaction to King's murder, as well as the killing of Bobby Kennedy two months later, may or may not mean anything. Whether or not cell memory and the experiences of one's parent can be passed to the child as a result of trauma, thereby influencing the person that child is to become, is something that will likely never be proven one way or the other. Even the possibility of such a thing is purely speculative and more than a bit romantic, but it makes for a good story; and I've never much believed in coincidences.

But even discounting cell memory, and even if we disregard the possibility that a mother may somehow transmit knowledge to a child during gestation, my experience with race predated my birth, if simply because being born to a white family meant certain things about the experiences I was likely to have once born: where I would live, what jobs and education my family was likely to have had, and where I would go to school.

On my third day of life I most certainly experienced race, however oblivious I was to it at the time, when my parents and I moved into an apartment complex in the above-mentioned Green Hills community. It was a complex that, four years after completion, had still never had a tenant of color, very much *not* by accident. But in we went, because it was affordable and a step up from the smaller apartment my folks had been living in prior to that time. More than that, in we went because we could, just as we could have gone into any apartment complex anywhere in Nashville, subject only to our ability to put down a security deposit, which as it turns out was paid by my father's father anyway. So at least as early as Monday, October 7, 1968—before the last remnants of my umbilical cord had fallen off—I was officially experiencing what it meant to be white.

I say this not to suggest any guilt on my part for having inherited this legacy. It is surely not my fault that I was born, as with so many others, into a social status over which I had little control. But this is hardly the point, and regardless of our own direct culpability for the system, or lack thereof, the simple and incontestable fact is that we all have to deal with the residue of past actions. We clean up the effects of past pollution. We remove asbestos from old buildings for the sake of public health, even when we didn't put the material there ourselves. We pay off government debts, even though much of the spending that created them happened long ago. And of course, we have no problem reaping the benefits of past actions for which we weren't responsible. Few people refuse to accept money or property from others who bequeath such things to them upon death, out of a concern that they wouldn't want to accept something they hadn't earned. We love to accept things we didn't earn, such as inheritance, but we have a problem taking responsibility for the things that have benefited us while harming others. Just as a house or farm left to you upon the death of a parent is an asset that you get to use, so too is racial privilege; and if you get to use an asset, you have to pay the debt accumulated, which allowed the asset to exist in the first place.

If you think this to be unreasonable, try a little thought experiment: Imagine you were to become the Chief Executive Officer of a multi-billion dollar company. And imagine that on your first day you were to sit down in your corner-office chair and begin to plan how you would lead the firm to even greater heights. In order to do your job effectively, you would obviously need to know the financial picture of the company: what are your assets, your liabilities, and your revenue stream? So you call a meeting with your Chief Financial Officer so that you can be clear about the firm's financial health and future. The CFO comes to the meeting, armed with spreadsheets and a Power Point presentation, all of which show everything you'd ever want to know about the company's fiscal health. The company has billions in assets, hundreds of millions in revenues, and a healthy profit margin. You're excited. Now imagine that as your CFO gathers up her things to leave, you look at her and say, "Oh, by the way, thanks for all the information, but next time, don't bother with the figures on our outstanding debts. See, I wasn't here when you borrowed all that money and took on all that debt, so I don't see why I should have to deal with that. I intend to put the assets to work immediately, yes. But the debts? Nope, that's not my problem."

Once the CFO finished laughing, security would likely come and usher you to your car, and for obvious reasons. The notion of utilizing assets but not paying debts is irresponsible, to say nothing of unethical. Those who reap the benefits of past actions—and the privileges that have come from whiteness are certainly among those—have an obligation to take responsibility for our use of those benefits.

But in the end, the past isn't really the biggest issue. Putting aside the historic crime of slavery, the only slightly lesser crime of segregation, the genocide of indigenous persons, and the generations-long head start for whites, we would still need to deal with the issue of racism and white privilege because discrimination and privilege today, irrespective of the past, are big enough problems to require our immediate concern. My own life has been more than adequate proof of this truism. It is to this life that I now turn.

AWAKENINGS

FOR WHITES, THE process of racial identity development is typically far slower than for people of color. As the dominant group in the United States, whites too often have the luxury of remaining behind a veil of ignorance for years, while people of color begin noticing the different ways in which they are viewed and treated early on. Recent studies suggest that even by the age of eight, and certainly by ten, black children are cognizant of the negative stereotypes commonly held about their group. Folks of color know they are the *other*, and pretty soon they learn what that means. What's more, people of color not only recognize their *otherness*, but are also inundated by whiteness, by the norm. Sort of like that kid in the movie *The Sixth Sense* who sees dead people, to be black or brown is to see white people often. It's hard to work around us.

But for whites, we often don't see people of color. To be white in this country has long been to be in a position where, if you wanted to, you could construct a life that would be more or less all-white. Although the demographic changes underway in the nation—which by 2040 will render the United States about half white and half of color—are making it more difficult to maintain racially homogenous spaces, in many parts of the country white youth grow up with very little connection to anyone who isn't white.

Even in 2011, I meet white folks all around the country who never really knew any person of color until they came to college; in some cases, they had hardly even *seen* people of color (other than on television) until then. Though perhaps it shouldn't surprise me, in part it does because such insularity is so foreign to my own experience.

Fact is, I remember the first time I ever saw a black person too—I mean *really* saw them, and intuited that there was something different about our respective skin colors. But that memory is not a college memory or a teenage memory; rather, it is my very first memory from my childhood.

I must have been about two, so it would have been perhaps the fall of 1970, or maybe the spring of 1971. I was in the living room of our apartment, gazing as I often did out of the sliding glass door to the porch, when about two hundred feet away, cutting across the rectangular lawn used as common recreation space by residents of the complex (which I would in years to come all but commandeer as my personal baseball diamond), came striding a tall, middle-aged black man in some kind of a uniform.

The man, I would come to learn, was named Tommy, and he was one of the maintenance crew at the Royal Arms. It is testimony to how entrenched racism was at that time and place that this man, who was at least in his fifties by then, would never be known to me or my parents by anything other than his first name. Even as a mere infant I would be allowed the privilege of addressing this grown black man with a family and full life history only as Tommy, as if we were equals, or perhaps "Mister Tommy," as my mother would instruct, since at least that sounded more respectful. But about him, I would need know nothing else.

As I gazed out the window my attention was riveted to him and the darkness of his skin. He was quite dark, though not really black of course, which led me to ask my mother who the brown man was.

Without hesitation she said it was Mr. Tommy, and that he wasn't brown, but black. Having developed a penchant for argument, even at two, I naturally insisted that he most certainly was *not* black. He was brown. I knew the names of all the crayons in my Crayola box, and knew that this man certainly didn't look like the crayon called "black." Burnt umber maybe, brown most definitely, but black? No way.

My mother acknowledged the accuracy of my overly literalistic position, but stuck to her guns on the matter, explaining something rather profound in the process, the profundity of which it took many years for me to appreciate. "Tim," she explained, "Mister Tommy may look brown, but people who look the way Mister Tommy does prefer to be called black."

And that was the end of the argument. Even at two, it seemed only proper that if someone wanted to call themselves black they had every right to do so, whether or not the label fit the actual color of their skin. Mine, after all, wasn't really "white" either, and so it was really none of my business.

This may not seem important, but think how meaningful it can be to learn early on that people have a right to self-determination, to define their own reality, to claim their own identity—and that you have no right to impose your judgment of them, on them. When it comes to race, that's not a lesson that most whites learn at the age of two or *ever*. Historically, white Americans have always felt the right to define black and brown folks' realities for them: insisting that enslaved persons were happy on the plantation and felt just like family, or that indigenous persons were the uncivilized ones, while those who would seek to conquer and destroy them were the practitioners of enlightenment.

At the level of labels, racism has long operated to impose white reality onto others. Whites found the assertion of blackness (and especially as a positive, even "beautiful" thing in the 1960s and 1970s) threatening because it was an internally derived title unlike "colored," or "Negro," terms which had been foisted upon black bodies by the white and European tradition. Likewise, many whites today react hostilely to the use of the term "African American" because it came from within the black community, and as such, stands as a challenge to white linguistic authority.

When whites tell black folks, as we often do, that they should "just be Americans," and "drop the whole hyphen thing," we're forgetting that it's hard to *just* be an American when you've rarely been treated like a full and equal member of the family. More to the point, it isn't our hyphen to drop. But it's always hard to explain such matters to those who have taken for granted, because we could, that we had the right to set the parameters of national identity, or to tell other people's stories as if they were our own. It's been that way for a while and explains much about the way we misteach history.

So at roughly the same time as I was being instructed by my mother on the finer points of linguistic self-determination, I was also beginning to read. I read my first book without help on May 5, 1971, at the

age of two years, seven months, and one day. That's the good and rea-
sonably impressive (if still somewhat freakish) news. The bad news is
that the book was *Meet Andrew Jackson*, an eighty seven-page tribute to
the nation's seventh president, intended to make children proud of the
nation in which they live, and of this, one of that nation's early leaders. Given that my mother had been quick to prohibit books like *Little
Black Sambo* from coming into our home because of the racial stereotypes in which the story trafficked, it was somewhat surprising that she
would indulge such a volume as this one, but she did, and I consumed
it voraciously.

Therein, I learned that Jackson's mom had admonished him never to
lie or "take what is not your own" (an instruction he felt free to ignore as
he got older, at least as it applied to indigenous peoples or the Africans
whom he took as property), and that when Jackson headed West as a
young man, he encountered Indians who "did not want white people in
their hunting grounds," and "often killed white travelers." This part was
true of course, if a bit incomplete: people whose land has been invaded
and is in the process of being stolen often become agitated and sometimes even kill those who are trying to destroy them. Imagine.

On page 46, I read that although "some people in the North were
saying it was not right to own slaves . . . Jackson felt the way most other
Southerners did. He felt it was right to own slaves. He called his slaves
his 'family.'" Well then, who are we to question his definition of that
term? Ten pages later, I learned that Jackson fought the Creek Indians
to preserve America and save innocent lives, though oddly there was no
mention that in order to get an accurate count of the dead they slaughtered at Horseshoe Bend, soldiers in Jackson's command cut off the tips
of Creek noses and sliced strips of flesh from their bodies for use as
bridal reins for their horses—surely an accidental editorial oversight.

At the end of the book, after recounting Jackson's rise to the presidency, *Meet Andrew Jackson* concludes by noting that when Jackson
died, his slaves cried and "sang a sad old song." To insert such a flourish
as this, though it probably struck me as touching at the time, is utterly
vulgar, and suggests as well as anything what is wrong with the way
children in the United States learn our nation's history. There is no
scholarly record of sad songs being sung by slaves as Jackson lay dying.

This kind of detail, even were it true—and it almost certainly is not—has no probative value when it comes to letting us know who Andrew Jackson was. It exists for the same reason the old fairy tale about George Washington cutting down the cherry tree and telling his dad because he "couldn't tell a lie," exists—because no fabrication is too extreme in the service of national self-love. Anything that makes us feel proud can be said, facts notwithstanding. Anything that reminds us of the not-so-noble pursuits of our forefathers or national heroes, on the other hand, gets dumped down the memory hole. And if you bring those kinds of things up, you'll be accused of hating America.

The way in which we place rogues like Andrew Jackson on a pedestal, while telling people of color to "get over it" (meaning the past) whenever slavery or Indian genocide is brought up, has always struck me as the most precious of ironies. We want folks of color to move past the past, even as we very much seek to dwell in that place a while. We dwell there every July 4, every Columbus Day, every time a child is given a book like *Meet Andrew Jackson* to read. We love the past so long as it venerates us. We want to be stuck there, and many would even like to return. Some say as much, as with the Tea Party folks who not only announce that they "want their country back," but even dress up in tricorn hats, Revolutionary War costumes, and powdered wigs for their rallies. It is only when those who were the targets for destruction challenge the dominant narrative that the past becomes conveniently irrelevant, a trifle not worth dwelling upon.

* * *

GOOD OR BAD, the past is a fact, and it often holds the keys to who we are in the present, and who we're likely to become in the future. This was certainly the case for me.

By 1971, it was time for me to begin preschool. Although I'm certain there were any number of programs in Green Hills or thereabouts in which I could have been enrolled, my mother made the decision (very much against the objections of certain friends and family) that I should attend the early childhood program at Tennessee State University (TSU), which is Nashville's historically black land-grant college. Her reasons for the decision were mixed. On the one hand, she knew that upon beginning school I would be in an integrated environment—something she had never had the benefit of experiencing—and she wanted me to know what it was like to occasionally find myself in a space where I might not be the taken-for-granted norm. On the other hand, I've long suspected that it was also something she did to tweak her family and mark her own independence from the much more provincial life she had led growing up.

TSU, the name of which had recently been changed from Tennessee A&I, is located in North Nashville, just off the foot of Jefferson Street—the epicenter of Nashville's black community. Although the Jefferson Street corridor had been recently devastated by the construction of Interstate 40 right through the middle of it—a part of "urban renewal" that occurred nationwide and contributed to the destruction of up to one-fifth of all black housing in the country by 1969—the city's black residents were rightly proud of the area and constantly fought to return it to its former glory. My grandfather had grown up on Jefferson Street as a teen, since the black community was one of the few places Jews could live unless they were of substantial means. Of course, he hadn't gone to school there. During the days of segregation, he would be sent to the white school downtown, Hume-Fogg, even though his neighborhood school was Pearl, one of the academic jewels among southern black high schools at the time.

Not to romanticize the days of segregation of course, but under conditions of formal oppression, black business districts like Jefferson Street had often managed to carve out a thriving subculture of black success. Forced to turn inward, African Americans across the nation spent their money with black businesses, and the children in the schools knew that the teachers and administrators loved them—they were, after all, their neighbors. While integration was clearly necessary to open up the opportunity structure that had previously been closed off, it also led to the firing of thousands of black teachers across the South, who were no longer wanted in the newly consolidated schools into which blacks would be placed (but as clear minorities in most cases). Integration would be of limited success because whites had been ill-prepared to open up the gates of access and opportunity wide enough for any but a few to squeeze through. Those few managed to leave the old neighborhoods and take their money with them, but the rest were left behind, access to suburban life limited, their own spaces transformed by interstates, office buildings, and parking lots, in the name of progress.

Just a mile or so from Fisk—the city's historically black private college—TSU was seen as the university for working class African Americans, and more to the point for local black folks, while Fisk (long associated with alum W.E.B. DuBois's "talented tenth" concept) attracted more of a national and international student clientele. At the time of my enrollment at TSU, the college was embroiled in a struggle with state officials who had been seeking to establish a branch campus of the University of Tennessee in downtown Nashville. Concerned that such a school would allow whites to avoid the mostly black campus by attending a predominantly white state institution in town, and thereby siphon resources from TSU to the newly-created UT-Nashville, TSU officials were battling valiantly to remain the flagship of public education in the city.

As a student in TSU's early childhood program, my classmates would be principally the children of faculty or families living in close proximity to the college, which is to say, they would be mostly black. Indeed, I would be one of only three students in the classroom who weren't black, out of a class of roughly twenty kids. Although several of the teachers who ran the program were white, the ones I remember most vividly were African American women. They seemed quite clearly to own the space. It was their domain and we all respected it.

I can't remember much about my time at TSU, although I can vividly recall the layout of the class, the playground, and the drive to and from our Green Hills home each morning and afternoon to get back and forth. But despite the vagueness of my TSU memories, I can't help but think that the experience had a profound impact on my life, especially as I would come to understand and relate to the subject of race. On the one hand, being subordinated to black authority at an early age was a blessing. In a society that has long encouraged whites to disregard black wisdom, for a white child to learn at the age of three to listen to black women and *do what they ask of you*, and to believe that they know of what they speak, can be more than a minor life lesson. It would mean that a little more than twenty years later, listening to African American women in public housing in New Orleans tell me about their lives and struggles, I would not be the white guy who looked them square in the face and inquired as to whether it might be possible that they had lost their minds. I would not be the white guy who would assume they were exaggerating, making things up, or fabricating the difficulties of their daily routine. I would go back to that early imprinting, and remember that people know their lives better than I do, including those whom the society has ignored for so long.

Attending preschool at TSU also meant that I would be socialized in a non-dominant setting, my peers mostly African American children. Because I had bonded with black kids early on, once I entered elementary school it would be hard not to notice the way that we were so often separated in the classroom, by tracking that placed the white children in more advanced tracks, by unequal discipline, and by a different way in which the teachers would relate to us. At Burton Elementary, with the exception of the African American teachers, most of the educators would have had very little experience teaching black children, and in some cases, very little interest in doing so. At one point in my first grade year the teacher would actually pawn off the task to my mother, who had no teaching background, but who knew that unless she intervened to work with the African American students they would receive very little instruction in the classroom.

While few white children at such an age would have noticed the racial separation going on, I couldn't help but see it. These were my friends, a few of whom I had been at TSU with. Even the black kids I hadn't known before were the ones with whom I would identify, thanks to my TSU experience. Although I hardly had a word to describe what was going on, I knew that whatever it was came at a cost to me; it was separating me from the people in whom I'd had some investment. Although the injury was far more profound to them—after all, the institutional racism at the heart of that unequal treatment wasn't aimed in my direction, but theirs—I was nonetheless the collateral damage. My mother had never tried to push me into whiteness or put me into a socially-determined space. But what she would not do, the schools would strive for, from the very beginning.

* * *

WHATEVER RACIAL SEPARATION the school system sought to re-impose, even in a post-segregation era, it was something against which I struggled for years. I had a few white friends, but very few. Albert Jones, who is still my best friend to this day, was among the only white classmates with whom I bonded at that time. Frankly, even that might have been a case of mistaken identity. Though white, his dad worked at TSU in the School of Education, so even he had a connection to the black community that made him different. But other than Albert, pretty much all of my friends at Burton were black.

Yet, as I would discover, interpersonal connections to racial others say little about whether or not one is having experiences similar to those others. Even when a white person is closely tied to African Americans, that white person is often living in an entirely different world from that of their friends, though we rarely realize it.

It would be early 1977, in third grade, that I received one of my earliest lessons about race, even if the meaning of that lesson wouldn't sink in for several years. The persons who served as my instructors that day were not teachers, but two friends, Bobby Orr and Vincent Perry, whose understanding of the dynamics of race—their blackness and my white-ness—was so deep that they were able to afford me the lesson during something as meaningless as afternoon recess.

It was a brisk winter day, and Bobby, Vince, and I were tossing a football back and forth. One of us would get between the other two, who stood at a distance of maybe ten yards from each other, and try to intercept the ball as it flew through the air from one passer to the next. Football had really never been my game. Though I was athletic and obsessed with sports, I was also pretty small as a kid; as such, I saw little point in a game that involved running into people and being tack-led. I preferred baseball, but since baseball season was several months away, the only options that day during P.E. class were kickball or foot-ball. Normally, I would have chosen kickball, but when Bobby and Vince asked me to play with them I had said yes. Because we were so often separated in the classroom, I treasured whatever time I could carve out with my black friends.

Our game began innocently enough, with Bobby in the middle, usu-ally picking off passes between Vince and me. Next it was Vince's turn, and he too picked off several of the passes between Bobby and me, though the zip with which Bobby delivered them often made the ball bounce off of Vince's hands, too hot to handle.

When it came time for me to be in the middle, I frankly had little expectation about how many passes I could intercept. My size alone virtually ensured that if Vince and Bobby wanted to, they could simply lob the ball over my head, and so long as they did it high enough and fast enough, there would be very little opportunity for me to pull the ball down. But strangely, I caught every one. Each time they would pass just a bit beyond my reach and I would jump to one side or the other, hauling their efforts into my breast, never dropping a single one or allowing even one pass in thirty to make it past me.

At first, I reveled in what I assumed must be my newfound speed and agility. What's more, I beamed with childish pride at the smiles on their faces, assuming that Bobby and Vince were impressed with my effort; and I continued to interpret this series of events as evidence of my own abilities, even as they both began to repeat the same refrain after every pass, beginning with about the tenth throw of the series. As the ball left Bobby's throwing hand and whizzed toward its destination in Vince's outstretched arms, only to be thwarted in its journey time and again by my leaping effort, they would repeat, one and then the other, the same exclamation.

"My nigger Tim!"

Pop! The ball would once again reverberated as it hit my hands and was pulled in for another interception.

"My nigger Tim!"

I would toss it back, and we would repeat the dance, Bobby moving left, Vince right, me following their steps and taking cues from their body language as to where the ball would be going next.

Pop! Another catch.

"My nigger Tim!"

After the first dozen times they said this, each time with more emphasis and a bit of a chuckle, I began to sense that something was going on, the meaning of which I didn't quite understand. A strange feeling began to creep over me, punctuated by a voice in the back of my head saying something about being suckered. Not to mention, I instinctively felt odd about being called a "nigger" (and note, it was indeed that derivation of the term, and not the more relaxed, even amiable "nigga" which was being deployed), because it was a word I would never use, and which I knew to be a slur of the most vile nature, and also, let's face it, because I was white, and had never been called that before.

Though I remained uncomfortable with the exchange for several minutes after it ended, I quickly put it behind me as the bell rang, recess ended, and we headed back to class, laughing and talking about something unrelated to the psychodrama that had been played out on the ball field. If I ever thought of the event in the days afterward, I likely contented myself with the thought that although their word choice seemed odd, they were only signifying that I was one of the club so to speak and had proven myself to them. Well, I was right about one thing: they were definitely "signifying"—a term for the cultural practice of well-crafted verbal put-downs that have long been a form of street poetry in the black communities of this nation.

As it turns out, it would be almost twenty years before I finally understood the meaning of this day's events, and that understanding would come while watching television. It was there that I saw a black comedian doing a bit about making some white guy "his nigger," and getting him to do whatever he, the black comic, wanted: to jump when he said jump, to come running when he was told to come running, to step 'n fetch' it, so to speak. So there it was. On that afternoon so many years before, Bobby and Vince had been able to flip the script on the racial dynamic that would, every other day, serve as the background noise for their lives. On that day they were able to make me not only a nigger, but their nigger. The irony couldn't have been more perfect, nor the satisfaction, I suppose, in having exacted a small measure of payback, not of me, per se, since at that age I had surely done little to deserve it, but of my people, writ large. It was harmless, and for them it had been fun: a cat and mouse routine with the white boy who doesn't realize he's being used, and not just used, but used in the way some folks had long been used, and were still being used every day. Today Tim, you the nigger. Today, you will be the one who gets to jump and run, and huff and puff. Today we laugh, and not with you, but at you. We like you and all that, but today, you belong to us.

As I thought about it, however, I was overcome with a profound sadness, and not because I had been tricked or played for a fool; that's happened lots of times, usually at the hands of other white folks. I was saddened by what I realized in that moment, which was very simply this: even at the age of nine, Bobby and Vince had known what it meant to be someone's nigger. They knew more than how to say the word, they knew how to use it, when to use it, how to contextualize it, and fashion it into a weapon. And the only way they could have known any of this is because they had either been told of its history and meaning, had been called it before, or had seen or heard a loved one called it before, none of which options were a lot better than the others.

Even as the school system we shared was every day treating Bobby and Vince as that thing they now called me—disciplining them more harshly or placing them in remedial level groups no matter their abilities—on the playground they could turn it around and claim for themselves the power to define reality, *my* reality, and thereby gain a brief respite from what was happening in class. Yet the joke was on them in the end. Because once recess was over, and the ball was back in the hands of the teachers, there were none prepared to make *me* the nigger.

It had been white privilege and black oppression that had made the joke funny in the first place, or even decipherable; and it would likewise be white privilege and black oppression that would make it irrelevant and even a bit pathetic. But folks take their victories where they can find them. And some of us find them more often than others.

* * *

I WAS NEVER a very good student. No matter my reading level or general ability, I had a hard time applying myself to subject matter that I didn't find interesting. In effect, I treated school like a set of noise-canceling headphones, letting in the sounds I was interested in hearing while shutting out the rest. By middle school I was struggling academically, finding myself bored and looking desperately for something else to occupy my time. Given the home in which I lived, it was hardly surprising that I would settle on theatre. Growing up in a home where my father was always on stage, even when he wasn't, had provided me with a keen sense of timing, of delivery, of what was funny and what wasn't, of how to move onstage, of how to "do nothing well," as Lorelle Reeves, my theatre teacher in high school, would put it.

I grew up memorizing lines to plays I would never perform, simply because my dad had saved all the scripts from shows he had done in the past. They were crammed into a small, brown-lacquered paperback book cabinet that hung in the living room of our apartment— one after another, with tattered and dog-eared pages, compliments of Samuel French, the company that owned distribution rights for most of the stage play scripts in the United States. I would pick them up and read them out loud in my room, creating different voices for different characters. The plays dealt with adult themes, many of which I didn't understand, but which I pretended to, just in case anyone ever needed a ten-year-old to play the part of Paul Bratter in *Barefoot in the Park*.

At Stokes School, in fifth grade, I would finally have the chance to take a theatre class as an elective. The teacher, Susan Moore, was among the most eccentric persons I've ever met. Had I been older, I may well have appreciated her eccentricity; but at the age of ten, eccentric is just another word for weird, and weird is how we students viewed her. All we knew was that she was an odd, fat lady (we weren't too sensitive on issues of body type, as I'm sure won't surprise you) with a dozen cats, whose clothes always smelled like cat litter and whose car smelled worse. One of my friends, Bobby Bell, who was not in the drama club but once got a ride from Ms. Moore, dubbed her wheels the "douche 'n' push," which we all thought was hilarious, even though I doubt any of us really knew what a douche was. In fact, once I learned the meaning of the word, calling her car a douche 'n' push seemed less funny than gross.

We didn't study much in terms of theatre technique. For good or bad, Susan thought it best to just throw us into the process of doing theatre, learning as we went. So she would pick a play and we would work on it for the better part of a year: reading it, learning it, and then finally producing and performing it. The good thing about this process was that it led to fairly sophisticated outcomes, at least for fifth and sixth graders. When you have ten- and eleven-year-olds pulling off Shakespeare's *Taming of the Shrew* and never dropping a line, you know you're doing something special. As the male lead in that production, I can attest to feeling significantly older and wiser than my years for having done it, for having successfully taken on a Shakespearian farce at such an age.

On the downside, unless you got one of the coveted roles in the play chosen for that year by Ms. Moore, your participation in the theatre group would be circumscribed. Occasionally, she would create a few characters and script a few lines for them, so that as many kids as possible could get a chance to be onstage, but this hardly flattened the hierarchy of the club. There were the actors and there was everyone else: the students who would work the lights, pull the curtains, or just hang out and perhaps help the actors run lines, or maybe just quit theatre altogether and find something else to do.

Having an actor for a father pretty well assured me of a prominent role in whatever production was chosen as our annual play. Ms. Moore could presume my talent, and although that talent may have been genuine, there were certainly no cold readings or auditions. A few of us would pretty much rotate: I would be the male lead in one play, and in the next production that honor would go to Albert. The female leads would also pretty much rotate between two of the girls in our class, Stacey Wright and Shannon Holladay. It was a fairly closed circle.

In sixth grade we would switch from Shakespeare to *You're a Good Man, Charlie Brown*, which, given that it's a musical and neither Albert nor I could sing, should have guaranteed that it would be our turn to pull curtains or some such thing. But despite our lack of ability, we were cast as Charlie and Linus, respectively. In my case, Ms. Moore actually agreed to take the song "My Blanket and Me" out of the play altogether, because I made clear that I was terrified to sing a solo in public.

My ability to force script changes was not about race of course, but my ability to be in the position I was, and therefore to make that kind of demand and gain the director's acquiescence, most assuredly *was* about race, at least in part. Had I been anything but white, it would have been highly unlikely that I would have gotten the parts I landed in any of the productions done at that or any other school. These were roles written for white actors. Shakespeare's work is not, to be sure, replete with black characters, and there are only so many times a school can do *Othello*. Likewise, *You're a Good Man Charlie Brown* was written before the introduction of the comic strip's one black character, Franklin.

Although Ms. Moore added a few lines to the script and had a black kid deliver them in the person of Franklin (and created an entirely new character for Carol Stuart, one of the few black students in the theatre class), this hardly altered the racial dynamic at work.

To be white at that school, as in many others, was to have a whole world of extracurricular opportunity opened to oneself—a world where if you were a mediocre student (as I was), you could still find a niche, an outlet for your talents, passions, and interests. To be of color at that same school was to ensure that no matter how good an actor or actress you were, or were capable of becoming, you were unlikely to be in a position to avail yourself of this same outlet for your creativity. Unless a theatre teacher is prepared to violate the aesthetic sensibilities of the audience, which is rare, and cast a person of color in a role traditionally played by a white person (like Romeo, Juliet, Hamlet, or Snoopy even), black, Latino, and Asian kids are just out of luck.

This, it should be noted, is no mere academic point. Theatre was a life raft for me in middle school, without which I might well have gone under altogether. My ability to access it, and the whiteness that granted me that ability, was no minor consideration. By the time middle school began, my home life was increasingly chaotic. My father's drinking had gone well past heavy, on the way to serious alcoholism. Though he was still technically functional—and would remain so, more or less, right up until he got sober eighteen years later—his addiction propelled his internalized rage and sense of failure forward, which would explode time and again in our small apartment, always aimed directly at my mother. Though she absorbed the nightly verbal blows and tried her best to shield me from the damage, each fight, each hateful word, each guttural expression of unhinged contempt cut deeply into my sense of personal security.

I took to closing myself off in my room after school most days. When he was around, I would only come out to eat dinner, always making sure to be back in my own personal space shortly thereafter, as the drinking continued and the fights were sure to begin. Then, on those occasions when he would go out to a bar to drink more, I would force myself to stay up late until I could hear the hall door open at the far end of our apartment building, followed by the sound of his heavy drunken footsteps moving closer to our unit, and I could know that at least for that night he wasn't going to kill himself while driving. I could go to sleep.

Things got so bad at one point that I began to keep track with hash marks on a page the number of days in a row that he had been drunk: twenty-one on the day I stopped counting. Though I longed for a closer relationship with my dad, I also breathed more easily whenever he was in a play out of town. By then I had learned that quiet loneliness is always preferable to amplified togetherness when the cacophony to which you're being exposed reverberates with the blaring notes of marital discord.

Only by escaping into the world of acting (a strangely ironic choice, I realize) was I able to make it through those grades at all. It was my refuge. I could lock myself in my room with a play script, avoid my father, escape the smell of Canadian whiskey or bad vodka on his breath, and avoid the verbal battles that were the hallmark of his relationship with my mother. The only times I would come out of my room were in those moments when I honestly felt that if I didn't he might kill her. Although my home was not one characterized by physical abuse—thankfully, my dad only struck my mom once (which of course was one time too many) by pushing her into a wall outside my room—when you're ten and eleven your mind has a hard time processing the distinction between verbal and physical violence, and knowing where that line is, and just how much it might take for the abuser to cross the metaphorical Rubicon. During this period, although I never had friends over—mostly because I didn't want them to see my father drunk—I also refused to go to their homes, at least not past dinner, feeling that I needed to be in the house as a way to deter my father from the inevitable leap to assault or even murder.

No matter the infrequency of physical abuse, in my mind the threat always seemed to hang like a thunder cloud over our home. At one point, I was so sure he would kill her that I began planning an escape route. If I could intervene and save her I would, but if it became apparent that I wouldn't be able to do much good, I knew how to get my bedroom window open fast, and exactly where I would run to get help, or to borrow the weapon with which I would end my father's life.

That my dad was not going to kill my mother was hardly the point.

When you hear him say that he's going to—like the one time he said it with a steak knife held three inches from her face, while I watched from perhaps seven feet away—and you're a child, you are in no position to deconstruct the context of his words. All you can do is spend precious moments of your youth trying to figure out ways to save your mom's life, or at least your own, on that day when your father has one drink too many and burns dinner because he wasn't paying close enough attention, or can't find his keys and flies into a rage, and reaches into the utensil drawer—and not for a spoon or salad fork.

So when I say that theatre was a life raft, I am not engaging in idle hyperbole. I mean it literally. Without it, I would have had no escape. While my physical existence may have continued—after all, my father never killed anyone in the end, and had he meant to, it's doubtful I could have dissuaded him with a sonnet—my already fragile emotional well-being would have likely taken a nosedive, with dire consequence in years to come. Theatre was how I released my frustrations; it was how I avoided falling into clinical depression; it was how I got my mind off other things, like killing my father before he could harm my mom, which I did contemplate in my more panicked moments.

Without theatre, which I could only access the way I did because I was white, it is a very open question how my life would have gone. If all the other variables had been the same, but I had been anything other than white, and thereby bereft of the diversion offered by acting, I feel confident that things would have gone differently than they did. As for my father, he should be grateful that we were white, and that I had an outlet.

* * *

NEXT TO THEATRE, my other obsession as a kid was sports. When I wasn't working on lines for whatever play we were soon to be performing at school, I was likely to be practicing either basketball or baseball.

As for basketball, I had begun playing competitively at the age of nine. By my fifth grade year, 1979, I was playing for what was undoubtedly the most feared team of eleven-year-olds in the city. Comprised of twelve guys, nine of them black, we had the advantage of racist stereotypes working in our favor. Most of the teams we would play were made up of private school white boys who had barely even seen a black person, let alone played ball against one. Psychologically we had won before we even stepped on the court in most cases. The only times we lost were because the white boys' coaches were smart enough to encourage their players to foul and force us to the line. Sadly, most of our guys could hit twenty-five-foot jumpers with no problem, but free throws from fifteen feet? Not so much.

Still, the racial lessons imparted by my basketball experience were profound. We would walk in the gym, part of the YMCA youth basketball program, in our black uniforms and our mostly black skin, and watch a bunch of pasty white boys damn near piss themselves. We'd win by scores of 40–8, 34–6, 52–9, and other absurd point spreads; and it wasn't because we were that much better. Fact is, our field goal percentage wasn't very high, but we'd always get multiple shots during each offensive possession because the other team was too afraid to fight for rebounds. It was as if they thought our guys might knife them if they even tried.

Because our opponents were so psyched out by the black players, they assumed they had little to fear from the few of us who were white. So whenever the other team got to the foul line, we would line up four black guys around the paint to rebound if they missed, and I would stand at the extreme other end of the court, literally on the opponent's foul line, completely unguarded, because they weren't afraid of the short white guy. Their players would miss their free throws, our guys would rebound, and throw the ball down court to me for an easy layup each time.

On the one hand, the stereotypes of black athleticism worked in our favor on the court, triggering in our opponents what psychologists like Claude Steele call "stereotype threat" on the part of the white players. According to this theory, which has been amply demonstrated in lab experiments and real world settings, when a person is part of a stigmatized group (thought to be less intelligent or less athletic, for instance), the fear of confirming the negative stereotype when forced to perform in a domain where that stereotype might be seen as relevant to performance, can drive down performance relative to ability. In other words, the anxiety spawned by fear of proving the negative stigma true can actually cause a person's skills to suffer, whether on a basketball court or a standardized test.

In most situations, stereotype threat affects socially marginalized groups, since they typically face more stigmatizing stereotypes than dominant groups. So black students do worse in academic settings than their abilities might otherwise indicate because of the anxiety generated as they try *not* to confirm racist stereotypes about black intelligence; women and girls do worse on math exams because they fear validating common stereotypes about female math ability or the lack thereof; and the elderly do less well when told they're taking a test of memory because of a fear that they may confirm negative beliefs about their abilities in that arena. But because of the widespread and anti-scientific belief that blacks are "natural athletes," superior to whites especially at basketball, in this particular case the stereotype vulnerability fell on our white opponents. For a brief thirty-two minutes on the court, the script was flipped.

But thirty-two minutes does not a day make, let alone a lifetime—a point worth remembering, lest we assume a parity of disadvantage between whites and blacks, simply because in one arena like sports (and even then, just a few particular sports), blacks occasionally get the benefit of the doubt and are thought to be superior.

A few years ago, I received an e-mail from a very thoughtful private school mom in Minnesota, who had been asked to read the first edition of this book, along with other parents at the school her child attended. Much of it she liked, but she felt compelled to tell me of at least one instance of "black privilege" in the school, and how it was, to her mind, negatively impacting her white son. Her son, she explained, was an excellent football player—a running back as I recall—and faster than several of the black guys on the team. Nonetheless, the coach (who was white) gave him less playing time than her son's black teammates. She attributed this to the coach's inability to believe that a white guy could be as good a running back as a black guy. In other words, because of the black athlete stereotype, inferior black players were getting more opportunity than her son.

Now on the one hand, I'm a parent, so I know something about the way parents tend to view our children. To put it mildly, we are not always the most objective judges of our own kids' talents: we tend to think their preschool scribbling is a sure sign of artistic genius, their first sentence evidence of pending literary fame, their ability to play a tune on the piano proof of their status as prodigies, and their successful

completion of a pirouette sufficient confirmation that they'll be dancing in the Joffrey in no time. So I take parental bragging about children
with a grain of salt. I would hope others would do the same when I get
to talking about mine; they're great, mind you, but they're just kids.

On the other hand, I was willing to indulge this mom's accolades
for her son. After all, she could be right—he really could be faster than
the black guys—and if she was (in other words, if the coach really was
making a racist decision in favor of the black players and against her
white son), there was an interesting lesson to be learned; but it wasn't
the one she imagined.

Let's assume the coaches on her son's team really did misperceive the
relative abilities of their players because of some pro-black stereotype
when it came to speed or agility. Where would that thought have come
from? How did it originate, and for what purpose? Well, of course, the
racist stereotypes of black physicality and athletic prowess have long
been constructed as the opposite of certain other abilities they are presumed to lack, namely, intellectual abilities. Interestingly then, whites,
having been considered intellectually superior to blacks, which works
to our benefit in the job market and schools, end up being seen as less
athletic, because we have long viewed the two skill sets (sports and academics) as incompatible. Ironically, what this means is that the racist
construction of an *anti-black* stereotype when it comes to intellect—
which includes as a corollary the idea that blacks are better athletes,
since brain power is believed to be inversely related to athleticism—can
have a negative consequence for those whites who play sports. They end
up the collateral damage of racism—not racism aimed at *them*, but a
larger mindset of racism long aimed at the black and brown.

Which is to say that if we'd like to see white football players or basketball players given a fair shot to prove themselves, free from the inferior-
izing assumptions that can attach to them because of a larger system of
racist thought, we have to attack that larger structure. We can't merely
deal with one of its symptoms. In other words, young men like the son
in this story will be viewed as equally capable running backs at precisely
that moment his black teammates are likely to be seen as equally capable
doctors or engineers, and not one second earlier.

* * *

BY MIDDLE SCHOOL, my closeness to my black friends had translated into a remarkable ability to code-switch, meaning an ability to shift between so-called "standard" English, and what some call "Black English," and to do it naturally, fluidly, and without pretense. Although my parents never minded this, even when I would forget to switch back, thereby remaining in black cadence and dialect around the house, there were others who found it mightily disturbing. Teachers were none too happy with the way they would hear me speaking in the halls to my friends. It was one thing for an actual black person to speak that way, but for a white child to do so was one step over the racial line, and one about which they were hardly pleased.

Adding to the general unease that some white folks seemed to feel because of my growing proximity to blackness, there was my musical taste, which included a growing affinity for funk and hip-hop, the latter of which was just then beginning to emerge on the national scene. I had long had strangely eclectic musical tastes, so although I was a huge KISS fanatic, I went to bed every night listening to WVOL, Nashville's so-called urban station, always making a point not to go to sleep until I had heard Parliament's "Theme From the Black Hole," or something, anything, by Kurtis Blow.

I had actually been the first person in my school, white or black, to memorize every word to the fourteen-minute version of "Rapper's Delight" (the first major rap hit, though purists dispute the legitimacy of its pedigree and performers, the Sugar Hill Gang). My friends and I would have rap battles to see who could get through the latest song without forgetting any of the words. I usually won these rather handily.

But all this cross-cultural competence didn't endear me to the white teachers, many of whom had been teaching long enough to remember (and prefer) the days when white faces were the only ones in front of them; and by God those white folks had known what it meant to be white—and what it surely *didn't* mean was beatboxing.

One teacher in particular quite clearly despised me. Mrs. Crownover, who was my teacher for Language Arts (literature and English class), spoke to me in a voice that barely concealed her contempt, and looked at me with an expression similar to that which one makes around rotting food. When she gave me a D in the class for the second grading

period of fifth grade, my mother was stunned. Given that it was a reading class and I had been reading since before I was three, it made little
sense that I would have done so poorly. Frankly, I hadn't been doing my
best work. I found the class boring and her lessons tedious, so I knew I
wouldn't be getting a good grade; but a D seemed extreme, even with
my lackadaisical effort.

When my mother went to meet with Mrs. Crownover to discuss my
grade and find out if there was anything she needed to be worried about
in terms of my own effort, focus, or reading skills, it became clear that
the grade had been largely unrelated to my effort or ability; rather, it
was principally connected to how she felt about my social circle. As Mrs.
Crownover told my mom, "Any white parent who sends their child to
public schools nowadays should have their heads examined."

As it turns out, this would prove to be a not-so-incredibly bright
career move on Mrs. Crownover's part. Standing up for my friendships and her own principles, my mother took action, getting together
with a few other parents and demanding a sit-down with the principal.
Within a matter of weeks, Mrs. Crownover had mysteriously and quite
unceremoniously disappeared, at first to be replaced by a series of sub-
stitute teachers, and finally, the next year, by someone else altogether. An
extended sabbatical, and I believe an early retirement (though not early
enough), was to be her much deserved fate.

On the one hand, an act of antiracist resistance such as this is worthy
of praise. My mom did what she should have done, and what any white
parent in that situation should do. But there is an interesting aspect to
this story that is equally worthy of attention, and which demonstrates
that even in our acts of allyship we sometimes miss the larger issues.
Yes, my mother had resolved to get the individual racist teacher in this
instance removed. So far so good. No longer would she be free to work
out her own personal damage on children. There would be one less
teacher at Stokes carrying around the deep-seated conviction that black
children were inferior to the white children she apparently felt should
have all fled to private schools at the first sign of integration.

But with that excision accomplished, there remained a far more
dangerous institutional cancer operating in the heart of the school that
I shared with those black friends of mine. When I returned to class

after Mrs. Crownover's removal, I was still attending a school system that was giving the message every day that blacks were inferior. The school had never needed this one teacher to impart that lesson; it was implicit in the way the school system had been tracking students for five years by then, placing blacks almost exclusively in remedial or standard level tracks while placing most all white students in advanced tracks, or so-called "enrichment" programs, as if those with privilege needed to be made *richer* in terms of our opportunities. And neither my mother nor I, with all those close friends, had said anything about *that* racism.

Even in sixth grade, when the racialized nature of tracking became blatant, I wouldn't catch it. My primary teacher that year, Mrs. Belote, would literally wave her hand, about mid-way through fifth period, signaling to the white kids that it was time for our V.E. class (which stood for, I kid you not, "Very Exceptional") down the hall. We would quietly rise and depart the integrated classroom like a receding tide of pink, leaving a room filled with black kids who couldn't have missed what was happening, even though we did. We never thought about it once at the time, friendships or no.

In other words, even as my mother had stood up against the obvious bigot, she had dropped the ball, just like everyone else, when it came to confronting *institutional* racism. My closeness with black people hadn't protected them from that system, and hadn't allowed me to see what was happening, let alone resolve to fix it, at least not yet.

ᴴ　ᴴ　ᴴ

OF COURSE, THERE were a few exceptions to the racialized tracking scheme at Stokes and throughout the Nashville public schools. Typically there would be one or two black females in the enrichment classes but rarely ever a black male. One of the black females in particular is worth reflecting upon, as her experience demonstrates quite clearly the absurdity of racism as a national and even global phenomenon. During that fifth grade year, she was the one black student who was consistently placed in the advanced track. Her name was Rudo Nderere, and she and her family had recently come to the United States from Zimbabwe, arriving, if memory serves, before it actually became Zimbabwe—when it had still been Rhodesia, a racist, white supremacist and apartheid state, much like South Africa.

White teachers *loved* Rudo, and on several occasions I would hear them commenting upon how intelligent she was (which was true), and how articulate she was (also true), and how lovely her accent was (absolutely inarguable, as the Southern African accent is among the most pleasant in the world). But of course there were also native-born blacks in that school, and in those same teachers' classrooms, who were every bit as brilliant and articulate. But the teachers rarely saw that, which is why their astonishment at Rudo's articulateness was so implicitly racist: it suggested that such a characteristic was somehow foreign to black people, that the ability to speak well was a white trait that no black person had ever managed to possess before.

In any event, what was fascinating about the way Rudo was viewed in that Nashville middle school is how utterly different the perception of her—the very same her, with the same intelligence, accent, and ability to string words together in coherent sentences—would have been, and indeed *had* been in her native country. In Rhodesia, from which place she had just recently departed, she would have been seen as inferior, no matter her genius. She would have been a second-class citizen, her opportunities constrained, all because of color. But in America, she could be viewed as exotic, as different, as capable. She could be contrasted with local black folks who were perceived as less capable, as aggressive, as uninterested in education, as inferior.

Many years later I would realize the process at work here—the way that foreign-born blacks are often played off against native-born African Americans in a way that has everything to do with racism and white supremacy. Reading a story in my local paper about a white church in town that had been working with Sudanese refugees to help them find jobs, child care, and various social services, I was struck by one of the statements made by the church's pastor. When asked why the church had gone to such lengths to help African migrants, but had never done similar outreach with local black families in need of the same opportunities, the pastor noted that in some ways it was probably because the Africans were so *grateful* to be here. They had chosen to come, after all. They had wanted to be *like us*, like Americans. Native-born black

folks on the other hand had made no such choice, and they regularly contested the dominant narrative about what America means and
has long meant. African Americans, in other words, were pushy and
demanding, and felt entitled (imagine that) to the fruits of their prodi-
gious labors throughout the generations. But African immigrants were
joiners, wanting nothing more than the opportunity to partake in the
American dream. They serve as validation for the greatness of the country; they give the lie to the notion that the U.S. is a place where racism
still exists. After all, were it so, why would any of them move here? That
Irish and Italian and Jewish migrants had long before come to America,
despite the prejudices they knew they might well face in their adopted
countries—in other words, they had come for economic opportunity,
racial and ethnic bias notwithstanding, much as Africans sometimes do
now—seems to escape us.

   That one place may be preferable to another in terms of opportunity
says little about whether that first place is as equitable as it should be.
But for many white Americans, like those teachers at Stokes, the presence of someone like Rudo confirmed everything they needed to believe
about their nation. She was like a soothing balm, allowing them not
only to push away concerns about institutional racism, but also to avoid
confronting their own biases, which played out against the other black
students in their classes every day.

MIDDLE PASSAGE

1980 WAS A horrible year for a lot of reasons, only one of which had to do with the election of Ronald Reagan that November—itself a cause for sincere political mourning in the Wise home.

Only twelve days into the year, my mom's father died at the relatively young age of sixty five, ending a life that had been of miserable quality for the past half-decade thanks to several strokes that had rendered him unable to care for himself. A few months later, one of my dad's old theatre colleagues died on stage, the victim of a massive heart attack. The next month, another family friend was killed in a car accident, and one of my classmates, Roger Zimmerman, was killed when a drunk driver plowed into him while Roger had been riding his bike.

And then there was life with my father. In May, dad and I started working on a few scenes from the play "A Thousand Clowns," which we would perform during my school's spring theatre showcase. Ultimately the show went well, but he had shown up to dress rehearsal so blind-running drunk that I had a complete emotional breakdown on stage. Even as I glared at him through a literal cascade of tears, he failed to comprehend the meaning behind the melancholy, incoherently mumbling something about how brilliant I was for being able to make myself cry, just like the character in the scene was supposed to. I guess he also thought my silent seething on the ride home was just a matter of staying in character, rather than what it really had been: the expression of profound embarrassment that he had exposed his illness for so many of my friends to see. Needless to say, as sixth grade came to a close, the combination of my tenuous connection to my father, my parents' combative relationship, and all the deaths in our little corner of the universe had left me far more exhausted than any eleven-year-old should be.

Summer made things a bit better. Although my baseball team had muddled through another miserable year, I had enjoyed a fantastic season individually, making the city's all-star team. My dad had been out of town for much of the summer, doing a play in Atlanta, which meant not only that he wouldn't be showing up to my games loaded (as he had for much of the previous season), but that evenings at home with my mom would be blessedly quiet. We would get together on many of those evenings to watch old Alfred Hitchcock movies, or *Twilight Zone* reruns, the latter of which were among my favorite things to watch on TV.

By July, baseball season was over (this was long before the days of traveling teams and forty-game summer schedules), and I was enjoying doing nothing. I'd sleep in late, go swimming in the apartment's pool most of the day, and then spend the rest of my time reading, adding to my baseball card collection, or hanging out at the local game room, trying to master Pac-Man, which had been released just two months earlier.

There were exactly eight weeks left before the start of Junior High School, that morning of July 6, when I was woken by the sound of my mother opening the apartment door to retrieve the Sunday paper from the hallway. Though I'd heard the door open, I tried not to wake up, preferring to linger in bed a while. I closed my eyes, hoping to fall back asleep, only to be shaken a minute later by my mother's cry.

"Oh no," was all she said.

I instantly knew that whatever was wrong had something to do with the newspaper she had just opened, and that whatever it was didn't concern national politics or the Iran hostage crisis, which was in its ninth month. I scrambled out of bed and opened my door, afraid to learn what had happened, but curious. When I got to the living room I saw my mother crying. She turned away, hardly able to look at me.

"What happened?" I asked, as my stomach tightened, clenching around an abdominal hernia I'd had since infancy. My heart was pounding so hard that I could feel its beat, throbbing throughout my body. Before she could answer, a ringing sensation began in my ears, as if my body was somehow trying to prevent me from hearing the reply to my question.

She looked up, her eyes welling with tears, and delivered the news. "Bobby Bell is dead."

I heard her but somehow the words failed to register. It simply made no sense that Bobby, with whom I'd been friends since preschool at TSU, could be dead. It wasn't conceivable that Bobby, the twelve-year-old who had coined that word, "douche 'n' push," to describe the middle school theatre teacher's car, could be gone.

Bobby was one of the people I'd liked best all through school. We'd become close friends by fourth grade, and by sixth we were constantly to be found in class, the halls, or the lunchroom playing "pencil break" or "thump," the latter of which was a typically absurd boy game, in which you'd coil back your middle finger in the crook of your hand and then flick it forward into your opponent's clenched fist over and again until one player conceded the match due to pain. Bobby had these wonderfully fat knuckles, which made an almost drum-like noise when you'd thump them. And while the fleshiness of his hand probably provided extra protection to him, it also protected the thumper, since hitting a bony knuckle by accident when aiming instead for the meat below could be painful. How could this child, my thump rival, be dead?

In fact I was so sure it wasn't the same Bobby that I immediately asked about another Bobby Bell we knew, who was a few years older than me, and a local Little League legend.

"You mean Fruit?" I asked, that being the nickname of the other Bobby Bell.

"No Tim, Bobby, *your* Bobby," she said.

"How?" was all I could think to ask, still completely unwilling to get my head around the loss. The answer would be even harder to accept.

"He was killed last night at his dad's store. Somebody shot him," she explained.

And that's when I knew it was real. It made sense, however horrifying. Bobby often helped his dad at one or the other of his father's stores: convenience markets that also sold some of the most incredible barbecue in town. Bob Bell's Market on Twelfth Avenue had not been held up even once in the eight previous years since its opening. Not once. But on that muggy July evening in 1980, part of the busy Fourth of July weekend, it would be. And although Bobby had done everything the robber had asked—stuffing money in a bag quickly even as he cried the frightened tears that any child would shed, looking down the barrel of a gun poised mere feet from his face—he was shot in the head anyway, at point blank range, and died in front of his father. As he fled the store, the shooter, Cecil Johnson—later identified by Bob Sr. and other witnesses—shot and killed two other men in a taxi outside.

Angry and confused I spun around and shoved my fist into the wall. Luckily, right before my hand met plaster I had started to ease up on the punch so that when contact was finally made it wouldn't hurt so much. I was so numb that I couldn't cry, and I would stay that way for days, weeks, months, even years. In fact the first time I think I ever really let myself cry about Bobby wasn't until five years later, when I would talk about what had happened during a speech class, in which the assignment would be to discuss something emotionally painful that we had experienced growing up.

Both Bobby and his killer were black, the former the victim of, and the latter a practitioner of, a kind of racial self-hatred that has sadly claimed the lives of far too many African Americans over the years. Only someone who had long since given up on the notion of brotherhood could do something like this. Only someone who had long since concluded that human life was disposable—in this case black human life much like his own—could think to fire a .45 caliber weapon at a child while his father watched, all for two hundred dollars and some change. And in turn, the state of Tennessee (represented by D.A. Thomas Shriver, whose daughter Susan was a classmate of ours) would return the favor, seeking and obtaining a death sentence for Cecil Johnson, a rare occurrence when the racial identity of both perpetrator and victim is black. Studies have long found that death sentences are far more likely when whites are killed, especially by blacks. And in Davidson County, no death sentence had been obtained between 1976, when the Supreme Court reinstated the constitutionality of capital punishment, and the time of Cecil Johnson's trial. But in this case, the death of such a caring and loving child, helping his dad from whom he had been inseparable, was enough to justify, in the eyes of the jury, ending the life of Cecil Johnson.

I cared deeply for Bobby, and was grieved by his death. So too, I understood why his father so steadfastly supported a death sentence for the man who had taken his only son from him right in front of his eyes. But even then, at the age of eleven, I never wanted Cecil Johnson to die. And even now, though I would want to kill, personally, anyone who murdered one of my children, I steadfastly believe that no matter how much a person may deserve to die, the bigger question is whether the state deserves to kill. And that calculation—given the inherent class and racial biases embedded in the justice system—is considerably trickier than a simple consideration of what a murderer has earned for him or herself.

On December 2, 2009, nearly thirty years after Cecil Johnson murdered three people, including my friend, the state of Tennessee intravenously delivered to him a lethal cocktail of drugs, ending his life, and bringing to a close this chapter in mine. The night of Johnson's execution, as I thought about the waste of four lives—Bobby's, the other two victims, James Moore and Charles House, and his own—I couldn't help but wonder what kind of a society we are that so readily inculcates the notion of human disposability, whether in individuals who commit such senseless crimes, or in the body politic, which believes against all evidence to the contrary, that by ratifying that same mentality, it will somehow render its citizens safer.

*　*　*

JUNIOR HIGH WAS hell. To begin with, it looked like an industrial building where a call center might be housed: one level, bland office park architecture, and hardly any windows. It was (and still is) just one big brick structure, capable of squeezing all the joy out of the educational process by virtue of its physical plant alone. Though internally it had been constructed as an experimental, even progressive attempt at "open classroom" learning—no walls between classrooms, the idea being that teachers would co-teach in learning pods, linking, say, a literature lesson with a history lesson, and then with a geography lesson—none of the teachers at John Trotwood Moore made use of the open classroom approach. They didn't seem to believe in it, so the internal architecture of the building, which could have been liberatory in the hands of the right teachers, became little more than a wall-less, open arena for noise.

Adding to the absurdity of the school, Moore was part of a larger campus, which included a Metro Nashville Parks and Recreation facility. This meant adults had access to the campus grounds at all times of the day, even when the kids were in session—a strange arrangement that led Moore to be considered one of the easiest places to buy drugs in the city. A national news program had actually done a feature on drug availability at Moore a few years after its opening, contrasting its iniquitous activities with the otherwise bucolic, upscale neighborhood in which it was located. After all (though I don't think the news special had mentioned this), the parents of squeaky-clean crooner Pat Boone (and grandparents of Debbie Boone, whose song "You Light Up My Life" would become the biggest hit of the 1970s) lived right across the street from the school. Whites had been shocked (and I'm sure the Boones were) to learn that there were drugs in their communities too, let alone that those who were selling them from their neighborhood school (and buying them) were mostly white like themselves.

On the first day of seventh grade, as we were trying to acclimate to the new surroundings of junior high, I noticed my old friend Bobby Orr headed my way. I hadn't seen Bobby since the end of baseball season (we played on the same team), and so I greeted him with a hearty, "What's up?"

I got no reply.

Thinking that he hadn't heard me, I repeated myself. "What's up?" I inquired.

This time he looked my way, and his words, spoken forcefully, stung.

"Hey man, ya' know I don't speak to white people anymore."

"What?" I replied, not understanding why Bobby might have said something like this to me.

He could tell I was hurt, and being a nice guy and a friend, he backed off his previous proclamation of racial separatism.

"You know I'm just kidding!" he said, laughing a bit.

"Oh, okay," I replied, frankly not sure if he *was* kidding, and thrown for a loop by this ad hoc discussion of race in what had started as a fairly simple greeting at the beginning of the school year.

As it turned out, that exchange would serve as a bit of a metaphor for the next two years at Moore. The school was so divided racially— with whites, regardless of intelligence, being placed overwhelmingly in advanced classes, and folks of color, regardless of theirs, overwhelmingly in the standard classes—that it's only a slight exaggeration to say that most days, we white kids would hardly see any black students. Perhaps a few in a class here and there, but for the most part, only in the halls between classes, or in the lunchroom. This, in a school that was about one-third African American.

For most white students this separation wouldn't probably have struck them as all that big a deal, but for me it was like social death. Most of my friends in those first six years of school had been African American kids, and with the exception of Albert and two other friends, Zach Vietze and Rob Laird (the latter of whom went to a different school), I wasn't really close to any white people. I was having to relearn everything: how to make friends, how to interact with people whose interests were different, and how to basically be white again. At first I probably blamed Bobby and other black students for pulling away from me, but that feeling wouldn't last long, since it was obvious that the institution was doing the dividing, not the black kids, or the white kids for that matter.

Years later I would understand the context of Bobby's words to me that first day, after traveling across the country and speaking with hundreds of people who'd had similar experiences: whites and blacks, typically, who had been close right up until about that same age, and then suddenly the students of color began pulling away, cleaving to themselves. In almost each story, the white person had been confused about why it had happened, but the people of color never were. It hadn't been personal, they would insist, as indeed it hadn't been for Bobby. It was just business; in this case the business of self-protection, and the business of developing a secure identity as a black person in a society built on whiteness. Our experiences had been so different, our treatment so disparate, that by junior high, we just didn't have much in common anymore. The institution had accomplished what we alone never would have. It had forced us into our racial slots, whether we liked it or not. And Bobby, like the other black kids, knew where his slot was, far before I would realize mine.

*   *   *

WITHIN MONTHS OF beginning school that year, even as I tried to carve out some time with my black friends down at the Metro Park Board, shooting hoops or playing ping-pong or pool, it was obvious that we were drifting in different directions. Still unclear at the time as to what was happening and why, it sent me into an emotional tailspin for the better part of the year. My grades suffered miserably, I failed a class for the first time, and generally, I had no appetite for school any more. My dad thought I was on drugs, which probably made sense to him because *he* was on drugs, but I wasn't. I was just lost.

I wasn't really sure how to be white, but I figured I could fake it. The music I listened to changed almost overnight, or at least I would claim that it had. When people would ask me what kind of music I liked, I felt compelled to lie, to say things like Foreigner, and Journey, and Cheap Trick, even though I hated the first, could only stomach two songs by the second, and knew nothing about the third. Albert was a huge Billy Joel fanatic but I couldn't abide him either, so when Al would rave about "Piano Man," or even occasionally break into the song himself, I would just roll my eyes. Alan Green and David Harvard tried to turn everyone on to various music—Alan had one of the most extensive record collections you'd ever want to see, while David seemed to wear a different concert T-shirt every day from the latest heavy metal show he'd been to—but I wasn't into any of that either. I was over KISS by then and as for hip hop, I got the impression that I wasn't supposed to like it. It wasn't what the other white kids were listening to, so I figured I should get with the program. In fact, for most of seventh and eighth grade, I think I just stopped listening to music altogether.

Adding to the general awfulness of junior high, Moore was the school where all the white teachers who had tenure and had steadfastly refused assignment in the blacker schools before busing, had insisted they be placed after it. By the time my class would get there, it was filled with a gaggle of right-wing teachers unlike any public school I've seen since. Though a taxpayer-supported institution, John Trotwood Moore's faculty and administration might as well have been culled from a directory of some evangelical Christian ministry. There was the teacher who told Albert that his father (a devout Christian and church deacon) was likely a communist for taking him to see the critically-acclaimed movie

Reds, in 1981, and another who penalized me on an eighth grade term paper concerning the subject of school prayer, for ostensibly blaspheming God. Why? Because I had titled the paper, "Our Father Who Art in Homeroom," which I thought (and still think) was pretty damned clever.

The only exceptions to the right-wing rule at Moore were the two black teachers I had while there, who were the only teachers in the school from whom I ever learned anything valuable: Milton Kennerly and Barbara Thornton. Mr. Kennerly, my geography teacher, made a lasting impression on me when explaining that Western concepts of "civilization" were subjective, and that the term should not be used when referring to the U.S. or the industrialized world, especially not in relation to non-Western societies who have their own social and cultural understandings of what a good society should look like. We use the word "civilization" to mean "materially wealthy" and technologically advanced, even though material wealth and technology are often used for uncivilized, unethical ends, he explained. It is the only lesson from junior high that I remember.

* * *

I WAS MISERABLE all throughout my two years at Moore, but never so much as the day we were corralled into the auditorium so as to listen to the personal testimony of some twenty-something fundamentalist Christian, who had been brought in to encourage us all to join Young Life, a Christian youth group. As one of seven or eight Jews in the school, I sat utterly amazed that we were being required to attend this modern-day equivalent of a tent revival. I looked around the auditorium, hoping to lock eyes with any of the other Jewish kids, wondering what they were thinking, but had no luck. Finally, after about ten minutes of the presentation, I could stand no more. I stood up and walked out of the assembly. A few seconds after exiting the auditorium, and not really knowing where I intended to go, I was met in the hallway by the principal, Paul Hood.

"Where do you think you're going," Mr. Hood asked, clearly agitated by my having exited the pep rally for Jesus that he'd thrown together, with little or no regard for such niceties as the Constitution.

Thinking as quickly as I could, I offered the only answer I could conjure on such short notice. "I'm going to call my lawyer," was my reply, offered confidently and without hesitation.

"You're twelve. You don't have a lawyer," Mr. Hood replied, calling my bluff.

"No, but my parents do," I responded, not really knowing if this were true, "and it's illegal for you to make us listen to that guy."

Mr. Hood stood like a deer in headlights in the hallway of the school over which he ostensibly had control. Frankly, I'd been scared to death to challenge his authority that way, but had done it because I knew my parents would back me up if I didn't get satisfaction—in this case, an apology and a promise not to let it happen again. And I knew I'd have their support because they had made certain things clear to me from the beginning of my school experience. As I stood there facing down the principal, I flashed back to my very first day of first grade—the day I'd been given the encouragement to do exactly what I was doing that afternoon at Moore.

On Tuesday, September 3, 1974, I had begun as a first grader at Burton Elementary, sent off to school with some very clear admonitions from my father. Rather than the traditional, "Be polite to your teachers," or "Have a great day," I was given two simple instructions: first, that I was to let no one spank me (corporal punishment still being quite legal all across the South at that time, and even now); and second, that I was to allow no one to make me pray—something that, despite Supreme Court precedent outlawing the practice for twelve years by that point, was still occasionally tried in public schools throughout the area. It's hard to put into words the degree of entitlement that comes from knowing *even at the age of five* that your parents have your back, and that if some authority figure gets out of line, your mom and dad will support *you*. But that is what I was told, before I was told anything else about this thing called school. My parents were letting me know that injustice happens, and that they wouldn't stand for it. And that I shouldn't either.

So standing in front of Mr. Hood, I felt powerful. And while I would like to take credit for the bravery that animated me in that instance, it was white privilege that made the difference, far more so than some inherent courage on my part. After all, how many kids of color would have felt empowered enough to stand up to the school administration to protest the academic tracking that was relegating most of them to lower academic tracks than their white counterparts? How many would have felt empowered enough to stand up to the unequal discipline being meted out to students of color, relative to whites, even when rates of rule infractions were indistinguishable between the various racial groups? Likely not many.

In a very real sense, white racial privilege had empowered me to stand up for myself and for social justice more broadly. Knowing that my parents would go to bat for me had meant everything. But the fact that they would have done so had nothing to do with their love for me (which love was surely rivaled by that of the parents of the black kids with whom I went to school). Rather, it was predicated on the privilege that allowed even a lower-income white kid like myself to feel certain enough about my rights so as to challenge those who would abuse them. Yes, the story had been about institutional Christian hegemony and the marginalization of me as a Jew. But it was equally about the way that even Jews, with our historically inconsistent and situationally-contingent whiteness, can still access the powers of our skin in ways that make a difference.

*   *   *

INTERESTINGLY, MY IDENTITY as a Jew had never really been something about which I'd thought until Moore. Around that time, in addition to the institutionalized Christianity that coursed through my school, there was also the day in May 1981, when a group of neo-Nazis and Klan members were arrested as they drove on to the grounds of the Temple with what they thought was a working bomb. They had intended to detonate it and blow up my house of worship in the process, only to discover that the device was a fake, planted by one of their number who was an FBI informant. Good times.

I was growing up in a mixed-faith home, in which my mom was a Christian, and my dad, though Jewish, was largely uninvolved in my religious upbringing. I would be sent off to Temple each Sunday (or Saturday, beginning in eighth grade), where the Rabbi would teach me what it meant to be Jewish; and if not the Rabbi, surely one of the several classroom teachers in the Hebrew school could accomplish it.

But I guess I wasn't a very good student, because I never learned much. I learned vaguely about Jewish perspectives on various social issues of the day, but it seemed as though most of the lessons were about victimization: the Holocaust of European Jewry, or mistreatment at the hands of the Egyptian Pharaohs. Besides that I can't recall much, except being constantly hit up for Tzedakah money by the school director, so as to help plant trees in Israel. Tzedakah is a Hebrew word often translated as charity, though actually it's meant to refer to justice. It's somewhat similar to tithing by Christians, although I've never heard of Catholic churches guilt-tripping eight-year-olds into coughing up a percentage of their allowances so as to plant trees in Vatican City. Not to mention, since those trees were likely being planted on land confiscated from Palestinians (whether in 1948 or 1967), Tzedakah money for such a purpose would likely run directly counter to the cause of justice. But as a kid, I would have known nothing of that.

I also remember being berated and bullied by the Hebrew teacher, who was fresh from her last job with the Israeli Defense Force. I simply could not learn the language, nor did I understand the importance of doing so. Even then it struck me as odd that Jews would be trying to recapture the language of the Torah for everyday use (as in Israel), when frankly, Yiddish had served most of our ancestors just fine for centuries, and before that Aramaic, following the Babylonian exile. Later, of course, I would learn that to many in the Zionist movement, Yiddish was a shameful peasant language, associated with the diaspora, and so it was to be spurned in favor of the language of King David. If we reclaimed the ancient language we could reclaim the ancient greatness, the ancient power, never to be oppressed again (or so the story went). The modern Hebrew movement, was, in a real sense born of a deep shame at having been so mightily oppressed throughout Christian Europe and exiled from our ancient homeland. At some level, the reclaiming of Hebrew and the post-*shoah* cry of "never again" both seemed as much internally-directed self-affirmations as outwardly-pointed warnings to the rest of the world.

I got along with virtually no one at Temple. Most of the kids there went to private school, and their dads were doctors, or attorneys, or professors, or businessmen. Most all of their parents had college degrees.

And while I played ball at the Y with my black friends, they played at the Jewish Community Center, surrounded by other Jews. It seemed a very cloistered environment, very clubby, and I couldn't stand it. The few kids there who I went to school with were okay, but I wasn't really close to any of them.

It took me years to figure out why I'd been so miserable at Temple, why I never felt as though I fit in. Though I wouldn't have known it at the time—nor even the meaning of the word to describe the problem—in retrospect I can see that it was principally the classism of it all. While there are far more working class and even poor Jews in the United States than most people realize—estimates place the latter number at around fifteen percent, or about one in seven American Jews—in places like Nashville, lower-income Jews are almost completely invisible. While working class Jewish communities and neighborhoods are common in larger cities like New York, in places with much smaller Jewish communities, economically marginal Jews are pretty much out of sight, out of mind. They can't afford the cost of Temple or Synagogue, or even if they can, they can't swing the additional expense of participating in the civic events put together by the Jewish Federation. So, absent the financial resources to make themselves people worth knowing, they are effectively excluded from Jewish life.

As one of the few Jews at Temple in those days from a lower-income, non-professional family, I struggled constantly with the nature of my Jewishness, as I think my father did. I'm certain that the reason he rarely ever set foot in the Temple, typically coming only for services on High Holy days, was that compared to all these other families, ours seemed a relative failure. The internalized oppression—a concept about which I would learn many years later as it relates to people of color victimized by racism—was, in this instance, finding a home in me as well. It was bad enough to be economically struggling when you were white, and expected to succeed. But to be white *and* Jewish, and still be struggling was a double-whammy. What was wrong with us, with me? Much like the Asian kid who isn't good at math or science and thereby finds him or herself coming up short in relation to the Asian archetype constructed largely by non-Asians, so too was I seeming to fail in relation to the archetype of acceptable Jewishness: good with money, successful, hard-working.

To be the broke Jew was to grapple with self-doubt as a matter of weekly routine. It was to fail to fit in within your own community, even as the other community—the gentile community—was reminding you, in any number of ways, that you weren't one of theirs either. My Jewishness wobbly at best, I would more or less abandon it in any formal sense after my freshman year of high school, right after Rabbi Falk (who had been something of a civil rights legend in Nashville) threatened to fail me in Hebrew school if I didn't attend at least seven Friday night services per school semester. Though I tried to explain to him that I couldn't attend that many Friday services—weekends were when I went out of town for debate tournaments, and debate was going to be my ticket to college, not being a Jew—he persisted in his threats. Having been taught not to sit idly by and suffer fools gladly, nor the petty injustices often meted out by said fools, I did the most Jewish thing I could think to do in that situation: I staged a walk-out, telling him I was done—with him and Temple, roughly in that order.

* * *

I COULDN'T WAIT for the first day of high school. To be done with John Trotwood Moore would make Hillsboro seem like heaven, no matter how much more inviting it actually proved to be. Yes, as a freshman I'd be on the bottom rung of the ladder, but I didn't care. There would be new people to meet, new activities in which to get involved, and since it had been the school to which both my parents had gone (and from which my dad had graduated), I felt like I belonged there. It was almost as if I could claim some ownership over the space, if only because a mere seventeen or eighteen years earlier my mom and dad had walked those halls, and some of their old teachers were still there.

Hillsboro was a "comprehensive" high school, which is just fancy talk for a school that viciously tracks its students, some into a college-prep track and others into a vocational track. I'll leave it up to the reader's imagination to guess the racial and class demographic of each in turn. Of course, the teachers there (as with most places) would deny to the death that there was anything the least bit racist about this arrangement, or their own disparate treatment of the students. Rather, they would have said (as teachers most everywhere do) that they "treat all kids the same and don't see color."

Putting aside the absurdity of the claim—studies indicate that we tend to make very fine distinctions based on color, and that we notice color differences almost immediately—the fact is, colorblindness is not the proper goal of fair-minded educators. The kids in those classrooms *do* have a race, and it matters, because it says a lot about the kinds of challenges they are likely to face. To not see color is, as Julian Bond has noted, to not see the *consequences* of color. And if color has consequences, yet you've resolved not to notice the thing that brings about those consequences, the odds are pretty good that you'll fail to serve the needs of the students in question.

To not see people for who they are is to miss that some but not all students are dealing with racism. It is to privilege the norm, which is white, by assuming that "kids are kids," and then treating the kids the way you'd treat your own. But with more than eight in ten teachers in the United States being white, the children in the care of teachers for eight hours a day often look very different from the kids to whom those teachers go home at night. To treat everyone the same is to miss the fact that children of color have all the same challenges white kids do, and then that one extra thing to deal with: racism. But if you've told yourself you are not to see race, you'll be unlikely to notice discrimination based on race, let alone know how to respond to it.

The consequences of artificial color-blindness would become apparent at Hillsboro a few years later, in my senior year, when we had a small scale race riot involving about three-dozen students—not white against black, but white and black on one side, against Southeast Asian students on the other, most of whom had come to America after 1975, in the wake of the Vietnam War. Had you asked teachers or the administration if there were racial problems at Hillsboro at the beginning of that year, they would have assured you there were not. They would have pointed to the generally positive relationships between people of different races and downplayed or ignored the extreme isolation of the Southeast Asian students, much to the detriment of the institution, as we would later learn when we had to have cops in the halls for three days, just to restore calm.

Having never been asked to think about how we viewed the newcomers among us (often quite negatively), or to consider how misunderstandings often flared because of language and cultural barriers, the school shut its eyes and pretended everything was fine. By stifling any discussion of racial and cultural bias—and certainly never expecting the rest of us to learn about Thai, Lao, Vietnamese, and Hmong cultures and interrogate our prejudices—Hillsboro's colorblindness created the conditions that gave rise to that riot.

But I'm getting ahead of myself here. So let's back up.

* * *

ALTHOUGH I STILL loved theatre, I didn't really want to do plays in high school. That had been my father's thing at Hillsboro, so there were any number of reasons why I figured I'd best go in a different direction.

Instead of getting involved with the Drama Club, I chose Forensics. When someone first mentioned it to me, I had no idea what they were talking about. The only time I'd heard that word was with regard to forensic science, as part of the introduction to the TV show *Quincy*, which my mom and I loved to watch. Not wanting to cut up cadavers or investigate crime scenes, I had said no thanks. Once I learned that this kind of forensics referred to speech competitions, I decided to take a look.

Though I would ultimately settle on debate as my principal activity, I hadn't thought that would be the case at first. Rather, Albert and I began doing *Inherit the Wind* as a dramatic interpretation piece at local and regional forensics competitions, winning several and placing at the others. Although I had also been signed up at my first forensics tournament to do "Extemporaneous Speaking"—which involved drawing a topic from a hat and then having thirty minutes to put together a six minute speech on whatever subject you'd drawn—I found the prospect terrifying. After drawing my topic, I totally freaked out, leaving the library after ten minutes of preparation, and walking around the building until well past my time to make my presentation. Thankfully, my coach made me go back in for the second and third rounds, and I've been speaking ever since.

Debate would become for me in high school what theatre had been in middle school: a place to put my energy and also an escape from the craziness that was my home life. The idea of throwing myself into an activity that allowed me to travel, to get away from home at least two weekends a month, was more than a little appealing. I was sure by now that my father was not going to kill my mother, so I didn't fear leaving them alone, and mostly I just needed a break from the fighting and the drinking.

There have always been debaters of color, and indeed, my high school's top debater when I arrived was a black senior, James Bernard. James, who would attend Harvard Law with Barack Obama several years later—and would be one of the founders and first publishers of the hip-hop magazine *The Source*—taught me a lot about debate as well as activism, the latter in his capacity as one of the key players in the Nashville Youth Network: a loosely-knit coalition of teens energized around a number of issues of relevance to young people at the time. But despite James's debate prowess, the activity was, and still is, extraordinarily white, not merely in terms of its demographic, but also in terms of its style, its form, and its content at the most competitive levels. Debate literally exudes whiteness and privileges white participants in a number of ways.

On the one hand, there is the issue of money. Debaters, in order to be nationally competitive, require funding: either a school with a huge budget to pay for trips to national tournaments, or families that can swing the cost of sending their kids away for three days at a time, often by plane, for the purpose of competing. I had neither, but between what minor help my parents could offer and the money I made working twenty hours a week sacking groceries at a local market, we managed to make it work.

Then there are the summer debate camps, which even in the 1980s cost about fifteen hundred dollars, and which run for three to four weeks. Those who can afford to go to these get a huge jump on the competition. In fact, I don't know of any nationally competitive team whose members didn't attend at least one camp during the previous summer. During the summer before my junior year, my family was unable to afford to send me to a debate institute, and being unable to go set me back considerably, in terms of my own skills, for several months at the beginning of the tournament season. It took me most of the first semester to catch up to the other national-circuit debaters who had been at the camps learning technique and the year's topic backwards and forwards, all with the assistance of college coaches and top-notch research facilities.

Obviously, given the interplay of race and socioeconomic status in this country, blacks, Latinos, American Indians, and Southeast Asians (all of which groups have much higher poverty rates than whites) are woefully underrepresented in the activity, relative to their numbers in the student population. But the cost of debate is hardly the only thing that causes the activity to be so white. The substance of the arguments made and the way in which the arguments are delivered also tend to appeal to whites far more readily than to people of color for whom the style and substance are often too removed from the real world to be of much practical value.

Those who haven't seen a competitive debate (particularly in the most dominant category, known as policy debate) may be inclined to think that such a thing is a deep discussion of some pressing issue. But if that is what you expected, and you then happened into a debate at one of the nation's top tournaments and watched any of the elimination rounds (those involving the top sixteen or thirty-two teams, typically), you would think you had walked into a world of make-believe. Even if you could understand a single word being said, which is unlikely since the "best" debaters typically speak at lightning speed (and I was among the biggest offenders here, able to rattle off five hundred words a minute), you still wouldn't really understand what was going on. The terminology is arcane and only of use in the activity itself—terms like *topicality, counterplan, permutation, infinite regression,* and *kritik.*

The purpose of competitive debate is essentially to speak faster than your opponents so they will "drop" one of your arguments, which you will then insist to the judge is the most important issue in the round, warranting an immediate ballot in your favor. Just as critical, debaters are to make sure that whatever the topic, their arguments for or against a particular policy must be linked to nuclear war or ecological catastrophe, no matter how absurd the linkage. So, for example, you might claim that your opponent's plan to extend the retirement age will contribute to global warming by keeping people in the workforce longer, thereby increasing consumption levels, thereby increasing energy expenditure, thereby speeding up climate change and the ultimate end of the world.

Though one can theoretically learn quite a bit from debate, especially during the research phase of the operation, the fact remains that superficiality, speed and mass extinction scenarios typically take the place of nuanced policy analysis, such that one has to wonder how much the debaters really come to know about the issues they debate at the end of the day. Learning is always secondary to winning, and for the sake of winning, debaters will say virtually anything.

My own debate experience serves as vulgar confirmation of this maxim. On the one hand, I ran cases (which in debate terms means the primary position taken by the affirmative team upholding the year's formal resolution) calling for cutting off weapons sales to Venezuela, and also for the restoration of voting rights to ex-felons: positions with which I agreed. On the other hand, I also ran cases calling for a program that would employ all poor folks who were out of work to build a missile defense system (possibly the most ridiculous idea ever advocated in a debate round), and for reinforcing the nation's water reservoirs against poisoning by terrorists. Although the idea of protecting soft targets from terrorism might make sense, the evidence we used to make our case was almost exclusively from the most disgusting of anti-Muslim, right-wing sources (and this was in 1985 and 1986 mind you, long before 9/11). I am still taking extra baths to wash off the ideological stench of having read evidence in debate rounds from people like Michael Ledeen or Daniel Pipes (the latter of whom would, several years later, post highly critical comments about me on his website, so I guess the feeling is mutual).

When we were on the negative side, I would argue, among other things, that poverty should be allowed to continue because it would eventually trigger a glorious socialist revolution (which isn't even good Marxist theory, let alone a morally acceptable position), or that civil liberties should be eradicated so the United States could transition to a society in which resource use was limited by force, family size was strictly controlled, and thus planetary destruction averted. These kinds of arguments, it should be noted, were hardly mine alone: they were absolutely typical on the national debate circuit, and they still are.

The reason I call this process a white one is because whites (and especially affluent ones), much more so than folks of color, have the luxury of looking at life or death issues of war, peace, famine, unemployment, or criminal justice as a game, as a mere exercise in intellectual and rhetorical banter. For me to get up and debate, for example, whether or not full employment is a good idea presupposes that my folks are not likely out of work as I go about the task. To debate whether racial profiling is legitimate likewise presupposes that I, the debater, am not likely to be someone who was confronted by the practice as my team drove to the tournament that day, or as we passed through security at the airport. In this way, competitive debate reinforces whiteness and affluence as normative conditions, and makes the process more attractive to affluent white students. Kids of color and working-class youth of all colors are simply not as likely to gravitate to an activity where pretty much half the time they'll be forced to take positions that, if implemented in the real world, might devastate their communities.

Because debaters are encouraged to think about life or death matters as if they had little consequence beyond a given debate round, the fact that those who have come through the activity go on to hold a disproportionate share of powerful political and legal positions—something about which the National Forensics League has long bragged—is a matter that should concern us all. Being primed to think of serious issues as abstractions increases the risk that the person who has been so primed will reduce everything to a brutal cost-benefit analysis, which rarely prioritizes the needs and interests of society's less powerful. Rather, it becomes easier at that point to support policies that benefit the haves at the expense of the have-nots, because others whom the ex-debaters never met and never had to take seriously will be the ones to feel the damage.

Unless debate is fundamentally transformed—and at this point the only forces for real change are the squads from Urban Debate Leagues and a few college squads of color who are clamoring for different styles of argumentation and different evidentiary standards—it will continue to serve as a staging ground for those whose interests are mostly the interests of the powerful. Until the voices of economically and racially marginalized persons are given equal weight in debate rounds with those of affluent white experts (whose expertise is only presumed because other whites published what they had to say in the first place), the ideas that shape our world will continue to be those of the elite, no matter how destructive these ideas have proven to be for the vast majority of the planet's inhabitants.

Privilege makes its recipients oblivious to certain things, and debate, as an activity, is one of its many transmission belts—one that I was able to access, to great effect, in my life. Lucky for me that I went to a school that offered it, that I had parents who somehow managed to help me afford it, and that its game-playing format wasn't yet a problem for me, ethically speaking. Lucky for me, in other words, that I was white.

* * *

DEBATE WASN'T THE only arena for white privilege in high school. There was also the entirely Eurocentric curricula, the ability to get away with cheating, or even skipping school in ways no student of color could likely have done, and of course, there was partying.

I can't even remember, because there are simply too many to recall, the number of parties I attended in high school at which hundreds of underage kids, including myself, were drinking and taking various types of drugs. These were parties with up to five kegs of beer, where guys were taking cover charges at the end of the driveway and stamping people's hands, right on the road, in plain view of everyone, including the police cars that would occasionally cruise by to make sure the noise wasn't getting too loud. On more than a few occasions the cops would even come onto the property in response to a noise complaint, and tell us to cut the music down. There is simply no chance that the officers didn't know alcohol was being served; likewise, they had to have been able to detect the smell of marijuana in the air. Yet not once did they arrest anyone, or even tell us to get rid of the booze and the weed, so as to warn us that next time we wouldn't be so lucky. Indeed, next time we *would* be that lucky, and the next time, and the next time, and the time after that, always.

These parties were at the homes of white people, surrounded by other homes lived in by white people, and attended almost exclusively by white people. There would always be a few people of color around, but for the most part, these were white spaces, which immediately gave law enforcement officials reason to cut us slack. Had these house parties been in black neighborhoods they would never have been allowed to go on at all, as large as they were, even without a single illegal substance on the premises. But for whites, in white neighborhoods, everything was different. Our illegality was looked at with a wink and a nod.

Criminal activity was also regularly overlooked on the debate circuit. When debaters at Nashville's prestigious boy's prep school, Montgomery Bell Academy (MBA), were caught destroying law journals at Vanderbilt University's law school in 1984, by using razor blades to cut out important evidence rather than take the time or spend the money to make Xerox copies, they faced no criminal penalties. Their parents probably repaid Vanderbilt for the damage, or perhaps MBA paid the bill, just to keep the activities of their elite team quiet. But whatever the case, no one ended up with a record, and MBA as an institution meted out no collective punishment either: no grounding their teams from competition for the year, no public *mea culpa*. With the exception of those of us in the Nashville area who knew the MBA debaters and considered some of them friends, most folks on the national circuit probably knew little of what had happened. Needless to say, if an urban team made up of black or Latino kids went into the library of their local college and defaced private property, things would go a bit differently.

When it came to drugs, the debate circuit was probably the best place to score. So everyone could identify the noise when the briefcase of one of MBA's top debaters accidentally opened up in the auditorium at Emory University in 1985, spilling its contents in front of 500 students waiting to hear which teams had advanced to elimination rounds. The clinking of dozens of nitrous oxide canisters upon the stage—canisters used for doing "whippets," an inhalant with a nasty habit of causing seizures and heart attacks—was hard to mistake for anything else. Everyone knew what the noise signified, and no one did anything but laugh, as the debaters scrambled to put the evidence of their recreational activity away.

That summer, I attended debate camp at American University in D.C. Upon arriving, I checked in, put my bags on the floor next to my bed, and spent the next two hours in the room of arguably the best debater in the history of the activity (who also, interestingly enough, went to MBA) getting baked into oblivion. Everyone knew what was going on in that room, yet no one did a thing. Even if you couldn't smell the weed, you couldn't miss the aroma of burning cologne—entire bottles of it— that had been poured out just inside the door and set on fire to cover up the real action that was taking place inside. No seventeen-year-old kid wears that much Polo.

And then there was alcohol.

When it came to drinking, I would venture to guess that pretty much every white student at my school who wanted a fake ID had one, many of them because of my own entrepreneurial efforts. Tennessee, lucky for us, had at that time what was probably the easiest driver's license in the country to fake. The state had only switched to a photo ID in 1984, so many of my classmates were able to use their paper licenses—the alteration of which took all of about fifteen minutes, a razor blade, and some glue—until their expiration dates; but even when the picture IDs came in, they were simple to replicate. All you needed was a poster board, some black art-supply-store letters for the wording, an orange marker for the TENNESSEE background at the top, a light blue piece of paper for the subject to stand in front of, off to the side of the board, and a clear piece of acetate (like for an overhead projector) onto which you could stencil the state seal, copying it from the encyclopedia. You would then place half of the seal on the bottom-left side of the board, and stand with your shoulder just behind the other half, hanging off the board, giving the appearance that the seal had been computer generated and stamped onto the picture. Although the methods and materials were crude, they worked.

I began my fake ID business out of my home, shuttling people in and out of my parents' apartment, with their knowledge I should add, occasionally a dozen in one afternoon. The process was simple: You brought a package of instant film, along with twenty dollars. I would take an entire roll. However many seemed usable were yours to keep, but you had to let them sit for 24 hours before cutting them to license size so that the chemicals in the paper would dry—otherwise, the paper would separate and the ID would fall apart. Then you had only to apply a white sticker to the back of the otherwise black instant camera film so as to mimic the plain white backing on a real license. Simple. Tennessee didn't laminate licenses in those days, so all you had to do was pop your fake into the little plastic holder that the state had provided you for your real driver's license and you were pretty much able to get into any club you wanted, and to drink at most bars.

My fake ID business provided me with a modest but welcome stream of revenue, and of course every one that I made was punishable by a five hundred dollar fine and up to sixty days in jail. Likewise, every occasion when I used one myself—which would have been probably three hundred times between the age of sixteen and the time I was finally able to drink legally in my senior year of college—was similarly punishable. That I thought I could get away with such an enterprise had everything to do with the cavalier way in which white youth view law enforcement in most cases. Because we know we can get away with drinking, and drinking and driving so long as we aren't hammered, and passing fake ID, we do it without so much as a second thought. The worst that's going to happen, we figure (usually correctly), is that we're going to get turned down by someone who knows that we're passing a phony. But they aren't going to call the cops. It's like the guy for whom I made an ID right before he left to go to college (he of the whippet canisters mentioned above), who tried to pass off my artwork at the door of some club in Georgetown, only to suffer the indignity of the bouncer taking the picture out of its plastic sleeve and bending it back and forth. It fell apart within seconds, owing not to my own shoddy work, but to the unfortunately crappy quality of instant film. The bouncer told him to get lost, but my client knew he wasn't going to jail that night. In fact, we both laughed about it when he had the occasion to tell me what had happened a year later.

I even showed my fake ID to cops on two different occasions, as did plenty of other folks I knew, and never got busted, even when I showed a phony Iowa license to a cop who was originally from Iowa and had to know the ID was phony, since I had just made up the template off the top of my head and it looked like crap. That was the same night that another of my friends, also white, showed the same cop an ID that was real, but which belonged to a guy who was in his late twenties or early thirties (my friend Rob was eighteen), with red hair (his was brown), and a beard (he was clean shaven). Not even close, but good enough for white boys.

* * *

IT WAS ALSO in high school that I began to develop my political sensibilities, aided in that process by the research I was doing for debate, but

also by the influence of punk music. Having spent several years listening to music hardly at all, by high school I had begun to gravitate to
punk, in part because it spoke to the sense of personal alienation I felt,
still ensconced as I was in my dysfunctional home situation, and also
because it resonated with my growing politicization.

Not all punk was political to be sure, and even the punk that was
wasn't always progressive. Bands like Fear had a deliberately offensive
right-wing tilt to their lyrics, and the Ramones, who I loved, were an
amalgam of two warring political factions—one led by Joey, the New
York Jewish liberal, and the other by Johnny, the far-right military brat
who stole Joey's girlfriend, inspiring the song "The K.K.K Took My
Baby Away." Punk had always had a bit of this political tension present,
with members of early punk acts occasionally sporting Nazi insignia on
their clothing or instruments just for shock value, though typically this
was more in keeping with the "fuck you" ethic of punk than due to any
real political sensibilities. That said, most punk acts leaned pretty clearly
to the left, at least if they had any discernable politics at all.

It was through punk records that I first became aware of any number
of burning issues at the time, especially those concerning United States'
foreign and military policy. After reading a political zine stuffed in a
two-record punk sampler—which I'd picked up at the only record store
in Nashville where you could find punk music (and even then, only in
the import bin)—I was instantly riveted to the growing anti-apartheid
movement in South Africa. The zine discussed, albeit briefly, the history
of U.S. support for the white racist government there—which although
representing only six percent of the population, oppressed the black
majority viciously—including Commerce Department approval of the
sale of "shock batons" to the South African Defense Forces for use on
black prisoners. It was also therein that I learned of the death of activist
and apartheid foe Stephen Biko, in police custody in 1977, which then
led me to seek out Biko's collected essays, *I Write What I Like*, which
remains among the most influential books in my own political and antiracist development.

In fact, I liked that title so much that I adopted it as a personal mantra of sorts. Though obviously I had never faced—nor would I ever
experience—oppression the likes of that which Biko had endured to

the end, the concept that one should write fearlessly and speak one's truth no matter the consequence was incredibly liberating. Of course, locally there were no injustices to combat that could rival what was happening in South Africa. But when you're sixteen, outrage comes easy. Soon enough, I'd discover an injustice about which to become animated. By comparison to matters of life and death—or even, frankly, the various forms of white privilege and racism that manifested at our school—the issue that emerged was minor. But all activists start somewhere I suppose.

And so in spring of 1985, when Hillsboro's administration suspended a freshman by the name of Anton Young for wearing a skirt, and threatened disciplinary action against any students who came to his defense, I put pen to paper and composed my first political screed: a short, sweet, 350-word polemic blasting the school's dress code and standing up for freedom of speech. Yes, Anton had been deliberately provocative—it was his style, and what made him such an iconoclastic element in the student body—but he hadn't been offensive. The skirt came down below his knees, and was more like a kilt than anything else, as I recall. The fact that there was another student (our resident skinhead wannabe) walking around daily with a leather jacket festooned with a swastika, and yet the administration had neither said nor done anything about *that*, seemed to indicate that the policy was not only horribly arbitrary, but enforced in a way suggesting that school officials were more concerned with ambiguous sexuality than racism. Not to mention, to threaten those who spoke out against the suspension of Anton was clearly an abrogation of our Constitutional rights.

My essay ran in the school's "underground paper." As a side note, any school that has an underground paper is a school with a lot of people who believe themselves to be writers (and of an especially hip and subversive type at that) against any and all evidence to the contrary—people for whom the regular school paper is too "establishment," and whose staffs are a bunch of ass-kissers, the literary equivalent of the Pep Club. It's a privileged concept, almost by definition, to think that what you have to say is so important that you can make your own paper, thumb your nose at the administration *and* the regular student press, and get away with publishing your truth, no matter who likes it.

Or in this case, who *doesn't* like it. I was sitting in third period government class with Mr. McMackin—the unofficial advisor to the underground rag—when a student worker came in from the principal's office and told me that Harry Brunson, the Assistant Principal, needed to see me. The paper had been out for roughly an hour, which meant there was little doubt it was the essay for which I was being summoned. I exited the room, as Mr. McMackin said something about the First Amendment under his breath, and headed downstairs, not knowing exactly what was going to happen.

When I got into Mr. Brunson's office and he closed the door behind us, I fully expected that I was going to be suspended or in some way punished. I also knew that if so, I would finally get to track down that lawyer I'd bragged about to the principal back at Moore when I'd threatened to sue him four years earlier.

Mr. Brunson cut right to the chase.

"I wanted to speak with you about that article you wrote. What would make you say such things?" he asked.

"Well, I feel that Anton was suspended for no good reason," I replied. "And meanwhile, Kon Moulder is walking around with a *swastika* on his jacket and nothing happens to him."

"I didn't know about this, this, what'd you say his name was? Kon?" Mr. Brunson said. "What does he look like?"

"He's sort of a big guy, bald, like a skinhead. He always wears a black leather jacket, and lately it's had a swastika on it. He's pretty hard to miss." I explained.

"Well, we'll look into that," he promised.

"Also," I continued. "My understanding is that you were threatening to discipline anyone who signed the petition in Anton's defense, by removing us from leadership positions in student clubs or student council. That's even worse than the original suspension for Anton."

"I'm not sure where you heard that, Tim, but it's not true. We would never do that," he assured me, though I didn't believe him. I had heard about this threat from teachers who had become aware of the plan from conversations in the teacher's lounge. It wasn't just some paranoid conspiracy theory spun by disgruntled teenagers.

"Okay then, great," I said, figuring that even if he was lying, he was now on record as opposing any such secondary punishment, so at least that much had been accomplished by the uproar.

"See Tim," he said, leaning in towards me as if he had something of the utmost importance to impart, "We're just concerned."

"Concerned about what?" I asked.

Mr. Brunson sighed, and then proceeded to make the one mistake no adult should ever make with a child—letting that child know that you fear them.

"I don't think you recognize your power," he began. "I think you could stand on a table in the lunchroom and tell the students to burn the building down, and they just might do it."

I laughed immediately, finding this to be the silliest thing I had ever heard, but it was apparent that he was completely serious.

"Well, I would never tell anyone to burn anything," I replied, "but seriously, if I did that everyone would think I was nuts. They would throw food at me. I mean, honestly, I'm really not that popular."

"Well, popular or not, I'm telling you, you have an ability to persuade," he said. "Last year when we had the presidential debate, I saw what happened. We've got twelve hundred students, and you got a standing ovation from two-thirds of them."

"Yeah but I was pretending to be Walter Mondale," I explained. "I mean, they were probably just grateful that I hadn't delivered the speech the way he would have."

"No, that's not it, Tim. I'm telling you. It's a real ability you have, but you have to be careful with it," he said, eyes locked on mine, apparently convinced that the revolution was just around the corner, and that I was Hillsboro's own Lenin, just returned from the Finland Station.

"Okay, well, is that it?" I asked, still floored by the seeming absurdity of the exchange.

"That'll be all," he replied.

And with that, I left the principal's office, knowing in ways I hadn't before what I wanted to do with my life. My road was becoming clear.

But as so often happens, there would be a detour.

* * *

THE SCHOOL YEAR was winding down. Prom was done, and weekends from mid-May until the end of the semester in early June were filled with parties. Though only a junior, I was suffering a pretty serious case of senioritis, more or less phoning in the remainder of my work, limping to the academic finish line and looking forward to summer, at which point I'd be going to debate camp in Washington, D.C.

The party for Saturday night, May 18, 1985, had been promoted all over campus the previous week. Fliers were everywhere, meaning that basically everyone was invited. It was going to be huge, and frankly, I needed the release. The week before, I had learned that my father was having an affair with a bartender at the dinner theatre where he had been doing the warm-up and running the lights for the current production. I'd learned of it by accident when one of the other employees at the theatre said something about their relationship to me after a show I'd gone to see there, assuming I knew already. I hadn't.

I'd gone home that night from the theatre angry, less about the affair than the fact that once again, my father was so drunk he could barely function. He had mumbled through the warm-up and made several lighting mistakes during the play. I was upset about the fact that he was cheating on my mom, of course. But I always figured he probably had been, so perhaps the lack of surprise at the official confirmation of what I'd long suspected led me to more or less shrug it off. When he stumbled in later that night, he woke me to apologize, not for being three sheets to the wind (he never apologized for that, nor even seemed to recognize the impact his alcoholism had on me), but rather for the affair. He'd thought that was why I stormed out of the theatre parking lot after the show, rather than hang out for a while as I sometimes did.

I didn't say anything. It was late and I didn't want to get into the real cause for my anger. I just wanted to go back to bed. My dad asked if I was going to tell mom about the affair. I said no, that it wasn't my job; it was his, and I thought he should do it soon if he intended to continue the relationship with Debbie. If he was done with the affair, I actually said he shouldn't tell her, because all that would do is hurt mom, while doing nothing to make amends; it would be for his benefit, his expiation of guilt and little else.

He didn't say anything to her that week about the affair, and I kept it under my hat, as I'd promised. By the time the week had ended, and I was gearing up for the party, I was glad for the ability to blow off some quickly building steam.

As it turned out, the party was pretty lame; lots of people, yes, but more or less just standing around drinking punch made with pure grain alcohol. I had one glass of the stuff and was almost immediately reminded of the last time I had made that mistake. It had been several months before, when having consumed five such glasses along with two beers and a rum and coke, I wound up puking all over the back of someone's car I didn't even know who'd offered to give me a ride home. Done with the punch, and remembering why I'd sworn never to drink that swill again, but not wanting to leave the party, I volunteered to go with a few other people, get some cash, and make a beer run.

From where the party was located, the closest ATM machine for my bank was about three miles away, in the shadow of St. Thomas Hospital, which sat up on a hill just off busy West End Avenue. So a bunch of us piled in one of the other kids' cars and headed down the road. I hopped out when we got there, inserted my bank card, and punched in my PIN. As the machine spit out twenty dollars, I heard a car honking as it sped down the road behind me. I turned to see what the ruckus was about just in time to watch a car, its hazard lights flashing, pass by the bank and enter the turn lane for the hospital. A strange feeling came over me as I stuffed the money deep into my pockets and climbed in the car to go get the beer we had promised to bring back to the party. I didn't say much on the way back to the festivities. Something about that car with the flashing lights, honking its horn, had unnerved me, though I couldn't explain why.

We delivered the beer, of which I proceeded to drink one, and then, tired and still largely non-conversational, I averred that it was time I got home. I asked my friend Jon, with whom I'd shown up to the party, for a ride. He wasn't happy to be leaving so soon, but when I told him I really needed to get home, the seriousness in my eyes and voice convinced him. Anyway, I told him, he could always come back. It would just take about twenty minutes round trip.

As I walked down the long hallway of E building at the Royal Arms—the place I had lived since I was three days old—I experienced vertigo for the first time. I was feeling dizzy, which made no sense given how little I'd had to drink. Maybe I was getting sick, I reasoned, as I put my key in the lock of our door, turned the handle on apartment E-7, and entered.

The only light on was a small lamp in the living room, putting off just enough of a glow to allow me to make out the physical presence of my mother, sitting on the sofa to the left of the table. She was lying down, propped up on a small pillow, with her left elbow up against the back of the couch, her left hand nestling her head. At my entrance to the apartment she had neither moved nor said a word. She wouldn't look at me, instantly taking me back to that morning five years before when we had learned that Bobby Bell had been murdered. Though I am far too given to catastrophic thinking—it comes with the territory when you have an alcoholic parent about whom you worry constantly—I knew that my hunch about something being wrong was likely to prove correct.

"What?" I asked, trying to keep it simple and get it over with.

"It's your dad," she replied. "He's in the hospital."

"What happened?" I asked with a sigh.

"He overdosed after the show tonight," she explained. "They just rushed him to the hospital an hour ago. I was waiting for you to get back to head over there. Let's go."

I can't recall if my mom already knew the details of my father's overdose before we got to the hospital, or if we only learned them upon speaking with the doctors; in any event, they weren't hard to figure out. The overdose hadn't been an accident. He had taken over two dozen anti-depressants, on top of a fifth of vodka. Almost immediately afterward, however, he had decided that he'd really rather not die. Panicked and regretful, he told his colleagues what he had done, at which point they had thrown him in the car and rushed to the nearest hospital, St. Thomas, which was nine miles away, up on the hill, overlooking the bank and the ATM machine where I had made my withdrawal at the very moment the car carrying him to the emergency room had passed by, lights flashing, horn honking. He had been conscious in that car, and when they got him to the hospital, he had walked in of his own accord, only to collapse in the waiting room.

When we got back to his bed in the ICU, he had a tube down his throat and was in a coma. The doctors thought he would likely make it, but it had been close. They had pumped his stomach of course, but the long-term effect of the drugs and alcohol on his body, and especially his brain function, was uncertain. On the side of his bed, sitting in plain sight on the table, was a six-inch strip of paper that had been ripped from the printout section of his heart monitor. It showed roughly ten to fifteen seconds of time, during which he had died—a flat line punctuated on either end by shallow heartbeats. It seemed a very strange thing to place next to a patient—like a macabre souvenir in case upon recovery he might like to take it home and put it in a scrapbook—but I left it there, after staring at it for what seemed like five minutes, considering what it signified.

The doctor explained everything to us about what had been in his system, and as he spoke I garnered a glance at my dad's chart, hanging up on the cabinet just outside his room. When he arrived his blood-alcohol content had been 0.41, to say nothing of the pills he'd swallowed. The booze alone had been enough to kill most people. Ironically, it would be his alcoholism and the tolerance that came with it that had likely kept him alive.

Within a day my father would leave the hospital, and the truth would finally come out as to why he had attempted suicide. Turns out, Debbie had broken up with him, and distraught over the ending of his year-long affair—and recognizing that the rest of his life wasn't going that great either—he had opted to check out, only to chicken out in the end. So now my mother knew. It hadn't been the way I had anticipated him telling her, but at least there were no more secrets to keep.

On the surface, this story might seem out of place in a book about race. After all, it doesn't appear to have much to do with such a subject. And yet, as I tried to piece together an understanding of my father's addictions—something that would take me many years, and wouldn't fully come until well after he got clean on my birthday in 1996—I came to understand how racial identity (and for that matter male identity and even Jewish identity) had all been a part of the larger picture.

Once my dad got clean and started attending AA, we would occasionally talk about what he was learning there. For the most part he seemed satisfied with the AA language and approach—it was keeping him sober after all—but there was something about it that seemed inadequate to me. It seemed as though the operative paradigm in AA was overly individualistic, as in *the addict* is powerless in the face of the disease, *the addict* needs to make amends, and *the addict* needs to give control over to some higher power (however defined). There was very little discussion about the social determinants of addictive behavior, and the way that individuals exist not in a vacuum but in a social context, which, under certain conditions, can make addictive behavior more likely.

After all, there must be a reason that the United States has so much higher a rate of drug and alcohol abuse than other nations, including other wealthy and industrialized nations. And there must be a reason that, according to the available research, white Americans have such a disproportionate rate of binge drinking and substance abuse relative to persons of color—contrary to popular perception—and why rates of suicide are also so high in the U.S. and among whites (and especially middle class and above whites), relative to people of color.

Though none of this was covered in AA, I began to see it the more I thought about my father's situation, and what I came to understand was this: To be an American and to be white is to be told in a million different ways that the world is your oyster; it is to believe, because so many outward signs suggest it, that you can do anything and be anything your heart desires. Although people of color and folks in other countries have rarely had the luxury of believing that mythology, white Americans have. And so when one's expectations are so high—and especially if you add to that the expectation of a Jewish man seeking to make it in a heavily-Jewish industry like comedy—and yet one's achievement falls well short of the aspiration and expectation, what happens?

In such a situation, in which the society is telling you that your failings are *yours*, your inadequacies *yours*, that there are no socially determined issues to examine—whether institutional obstacles in the case of oppressed groups or the dangerous mentality of entitlement and expectation that comes with privilege—what *could* certainly happen is that one might well capitulate to a self-destructive rage; either that, or project one's rage outward onto others in the form of abuse (which, on the verbal level, my father had also done). This is not to excuse the abuse, be it directed inward or outward, but it is to explain it in relation to a social context and not merely as the personal failing of millions of individuals acting in isolation. This is not to say that all addiction is the result of frustrated expectations—social pathology can have many different triggers, of which this would be only one—but it is to say that we can't ignore the way that such a phenomenon may be part of the larger mix, about which we need, desperately, to be aware.

It strikes me that unless we get a hold of this, unless we begin to address the way that privilege can set up those who have it for a fall—can vest them with an unrealistic set of expectations—we'll be creating more addicts, more people who turn to self-injury, suicide, eating disorders, or other forms of self-negation, all because they failed to live up to some idealized type that they'd been told was theirs to achieve. We'll keep creating for millions of families the pain that I'd grown up with, and the physical embodiment of that pain, which embodiment lay comatose in the bed that night, that little strip of paper at his bedside reminding us all of how close he'd come.

HIGHER LEARNING

FOR MOST OF my senior year, I was able to breathe far more easily than I could remember ever having done. My dad had left that summer after the suicide attempt, and although he and my mom remained married, the separation gave me a respite from the insanity that had been my home environment for the previous seventeen years.

We had a successful year in debate, which was a good thing, since debate was likely to be my key to getting into a good college. My standardized test scores were awful, barely cracking 1000 on the old 1600-point SAT, and my grades were a rather mediocre 3.3 on a 4-point scale, so I knew I'd probably need to wrangle a debate scholarship somewhere. Initially, I had wanted to go to Emory, in Atlanta. They had a great debate team, and Atlanta, though away from home, was still close enough to get back easily for visits.

But as the year progressed, it became apparent that Emory wasn't going to be an option. Over the summer I had fallen in love (or so I thought) with a debater from Lafayette, Louisiana. I'd met her at the American University debate camp, and she was going to be attending Louisiana State University. When she told me in no uncertain terms that I simply had to go to Tulane, in New Orleans, my emotions quickly trumped whatever previous plans I may have had. If I went to Emory, Monica explained, we would never get to see each other. It would be tough enough, she insisted, with her in Baton Rouge, and me seventy-five minutes down the road in New Orleans. But at least it would be workable. So I filled out my application to Tulane—a school about which I had never even thought once—and kept my fingers crossed, my academic and romantic future hinging on the decision to be made by their admissions officers. I wasn't confident about getting in. Aside from my mediocre academics, Tulane didn't have a real debate team at that time, let alone debate scholarships to give out. So my accomplishments in the activity weren't as likely to matter as they would have at Emory.

Fortunately, it must have been a down year for applicants, and so Tulane said yes. There was only one problem remaining; namely, how to pay for it. Although its cost is far greater today, as with all colleges, in 1986, with tuition at $12,950, and all costs combined coming in at around $20,000, Tulane was far pricier than anything my folks could afford. Complicating things further, I am notorious for procrastination, and so I had screwed around and not gotten my financial aid forms in on time. Since being late with financial aid forms means that one won't get as much assistance as might otherwise have been offered, how does one get to go to a place like Tulane? It helps—and this is surely an understatement of some significance—when one's mother is able to go down to the bank and take out a loan for $10,000 to fill the gap between what the school was offering in assistance and the overall costs for my freshman year.

But how does one's mother get such a loan? Especially when, as was true for mine, she had never owned a piece of property? When you've been living paycheck to paycheck, driving cars until they stopped running, taking few if any vacations because you just couldn't afford them? It helps (again with the understatement) if one's mother's mother can co-sign for the loan. While banks don't typically lend money to folks without collateral, like my mom, they are very willing to lend the same money to someone with it, like my grandmother, who was able to use her house as a guarantee against the loan.

The house, in which she lived until her death in December 2009 (and in which my mother still resides), was the fourth home she and my grandfather had owned. Although they had been of middle-class income—my grandfather having been in the military and then civil service for his entire adult life—they nonetheless were able to afford several nice homes in "good" neighborhoods, all of which had been entirely white, and as with the apartment complex where I'd grown up, not by accident. Although the Supreme Court, in 1948, had outlawed restrictive covenants barring blacks from these neighborhoods, it had remained legal to discriminate in other ways until the late sixties. Even then, there was little real enforcement of the Fair Housing Act until teeth were added to the law in 1988, and even now, studies suggest there are at least two million cases of race-based housing discrimination against people of color every year.

So in a very real sense, my grandmother's house, without which I could not have gone to Tulane, or to any selective (and thus, expensive) college, was there to be used as collateral because we were white. Not only did we have a house to use for this purpose, but it was a house in a desirable neighborhood, which would continue to appreciate each year. In other words, we'd likely make good on the loan, but if we defaulted, so what? The bank would have a nice piece of property, worth more than the money they were giving my mom. They couldn't lose, and neither could I. Whiteness, institutionalized and intergenerational, had opened the door for me. After nearly eighteen years of dysfunction and chaos, I was ready and willing to walk through it.

* * *

MY MOTHER, HOWEVER, was not nearly as ready for me to do so. Like many parents who have kids about to go off to school, she was sliding into a deep depression. For her, the notion of an empty nest was of no small concern. Now that my father was also gone, she would truly be on her own.

One day in the summer of 1986, while I was preparing for my move to New Orleans, Albert called and suggested we go to the Nashville Peace Fair, an annual festival with music, crafts, and dozens of information booths set up by various non-profit organizations from throughout the region. Given my increasing politicization, I was excited to go, and Al clearly needed the progressive inoculation that the Peace Fair would provide; after all, he was about to head off to the University of Mississippi, where he'd be unlikely to see so much as a Democrat in four years (at least among white folks), let alone anyone truly to the left of the political spectrum.

Upon returning to the apartment in late afternoon, I found my mother drinking. Actually, I found her completely in the can, and this was alarming because although my mother occasionally drank too much, it was rare for her to get started in the daytime. Even though I wanted to tell her about the Peace Fair, once I realized she was in no condition to talk, I decided to wait. It just didn't seem like the right time.

Unfortunately, my mother felt otherwise. Not only did she want to discuss the Peace Fair, and politics more broadly, she was itching to pick a fight, which is something she had never done before. It started slowly, with her asking me about the event, and though I tried to brush it off, she seemed genuinely interested. I began to tell her about some of the information I had picked up about U.S. foreign policy in Central America, and about apartheid in South Africa and how American corporations were helping to prop up the racist regime there.

I am not exactly sure how the discussion descended into the mess it would become. The whole episode was so bizarre, I think I was too shocked to take it all in. What I recall is that at some point we got on the subject of welfare and welfare recipients. And when one speaks of welfare in this country, whether or not one wishes to acknowledge it, one is almost always speaking of black people, not because black people are the only folks receiving state aid (indeed more whites receive benefits from the myriad social programs than do blacks), but because that is the image we have been encouraged to have when we hear the term. It's an image that has become implanted in the minds of Americans, especially whites, to such an extent that it's almost automatic, and it allows politicians to criticize "welfare" and its recipients without mentioning race, knowing that their constituents will get the message.

However we managed to get on the subject, it was obvious that my mom, angry at me for preparing to leave her nest, was going to use this issue—the one she knew would injure me because antiracism had been such an undercurrent in our home—as a way to lash out. The next thing I knew, she was spewing one after another nonsensical statement about lazy black women and their illegitimate children, and then launching into some extemporaneous diatribe about a particular black woman with whom she had worked (and with whom I always thought she'd gotten along pretty well), who in today's white zinfandel-induced haze, had become incompetent, pushy, a bigot.

In other words, we had gone from talking about a Peace Fair to talking about welfare to talking about a colleague of hers in a matter of minutes, and now things were getting heated, and I was firing back, which is exactly what she wanted. I was watching her use racism in a way that would have sickened her in her sober moments, as a tool to express some totally unrelated angst—as a way to work out the existential crisis she was experiencing at that moment. It was ugly, and not really understanding what was going on—in fact at one point I contemplated that my mother was either having a total nervous breakdown, or had been a fraud all of my life when it came to race—I lit into her, and told her never to speak that way in front of me again.

It was finally at the point where she began to utter the word, the word that was the only word I knew, growing up, never to say, that I exploded, not allowing her to finish it.

"Goddamn nig"- she started.

"Shut the fuck UP!" I screamed.

And that's when she swung at me, for the first time in my life, but slowly, not as though she really wanted to hit me. Her right arm came up in a sad and pitiful arc toward my cheek, palm open, her face contorted in pain—a pain deeper than any I had ever seen there, even as she had stood over my father's hospital bed on the night of his suicide attempt. The look that night had been a look of exhaustion, of resignation to the not-so-fairy-tale ending of her none-too-fairy-tale marriage. But this was not resignation I was seeing now. She was imploding, and in the process burning away all illusions. She was going to make me hurt, not physically—as she surely knew I would stop her arm long before her hand could make contact with the side of my head—but at the core of who I was, by making me question who *she* was.

And for that experience I thank her, because without it, I may never have really seen how distorted white people could be as a result of racism. My mom, after all, had been my model when it came to things political. She had been consistent, she had been clear, and she had never given me any reason to doubt her. But that confidence, that faith in her perfection was unhealthy; it was downright dangerous, because that is not the real world. That world of bedrock principle and never-wavering resistance in the face of social conditioning is not the world in which real people reside.

Racism, even if it is not your own but merely circulates in the air, changes you; it allows you to think and feel things that make you less than you were meant to be. My mother, by proving her own weakness and exhibiting her own conditioning, taught me that one can never be too careful, can never enjoy the luxury of being too smug, of believing oneself so together, so liberal, so down with the cause of liberation that it becomes impossible to be sucked in, to be transformed. We may only do it once, or perhaps twice, but it can happen. So long as that is true, we mustn't romanticize our resistance, but fight to maintain its presence in our lives, knowing that it could easily vanish in a moment of weakness, anger, insecurity, or fear.

Those moments are the ones that matter, after all. People never hurt others in moments of strength and bravery, or when we're feeling good about ourselves. If we spent all of our time in places such as that, then fighting for social justice would be redundant—we would simply *have* social justice and be done with it, and we could all go swimming, or dancing, or whatever people do. But it is because we spend so much of our time in that other place—a place of diminished capacity and wavering commitment—that we have to be careful. And it is for that reason that we need these reminders, however ugly, of our frailty. Knowing the horrors of which we're capable is the only thing that might keep us mindful of what and who we'd prefer to be.

* * *

I ARRIVED IN New Orleans with my parents and Monica in late August, though it felt more like early Hell, the mercury permanently stuck somewhere between ninety-five degrees and heat stroke. Worse still, the humidity was congealing into solid form, enveloping me like a tight-fitting coat of phlegm, and causing me to wonder whether this girl standing next to me on Bourbon Street, for whom I'd made the decision to come to Tulane, was really worth it. I was starting to have my doubts, allowing my mind to wander to thoughts of college up North, where it would be cooler. I'd be alone, but at least I wouldn't be covered in sweat.

As we walked along the heavily-trafficked tourist corridor—part of the roughly eighty square block area that had been the core of the city at its founding in 1718 by Bienville, the French Governor of Louisiana—I had to admit to having never experienced anything like it. From the ubiquitous smell of booze and seafood to the strip clubs to the architecture, it was certainly unlike my home town—a city also known for music and entertainment, but of a decidedly different kind. Lower Broadway, in Nashville, was certainly seedy at the time, but the French Quarter, even at its seediest, had *style,* it had culture, it had, above all else, *history.* Though I didn't yet know the racialized component of that history, I would learn soon enough. In fact, I would begin learning a little something about it that very day.

"Hey mister," a young squeaky voice cried out from behind me and to the right. I spun around, not sure that the words had been meant for me—after all, I hardly thought of myself as a mister, being only seventeen—and saw a black kid, perhaps ten, hopping off his bike and coming towards me.

"Yeah," I replied. "What's up?"

"I betcha' dollar I can tell you where you got 'dem shoes," the child answered.

"I'll take that bet," I replied, confident that there was no way this child in front of me could really know where I had purchased my footwear. Little did I know it at the time—I had, after all, been in the city for all of two hours—but I had just walked into the biggest trap in the history of traps. Being a big, bad *Tulane* student, however, I was cocky enough to assume that I had just won a dollar off some kid in the Quarter, not thinking for even a second that no one would have offered this bet if he didn't already know that he had me from the get-go.

As it turns out, of course, and as I would soon learn, the young man had never actually claimed to know the point of origin of the shoes on my feet. He had merely offered to tell me where I "got 'dem," as in had them, at that particular moment, owing nothing whatsoever to the location of the department store in which they had been purchased, the name of which meant no more to him than my own, and neither of which he had any real desire to learn. This was business, after all, not personal.

He asked me to show him the money, which I did, at which point he sprang the trap. "You got your shoes on your feet, you got your feet on the street, on Bourbon Street, now give me a dollar." It was a logic with which—once I learned the hyper-literal meaning of his initial challenge—I could hardly argue. I was indeed on Bourbon Street, between St. Peter and Iberville to be exact, my shoes planted firmly on my feet, my feet on the steaming, summer-scorched asphalt, damn near melting in the sun. I gave him the money gladly, and in the process learned more than the value of a dollar alone. Transaction completed, the wordsmith and street hustler, whose linguistic machinations had probably worked on a hundred tourists before, not to mention more than a few Tulane students and their parents, headed down the street in search of the next mark. It was a search that couldn't have taken long, filled as the streets of the Quarter typically are, and mostly with persons whose gullibility rises in direct relation to their blood alcohol levels, the latter of which remain dangerously elevated most of the time. Taking money off persons such as this was quite literally what the metaphor writer must have had in mind when first coming up with the phrase *like candy from a baby*.

There's something to be said, I thought to myself, about any place where poor folks, rather than just stealing your money, or simply begging for it, instead earn it by way of winning an entirely voluntary game of wits, outsmarting those who are typically far more educated and no doubt more socially respected than they. Street hustling of this sort—the kind that makes a riddle into a commercial transaction—is uniquely American in that regard, evidence of the ability of those who have been long neglected by the political and economic system to once and again turn the tables on those for whom the rules of the game were set up in the first place.

Of course, it's made all the more sweet by the realization that the kids who pull these scams know full well that the only reason anyone falls for it, *and most everyone does at least once*, is precisely because they are black and poor, and therefore presumed to lack the brainpower to pull one over on those who are white, more affluent, and imbued with (at least in our own minds) superior intellects. Yet they do, over and again, demonstrating the limitations of scholarly competence, which ultimately shrivels up like a dead leaf in the face of a far deeper intellect possessed by children who are seen as uneducable by the larger society, which tells us little about those so doubted, but quite a bit about the society that doubts them.

*   *   *

WHEN I GOT to Tulane, I considered myself a hip liberal, aware of racism and committed to fighting it. Within a few weeks of my arrival, however, I had largely missed the meaning of two different incidents— one fairly minor, the other pretty significant—and thereby missed an opportunity to respond in a forthright manner.

The first took place during freshman orientation, when all the bright seventeen- and eighteen-year-olds who had come to Tulane sat in a hot auditorium and listened to the typical "welcome to our school" routine given to all students at all colleges in the country. There were the expected platitudes about the history of the university, and about the importance of adjusting to life away from home, and warnings about the pitfalls of going to school in New Orleans. Among these snares was the ubiquitous problem of heavy drinking. The drinking age had just been raised to twenty one, but most students (though not me) had birthdays that fell within the grandfathering period. We were also warned to stay away from certain neighborhoods and to travel in groups because not all of New Orleans was as safe as Uptown, where the university was located.

At first glance this may seem like nothing more than good advice, but to the extent the warnings were all regarding black and poor neighborhoods, it was highly racialized and selective in a way that prioritized the well-being of whites to the exclusion of persons of color, the latter of whom might well have been at risk in certain white spaces. This was made all the more obvious by the second thing that happened, within a month or so of the beginning of school: namely, the announcement by the sheriff of neighboring Jefferson Parish that he had instructed his deputies to stop any and all black males driving in the Parish in "rinky-dink" automobiles after dark, on suspicion of being up to no good, as he put it.

At no point had Tulane officials suggested that students, even black ones, stay away from Jefferson Parish, even though it was understood to be less than hospitable to black folks. Sheriff Harry Lee—a Chinese

American loved by good old boys from the white flight suburb in large part because of his anti-black biases—had been profiling African American males for a long time before he ever went public with his law enforcement techniques, and Tulane had thought nothing of it. School officials had sought to make sure we didn't make the mistake of straying into the black and mostly poor parts of town, out of a concern that we might become victims of random street crime, but at no point did they warn students of color of the many areas in the metropolitan vicinity where they might have been endangered.

This was among the first examples of how whiteness was privileged in the educational environment of my school, but despite thinking that Harry Lee was a real asshole, especially when he went on *The Today Show* and tried to justify his racist policies to the nation, I did nothing to protest those policies, even as they privileged me, by signaling that I (and persons like me) would be allowed to come and go as we pleased, in and out of any part of the metropolitan area we felt like visiting. I failed to recognize how personal this system of privilege was, no matter how hip I fashioned myself.

Who was I kidding? My very presence at Tulane had been related to whiteness. During my time there I would come to learn that the same school that ultimately traveled 540 miles to pluck me out of Nashville had not been recruiting for several years at Fortier High, the basically all-black high school located about five hundred yards from the entrance to campus on Freret Street. There was a presumption that Fortier students, as well as those from several other New Orleans–area schools, were incapable of being successful at Tulane, so the attempt to recruit them simply wasn't made. Meanwhile, there I was, with an SAT score roughly 200 points below the median then (and 300 or more below it now), being admitted without hesitation and given financial aid. Better to spend money and resources on hard-drinking white co-eds from Long Island, Boston, Miami, the North Shore of Chicago, or Manhattan than to spend some of the same on local blacks, whose parents were good enough for cooking Tulane food, and cleaning Tulane toilets, and picking up Tulane garbage, but not for raising Tulane graduates.

Whiteness, as I was coming to learn, is about never being really out of place, of having the sense that wherever you are, you belong, and won't encounter much resistance to your presence. Despite my lousy test scores and mediocre grades, no one ever thought to suggest that I had somehow gotten into Tulane because of "preferential treatment," or as a result of standards being lowered. Students of color, though, with even better grades and scores, had to regularly contend with this sort of thing, since they were presumed to be the less-qualified beneficiaries of affirmative action. But what kind of affirmative action had *I* enjoyed? What preference had I received? Of course it wasn't race directly. It's not as if Tulane had admitted me *because* I was white. Clearly, my admission was related to having been on one of the top debate teams in the nation, but that wasn't even a talent that I'd be putting to use in college, so why had it mattered? And my academic credentials *had* been overlooked. Standards had been lowered for me, but no one cared.

Nowadays, I lecture around the country in defense of affirmative action and meet plenty of whites who resent the so-called lowering of standards for students of color but swallow without comment the lowering of standards for the children of alumni. Each year, there are thousands of white students who get "bumped," in effect, from the school of their choice, to make way for other whites whose daddies are better connected than theirs. Studies indicate there are twice as many whites who fail to meet normal admission standards but who are admitted anyway thanks to "connection preferences" as there are persons of color who receive any consideration from affirmative action. Yet rarely do the critics of affirmative action seem to mind this form of preferential treatment.

Most everyone I met at Tulane who was truly stupid was white and rich, like the guy who thought he was supposed to start every research paper with a thesis statement, the way he'd been taught to do it in seventh grade, or the young woman on my hall during sophomore year, who was stunned when she received an overdraft notice from her bank—after all, there were still checks in her checkbook. I never heard anyone lament the overrepresentation of the cerebrally challenged white elite at Tulane, and I doubt anyone is challenging the latest round of similarly mediocre members of the ruling class now. That's what it means to be privileged: Wherever you are, it's taken for granted that you must deserve to be there. You never spoil the décor, or trigger suspicions of any kind.

* * *

IN FACT, EVEN when you should trigger suspicions, or at least a side-ways glance or two, whiteness can protect you.

My freshman year was not a good one, academically speaking. In part, my struggles were in keeping with a longstanding tradition, whereby I always started slowly at each new school I attended. Whenever there had been a physical transition from one institution to the next—Burton to Stokes, Stokes to Moore, or Moore to Hillsboro—I had had a lousy first year in the new place. This time there were other distractions. Although I avoided many of the traps into which my fellow first-year students fell—I simply didn't have the money to go out and drink as much as they did, nor did I make friends easily enough to smooth the way for heavy partying that first year—I had other distractions that kept my mind off of schoolwork. First and foremost was Monica, who started that year at LSU but would transfer in the second semester to the University of Southwestern Louisiana, in Lafayette, to be closer to her family.

Between traveling to Lafayette two to three weekends per month by bus, going out the little bit that I did, and becoming involved in a number of campus political activities, I found little time to devote to my studies. Though I desperately needed to keep up my grades so as to maintain the meager scholarship I'd managed to wrangle, and hopefully to get the amount of the award significantly increased, I did quite the opposite. In my first semester, thanks to a particularly awful grade in French class—I had taken six years of French, but as I learned once I arrived at Tulane, couldn't speak a word of it—and a few mediocre marks in other classes, I pulled a 2.1 GPA.

My barely average performance in class was punctuated by two monumental screw-ups, which turned out alright, but could have been catastrophic. First, I overslept for an Environmental Science exam, showing up an hour late into a three-hour test, and then I missed a Political Philosophy final altogether, showing up in the afternoon for a test that had been given at 10 AM In the first instance, I was allowed to enter the testing room, even though students weren't supposed to come in after the test had begun; in the second case, despite the fact that missing the exam had been my fault, I begged the teacher to let me make it up and he did, in his office, right then and there.

I didn't give it much thought at the time, except to conclude that I had been lucky, and that I needed to make sure nothing like that would happen again. I certainly didn't think at the time about either of these fortunate breaks having to do with my being white. But in retrospect I do wonder how things may have been different had I been a person of color, and especially black. Might either or both of the professors have taken a more skeptical view of my seriousness as a student? The first might well have looked at me as irresponsible and not allowed me to enter the room. That *was* the policy after all. And the second professor could have viewed me as just not having what it took to be a successful Tulane student—a commonly held stereotype about black students there, even when they did well. So I can't know for sure, but I also can't doubt that in a situation like either of those, I'd rather have been white than anything else.

Perhaps this is the most important point though: No matter what my professors might have thought about my miscues, about oversleeping or missing an exam, one thing I would never have been forced to consider was that they might take either of those things as evidence of some racial flaw on my part. In other words, I would not have to worry about being viewed through the lens of a racial stereotype, of having one or both of them say, if only to themselves, "Well, you know how *those* kinds of students are," where "those students" meant white students. I could rest assured that my failures would be my own and would never be attributed to racial incompetence. For people of color, the same experience would have been different. They would not have been able to assume that their race would be irrelevant to the evaluation given them by a white professor, just as students of color must always wonder if whites will view them through the lens of a group defect if and when they answer a question incorrectly in class—something else I never had to sweat. Black or brown students in that situation would not only bear the pressure of having dropped the ball, they would further carry the burden of wondering whether they had dropped it, in the eyes of authority figures, on behalf of their entire group. If we understand nothing else, let us at least be clear that such a weight is not an incon-sequential one to bear. By the same token, to be able to go through life without ever having to feel as though one were representing whites as a group, is not an inconsequential privilege, either.

*   *   *

ALTHOUGH I DIDN'T have the dough to go out drinking much, even at the ridiculously cheap places around campus like The Boot or the Metro (where they had one dollar draft nights pretty regularly), I still did my share, using the fake ID I'd made myself, or when that one fell apart, a replacement that another student made for me, which looked a lot better than my own work. Frankly, the fake ID was barely necessary in New Orleans. Although the drinking age had been raised to twenty-one the year I got there, few places really carded. And because the laws in Louisiana didn't hold bars responsible for the actions of their inebriated patrons, the way laws in many other states did and still do, there was lit-tle incentive for them to refuse service to anyone.

Beyond drinking though, the real game at Tulane was weed. Although drugs were every bit as illegal in New Orleans as anywhere else—at least if you were black and poor—if you were lucky enough to be living at Tulane, which was (and is) a pretty white space contrasted with the city in which it's located, you were—and I'd venture to say, still are—absolutely set.

My freshman year, I lived on the eighth floor of Monroe Hall, next door to the biggest dealer on campus (white and from Long Island), and by reputation one of the biggest in the city. He would drop quar-ter-ounce bags in the hallway and not miss them. And being a dealer who, unlike most, liked to smoke his own stash, he would just write it off to being high, and never get too mad about it. I should say that I very much liked living next door to him, for obvious reasons. I couldn't afford his product myself, but between the misplaced freebies and the steady supply that others on the hall purchased from him, and were all too willing to share, I did alright.

There were two black guys on our hall, both on the football team. One of them smoked and the other didn't, but even the one who did looked at us like we were nuts. The sheer volume of grass being consumed dwarfed anything he was used to, and the way we were smoking it—out of two-foot bongs with a gas mask attached, so as to provide that all-important *third foot* of chamber—he found bizarre. "Can't y'all just roll a joint, man?" he would ask, not realizing that no, we couldn't just roll a joint. Privileged people like to overindulge. It comes with the territory. We weren't afraid of getting caught, as he was—since things would probably turn out differently if he were busted, on a lot of levels—so concealing our habits wasn't foremost on our minds.

I saw far more drugs at Tulane on my dorm floor alone in any given week than I ever saw in public housing projects, where I would work as a community organizer many years later, and as with the drinking and drug use in high school, it was overwhelmingly a white person's game, meaning either that whites have some genetic predisposition to substance abuse (for which there's no evidence), or there's something about being white that allows and encourages one to take a lot of risks, knowing that nine times out of ten everything will work out. You won't get busted and go to jail, neither of which black or brown folks can take for granted in the least.

Perhaps this is why national studies have found that next to having a Division I sports program, the most highly correlated factor with alcohol and substance abuse on campuses is the percentage of students who are white. The whiter the school, the bigger the problem—not because there's something wrong with whites, *per se*, but because privilege encourages self-indulgent (and often destructive) behaviors, and allows those with privilege to remain cavalier about our activities all the while.

* * *

WHEN I WASN'T getting high or visiting Monica, I was deepening my political involvement on campus and around the city. Although I first got involved with College Democrats, my political sensibilities had moved well to the left of the Democratic Party, and especially its conservative Louisiana contingent. Most of my activist time and energy was instead thrown into Central American solidarity work, opposing the arming of the contra rebels in Nicaragua who were seeking to overthrow the nominally socialist Sandinista government there, and opposing U.S. support for the governments of El Salvador and Guatemala, both of which had a penchant for murdering civilians in the name of anti-communism.

In the case of Guatemala, its dictator in the early eighties had been Efrain Rios Montt, whom Ronald Reagan insisted had "gotten a bum rap on human rights" and was "dedicated to social justice," despite his policies of bombing peasant communities and other atrocities, which ultimately took the lives, in his term alone, of over seventy thousand Guatemalans. When I wrote an essay on the matter for the campus paper in the first semester of my freshman year, I received my very first (though certainly not my last) death threat, phoned in to my dorm room by someone whose family was closely connected to the military there and who promised that he could make me disappear. Undaunted, and even slightly amused, I threw myself into the work full-bore.

Working with the Movement for Peace in Central America (MPCA), I got my first taste of real left activism by organizing protests, teach-ins and other activities with a mélange of seasoned radicals, spanning the full spectrum of the ideological left. Having come from Nashville, where liberal Democrats were rare, to be in a place where we had the luxury of five different types of Marxists was interesting and a bit bizarre.

I never really considered myself a Marxist, mostly because I rejected the notion of any proletarian/workers dictatorship, which for most Marxists is a requisite component of their belief system. I was certainly anti-capitalist and still find the profit system inherently exploitative. But having never seen its opposite work either, I have remained agnostic on the issue of socialism. I am far more positively disposed to it than to capitalism, but am unconvinced that such a system can avoid falling into heavy-handed statist oppression, ultimately no better than the heavy-handed corporate plutocracy it would replace.

I also have to say, I wasn't impressed with the organizational acumen of those who were proudly calling themselves communists. They had a hard time keeping MPCA functioning, so I never could figure out how people such as this were going to be able to run a government or society. The bickering about each faction's particular dialectic made for tedious meetings and strategy sessions, which revolved around some of the most inane bullshit you can imagine. It was Marx versus Lenin versus Trotsky versus Mao versus Che Guevara versus Stalin (yes, there were actually some committed Stalinists in the bunch who always gave me the creeps and who believed Enver Hoxha's dystopian regime in Albania was the only truly legitimate government on Earth). Even when you exclude from the group those members who were FBI plants—part of the ongoing disruption of the New Orleans–area CISPES (Committee in Solidarity With the People of El Salvador), which had been exposed the year before I arrived in the city—there was still an amazing array of folks with whom one could choose to associate, or disassociate as the case may be.

By sophomore year, I was growing tired of MPCA, mostly because of the sectarian infighting, but also because I was becoming focused on a different issue that had been burning around the nation at the time on college campuses—namely, the anti-apartheid struggle, and the fight to get universities to divest of stock held in companies still operating in South Africa, thereby propping up the white minority regime.

Under apartheid, twenty-six million blacks in South Africa were denied the right to vote and were restricted in terms of where they could live, work, and be educated. The white racist government also routinely tortured anti-apartheid activists and had engaged in military subversion campaigns in surrounding nations like Angola, Zimbabwe, and Mozambique. All of this it had done with substantial economic and even military support from the United States government and multinational corporations. In the case of corporate support for apartheid, anti-apartheid activists noted that not only did the presence of these companies in the country send a signal that apartheid was acceptable to them, it also resulted in the economic support of the racist state and the transfer of technology and capital, both of which helped maintain the system.

Although Tulane was unwilling to expose its portfolio to scrutiny, the administration acknowledged that it continued to hold shares in roughly 25 companies that were still doing business with the apartheid government. This, combined with the offer of an honorary degree to South African Anglican Archbishop Desmond Tutu (who had won the Nobel Peace Prize for his anti-apartheid efforts in 1984), was too much for some of us to stand. To offer a degree to Tutu, making him part of the Tulane family, while we continued to turn profits from companies that were propping up the system he had dedicated his life to ending, struck us as hypocritical, to say the least.

In March 1988, a coalition of organizations joined forces to form the Tulane Alliance Against Apartheid. The Alliance made three demands: divestment from companies doing business in South Africa; the creation of an African American studies department at Tulane; and the intensification of affirmative action efforts, both for student recruitment and faculty hiring. The last of these was especially necessary, since in the 1987–'88 academic year there were no African American faculty in the College of Arts and Sciences or Newcomb College, the two principal undergraduate schools.

In the days following the announcement of the new organization, those of us in the Alliance constructed makeshift shanties (reminiscent of the dilapidated housing in which millions of South African blacks lived) on the main quad in front of the University Center, so as to raise awareness of the issue and to pressure the Board of Administrators to divest. A few days after the beginning of the shantytown occupation, we demonstrated at the Board's quarterly meeting to demand divestment and to decry the offer of an honorary degree to Tutu so long as the school remained invested in apartheid-complicit firms. The Board was especially unhappy about the co-optation of their meeting agenda that day, as they had gathered mostly to announce the reinstatement of the school's basketball program, suspended three years earlier by President Eamon Kelly, due to a point-shaving scandal. While they had been hoping for a celebratory meeting and media splash, we had tried to steal (and had at least partially succeeded in stealing) some of their thunder that day.

During this time we also sent the Archbishop a packet of materials concerning Tulane's investments—what little information we had—and requested that he make a strong statement condemning the school's role in supporting, even if mostly symbolically, South Africa's racist system. We hoped he would either turn down the degree and boycott the school, or come as planned and deliver a withering indictment of the university's investments. Either way would have been fine with us.

A few weeks later, I was awoken in my dorm room by a call from a National Public Radio reporter. "What do you think of the Archbishop's announcement today that he would be turning down the degree from Tulane because of the school's investments?" she asked.

Groggy from too little sleep—we had only torn down the shanties a few days before, in preparation for the end of the school year—I wasn't sure whether the call was real or part of a dream.

"Excuse me?" I replied

"Yes, I was wanting to know if you'd heard the news," she said, "and if so, do you have anything to say about it? Archbishop Tutu is traveling in Canada right now, and last night at McGill University he announced that he would be turning down the degree from Tulane."

I was stunned, but pleased. The administration was shaken as news spread worldwide of Tutu's boycott, and a few days later, his subsequent announcement that he would return all honorary degrees he had ever accepted from schools with investments in South Africa unless they divested fully within one year. Clearly, the university had been denied the moment they had hoped for, in which Tutu would be honored by the school and thereby lend anti-apartheid cover for their otherwise morally indefensible investment practices. Although Tutu's boycott didn't change the board's mind about divestment, we anticipated that upon returning to campus in the fall, the movement would hit the ground running having obtained such a high-profile victory.

As it turned out, our optimism in this regard was entirely misplaced. Summer sapped the energy of the movement considerably as several of the key movers within the group graduated. Although I returned as a junior, and there were others of the original membership back that next year, we struggled from the outset to replicate the success of the previous semester. Membership waned and our direction seemed unclear. Although we continued to educate the university community about South Africa and the role of corporations in propping up the apartheid system, we stalled when it came to making any progress with the board. Most importantly, the organization in that second year became almost entirely white, and the alliance between the mostly white activists and the black-led organizations that had created the movement in the first place fell apart entirely, in a quiet but noticeable fashion.

Of course, none of us white folks were prepared to confront the reasons why such a racial split had opened within the organization, and why African American students, though clearly supporting the divestment struggle, had little to do with the formal organization pushing for that end. We did come up with some convenient excuses for it though, all of which let us off the hook entirely. As one white member put it, getting no argument from me in the process, the black students at Tulane were mostly "bougie," from upper-middle-class families, and didn't want to make waves. Aside from the fact that this was utterly untrue, who the hell were we to call anyone bougie? As if we were some hardscrabble working-class offspring of West Virginia coal miners or something.

Never did it occur to us that maybe black folks at Tulane were turned off by the way a handful of whites (myself included) had been elevated to the status of spokespersons by the media, and how we weren't savvy enough to avoid the trap of our own mini-celebrity. Maybe they were pissed because the original focus of the group—which had involved not only divestment but also black studies and affirmative action—was slowly replaced with a single-minded focus on the one issue that was easiest for white Tulanians to swallow and would call for no sacrifice on our part, or alterations in the way the campus looked and felt. Maybe they fell away because we were so quick to jump to cavalier methods of protest like taking over board meetings and openly inviting arrest if necessary, without consulting anyone, and without discussing the privileged mindset that treats going to jail like just another rite of passage for students to experience.

Whatever the case, the movement floundered that next year, and white privilege got in the way of our seeing why.

*   *   *

IN THE SUMMER between my junior and senior years at Tulane, living back in Nashville, I worked for Greenpeace Action, the canvassing arm of the international environmental group, famous for its "Save the Whales" campaigns. I had worked there the previous summer too, and although the pay was lousy (and I was a tragically awful canvasser), the camaraderie of the group was worth the shitty income. It was a relief just to be able to hang out with progressives in Nashville, few of whom I had known before those days.

By that second summer though, I was starting to have serious doubts about the work we were doing, and even the people in the organization with whom I was working. Having thrown myself into the study of the civil rights movement in school the previous year—and having had the honor of meeting several movement legends at a conference held at Tulane in spring of 1989—I was finding myself wondering why the environmental movement (and especially its overly-white organizational arms like Greenpeace) said so little about environmental racism, meaning the disproportionate impact that toxic waste dumps and other forms of polluting activity were having on communities of color. And why were our tactics so utterly lame when compared to those of the civil rights struggle?

Never were the movement's tactics—and issue focus—more self-evidently absurd to me than on the day that summer when it was announced we would be staging a protest at the Burger King restaurant across the street from Vanderbilt University. Specifically, we would be protesting the fish sandwich at Burger King because the fish came from Iceland, and Icelandic fishermen were known for killing whales. So naturally, the 21st Avenue Burger King was complicit with the whale slaughter and we were going to let them know it. Simple, and quite possibly the most ass-backwards demonstration in the history of any social movement. In fact, from a purely tactical perspective it had been ridiculous. Who even knew that Burger King *had* a fish sandwich? Probably nobody until we alerted them to that fact, meaning that we had probably helped them sell more fish sandwiches in an hour than they had sold in the previous week. Way to go hippies.

Thankfully, I would soon get a chance to be in the presence of veteran activists with a far more laudable history and focus. That summer was the twenty-fifth anniversary of the Freedom Summer campaign in Mississippi—the voter registration, educational and direct action effort organized by an amalgam of civil rights organizations to break the back of apartheid there. As those with a sense of history will recall, it was during Freedom Summer that three civil rights workers, James Chaney, Michael Schwerner and Andrew Goodman—the first black and the latter two white—had been murdered by Klan members on the police force and their confederates, and buried in an earthen dam outside of Philadelphia, Mississippi. They had not been found for roughly a month.

An organization called the Philadelphia Coalition had formed to commemorate the anniversary and to renew the calls for justice that had long since been denied in the case, with several of the key participants in the murders never having been punished for their roles in the crime. Hearing of the commemoration and needing to connect to something more substantive than a fish sandwich protest, my mother and I decided to make the drive to Philadelphia.

My mom had been just a bit too young to volunteer for Freedom Summer, though her heart had been with the effort, no doubt to the chagrin of her parents, who came from the "why do they have to go and stir things up?" school of segregationists. They weren't bigots by a long shot; they just thought Dr. King and the others should have left well enough alone. In their world, whites and blacks had always gotten along so well.

In some ways, perhaps that ho-hum indifference had been almost worse than open displays of racist contempt. After all, to have heard your parents cast aspersions upon Dr. King could be seen as almost pathetic, given the towering greatness of the latter and the rather ordinary mediocrity of the former. But to have had his greatness and that of this movement met with blank stares, with *nothing*, must have been maddening. It's not unlike the difference between the person who seeks to openly justify the death of civilians in war time with bloodthirsty logic, on the one hand, and the person who blankly stares at the TV screen as it projects images of the death and destruction while not even blinking, on the other. The latter may not openly celebrate the carnage, but their refusal to show any emotion whatsoever is somehow more troubling. At least the celebrant of death is willing to demonstrate by virtue of his agitation that he is indeed alive and capable of feeling something, however grotesque. I have long thought I would prefer a land filled with angry and hateful people than one populated by spectators who watch the drama unfold, and no matter how bad it gets, never miss a single beat of their predictable lives.

Kids dying in Mississippi? Gotta remember to call Betty and make my hair appointment. Water cannons being turned on black people in Alabama? Gotta pick up the dry cleaning and grab a few things at the grocery. Medgar Evers shot down in his driveway? Did I remember to feed the cat?

So far as I know, the only reaction my grandmother ever had to the civil rights movement had been to express concern about shopping downtown during the sit-ins, which hit Nashville in February, 1960. She feared that the completely nonviolent black and white kids who were sitting in at the lunch counters might riot. That the only folks threatening to riot were white segregationists, and that the only violence came from them as well, didn't occur to her, nor did it alter her perceptions about who the good guys were and who the bad. Even her concern— feeling put out at the limitations placed upon her ability to shop downtown—bespoke numbness. She hadn't expressed openly contemptuous remarks about the protesters, but simply viewed the whole episode as an inconvenience. At one of the most important moments in the history of her country, she, like so many of her compatriots, had had no idea what was happening, nor had she particularly cared.

But my mother had, and she had passed it on to me. Now, a quarter-century after that fateful day when Goodman, Chaney, and Schwerner had met death at the hands of those whom—although they couldn't have seen it at the time—the three had been trying to save, she would finally make that trip to Mississippi.

We drove to Philadelphia for the anniversary gathering, which took place on the very site, just outside the city, where once had stood the Mount Zion Baptist Church, the burning of which Schwerner had gone to investigate that day in June of 1964. It was that visit to Philadelphia that ultimately had brought Schwerner and his comrades to the attention of Sheriff Rainey, Deputy Cecil Price, and their assorted Klan brothers.

The drive from Nashville takes about six hours, and we made it in almost complete silence. I can remember the miles ticking by as we headed south, and noticing the ubiquity of the kudzu, consuming everything to the side of I-59: trees, shrubs, old highway signs, everything. Kudzu, for those who haven't spent much time in the South, is a particularly tenacious vine that is every bit as common in Mississippi as the state flower, the magnolia. It is everywhere, thick, dense, and dark green. It spreads over the ditches and gulches just off the shoulder of the roadway. If you were to fall asleep while driving and had the misfortune of hurtling your car into a thicket of the stuff, there is a better-than-average chance that you might never be heard from again. Kudzu is more than a vine though, and it's no coincidence, I think, that it is to be found almost exclusively in the southern United States. It is the perfect vegetative metaphor for the way in which we southerners have so long sought to cover up our crimes, crimes that are not ours alone but which we, in so many ways, perfected and turned into an art form. Lynchings happened in all parts of the country to be sure, but Mississippi was an entirely different geographic, and, for that matter, historical species. It was the nerve center of white supremacy.

This was so much the case that later that year when I did honors thesis research in the state, I would find black folks still afraid to talk about the events of 1964 for fear that they could even now disappear if word got back to the wrong people—people who were still there, and who knew exactly how those black bodies that would occasionally float to the surface of rivers and lakes had arrived at their final resting places; people who still knew the location of the deepest point in the Tallahatchie; people who had never forgotten, in all those years, how much weight was needed to keep a body submerged until it became impossible to identify it. Mississippi was different, and it still is.

We arrived in Philadelphia just in time for the beginning of the day's events and had to park well away from the site of the old church and walk the rest of the distance. It was unbearably hot, and there were a few thousand people there already, many from out of state (including actors Jennifer Grey and Blair Underwood who were to star in a made -for-TV movie about the murders the next year), as well as many from around the Philadelphia area, including those who had decided to capitalize on the events by marketing T-shirts to commemorate the festivities. Whether or not the locals had cared about Goodman, Chaney, and Schwerner twenty-five years earlier, now, all were quick to wrap themselves in only the finest cloaks of racial ecumenism.

Despite some of the cynicism inherent to the local embrace of this civil rights reunion, the event was incredible, and more than compensated for the heat or the tacky commercial exploitation of the tragedy. I had never in my life been in the presence of so many heroes and sheroes, who had put their lives on the line for justice, and especially never so many white allies in that struggle. Growing up in this country, one learns very little about the role played by such persons. Not only are the contributions of people of color to this nation's history minimized in favor of a narrative that prioritizes the things done by rich white men, but those whites who resisted and joined with black and brown folks to forge a better way are similarly ignored. Growing up, and even having attended one of the "good" schools in my community, in which I took Advanced Placement American History, I had learned nothing of these people among whom I now stood, and whose contribution to human freedom had been so dramatic, far more so than that of Andrew Carnegie, J. P. Morgan, or Andrew Jackson, for example, about whom I had learned plenty in the same class.

To have taught us about these people—and not merely the ones who had died, but the ones who had lived and continued the struggle—would have been dangerous. It would have signaled to those of us born in the years after the height of the movement that we had a choice to make. It would have dared those of us who were white to dream of different ways to live in this skin. It was no coincidence that school boards and principals and the lawmakers who make educational policy wanted no part of such an enterprise, and still don't.

To see this collection of black leaders and white allies and to be in community that day with them was a source of great inspiration to me at twenty, as it appeared to be to my mother, there with me, at the age of forty-two. That she had been unable to participate in the battle we were celebrating was unfortunate. That she had raised a son to join that battle a quarter-century later had made her contribution every bit as vital.

* * *

IMMEDIATELY BEFORE WE had left for Philadelphia, my mother and I had been out at the home of my dad's folks, visiting for Father's Day. We knew that nine days later, my grandfather would be going into the hospital for prostate surgery, was none too happy about it, and could use some cheering up.

Paw Paw had never been in good health. His leg had been amputated at the age of sixteen, the result of an infection that had set in after he was kicked by a horse, and throughout his life there had been various complications from the amputation. Also, his diet was atrocious, consisting so far as I could tell of lox, gefilte fish, butter, and saltines. He also smoked unfiltered Lucky Strikes and drank more Chivas Regal than he probably should have. That he had made it to seventy was more than a bit surprising to some.

Two years earlier I had become aware of how rapidly his health was declining when he had come to New Orleans for college basketball's Final Four. He had driven the eight hours with one of his best friends, Cornelius Ridley, a basketball legend in his own right. Ridley had coached Pearl High School in 1966, the year they became the first black team in Tennessee history to win the state championship against white players, with Ridley becoming the first black coach to win a state title.

Coach Ridley, Paw Paw, and I had gone to the games, which included one of the most exciting finishes in championship history, in which Keith Smart of Indiana hit an improbable baseline jumper at the buzzer to beat Syracuse. But my grandfather had actually missed the ending, having become ill shortly after halftime, his blood pressure spiking and causing him to become so disoriented that he'd wandered back on his crutches to the hotel, thinking the game was over. Coach Ridley and I would find him there an hour later, after both of us had begun to panic about his whereabouts. Though his health stabilized in the months following his trip to New Orleans, by 1989 he was struggling, his kidneys malfunctioning to the point of requiring dialysis, and his blood pressure dangerously high.

During the Father's Day visit, I brought him a folder with every article I'd ever written to that point from the school paper and the alternative zine I was writing for in New Orleans. He had been a journalist in college, and because he appreciated my politics, I figured it would mean a lot more to him than another pair of socks.

We had no idea that he wouldn't be coming out of the hospital. Though he definitely wasn't in good shape, there was nothing to indicate that this would be anything other than a routine operation. After handing him the folder with my essays, I expected him to put it aside and read it later, perhaps in a week or so, after returning from his surgery. But he read the entire thing, methodically consuming a few dozen short pieces, leaving my mom, Mabel (who we called Maw Maw), and me to visit with one another. It was as if he knew that if he didn't read them then, he wouldn't be getting the chance.

Looking back, I should have known something was up with him. A few weeks earlier I had stayed at Leo and Mabel's house—I still liked to go and spend the night there sometimes when I was home from college, to take advantage of the peace and quiet—and had had a conversation with him unlike any I had ever had before. I remember him, for the first time, beginning to speak of his father. He was trying to tell me stories of what his dad had experienced in Russia, and about his journey to America (a story we only knew little bits and pieces of, principally the ones I shared earlier). But every time he started to tell a story, to actually provide me with a specific piece of information, his voice would trail off, and he would start again, usually in a different place, and on some totally different subject.

He repeated the process a few times until it became obvious that he wasn't going to get much out. It wasn't that his mind was going or his memories were fading. Though his body was at the end of a journey, his mind was strong. The problem was that he literally didn't have any stories to tell, at least not complete ones. And the reason he didn't have any stories was because tales about the old country and a connection to that immigrant past were often the first casualties of whiteness, the first things that had to be sacrificed on the altar of assimilation. To hold on to those stories, let alone to pass them down, would be to remain stuck, one was told; it would stifle one from becoming fully American (which meant white American at the time of entry for European ethnics). So one had to begin the process of transformation: Don't seem too Jewish, don't teach your children the language of their forbears, nor the customs, don't talk about the old country. Put all that behind and become a new man—a white man. Only by giving up one's past could a person like Jacob Wise win a future for his children, or so he was led to believe. Only in that way could he make others comfortable enough with his presence that they might welcome him and his brood into the American fold.

It had begun innocently enough, or so it seemed, there on Ellis Island, being told by some immigration official that they couldn't understand the thick Yiddish coming off your tongue, and so it would be necessary to give you a new name, to simply make one up. What was that, after all, which you were garbling? Shuckleman, Sheckman, Shuckman, Shankman? Ah, to hell with it, your name is now Wise; not Weiss, but Wise, whitened and sanitized for your protection—with all due apologies to Alex Haley, a Jewish Toby.

Had the name been the only thing lost, perhaps it wouldn't have mattered. What's in a name, after all? Well nothing except one's past; nothing except the intergenerational fiber that had kept your people together for generations; nothing except the story of how you survived. Nothing but *that*.

So the process of whitening had begun and now it was culminating in the inability of my grandfather, Jacob's son, to pass down any story, anything at all about his father, his mother, his grandparents, or the place from which we came. To know those stories would first have required that he had been taught them; and for him to be taught them would have required that Jacob had been willing to do so; and for his father to have been so willing would have meant that he had been able to resist the pull and lure of whiteness; and to do that had been unthinkable.

So my grandfather joined our ancestors, about whom neither I, nor oddly enough, even he, knew much of anything. With him went my connection to the past, leaving me—and now my daughters—with nothing other than one-half of a set of gold candlesticks, the only items smuggled out of Russia on that ship Papa boarded so many years ago. I don't even know the story that goes with the candlestick, but sadly it is all I have left.

All, that is, except for my white skin. And though that skin provides me with innumerable benefits, it is hardly better than the candle in the candlestick at keeping me warm at night, because I know its true price; I know how much my family paid for it, and for my name. I know, because I saw in Paw Paw's eyes that day, what the cost of white privilege had been for my people, what it had exacted of my kinfolk as they hit the reset button on the game of life and stifled their traditions and cultures so they might find a place in this land. I know the cost incurred and the penalty paid by those who had to give up who they were and become something they were not—white. I know because I saw the bill of sale, saw it in the silence between my grandfather and myself. It was a silence louder than any scream I had ever heard.

* * *

SENIOR YEAR BEGAN, and as usual, I was distracted from my studies. As had been true my freshman year, I was once again in a long
distance relationship—this time with a woman at Vanderbilt whom
I'd met working at Greenpeace—and so every other weekend for the
several months that our relationship lasted, I was back and forth
to Nashville. Luckily, by this point I had enough credits under my
belt to take a light load academically, including only three courses
in my last semester, along with finishing up the honor's thesis on the
Mississippi civil rights movement. So even with the distractions, I
managed to do alright.

When the year started off, I had planned to focus most of my activist attentions on reinvigorating the anti-apartheid movement that had
faltered the year before. But even before a month had gone by, the campus was rocked by a racist scandal quite a bit closer to home. In mid-
September, a cross was burned on the lawn of the Delta Tau Delta
house. Apparently, the fraternity had been targeted because it had just
extended a bid to a black student, Donnell Suares, for the first time in the
chapter's history. Someone, perhaps an alum, wasn't too pleased about it.

When the campus paper broke the news (which had been covered up
for roughly two weeks by the fraternity itself, and then by the administration once they learned of it), all hell broke loose. It was bad enough
that a cross had been burned, but the fact that the Delts hadn't seen fit to
notify the proper authorities—a move that the head of campus security
blamed for hampering the investigation—was damned near criminal.
That the president's office had further attempted to keep the incident
underwraps, thereby losing the opportunity to make a clear public statement condemning the hate crime, only compounded the offense. The
fraternity clearly failed to appreciate the magnitude of the incident. At
a press conference called by myself and several members of the school's
black student group, Chet Givens, the frat's president explained they
had remained silent about the hate crime because they "didn't believe
it was racially-motivated or a campus issue." Interestingly, one of the
members of the fraternity who remained stone silent for the two weeks
of the initial cover-up, was Andrew Breitbart, now one of the nation's

most notorious right-wing commentators. That Breitbart now claims to have been the person who pushed for Suares' membership in the first place makes his silence and unwillingness to quit the group in the wake of their non-chalance even more pathetic. Some friend was Andrew.

As for the administration, protecting the public image of the school took priority over forceful action, much as it had three years prior, when the Delta Kappa Epsilon fraternity had marched through the middle of campus in blackface, taunting black students with lit torches in a mock Mardi Gras parade. At the time, the president's office had said they were unable to punish anyone (despite the fact that the fraternity had been banned from campus and the torches were weapons being thrust in the faces of black students) because they couldn't identify the perpetrators under all that greasepaint—an interesting twist on the "all blacks look alike" trope. The fact that the yearbook staff had no problem identifying each and every one of them a few months later, changed nothing.

In any event, and in keeping with the inventive ways in which white folks so often manage to deny the existence of racism even when its presence is obvious, there were many beyond merely Givens and the Delts who claimed the cross-burning might not be racially-motivated. Because the cross had only been two feet tall, they speculated, it might have had nothing to do with racism. Of course, because the way to discern the motives of people who burn crosses is always by use of a handy slide rule.

Though many of us blasted the administration's handling of the incident and gave them a much needed public battering for it, nothing much happened. No one was ever caught or punished for the act, and thus, there was nothing to deter others from doing it again. As such, in January, three members of the Kappa Alpha Order fraternity (the KAs), which celebrates the "Old South" and considers Robert E. Lee their spiritual founder, burned a cross in their own backyard. This time the story got out as soon as it happened, thanks to other members of the fraternity who hadn't been involved in the incident and reported those who had.

But then too, the denial was creative. The frat boys who had burned the cross actually went so far as to say they had had no intention to do so, but were merely adding wood to a bonfire in their backyard when two pieces "happened to fall in a cross-like position" in the flames. It

was all a big misunderstanding. Yes, we dress up in Confederate uniforms and march down St. Charles Avenue every year, all the way to
Robert E. Lee circle, waving confederate flags, but we're not *racists*, and
that cross thing was just a coincidence. When it was pointed out that a
Martin Luther King Jr. Boulevard sign had been tacked to the horizontal
bar on the cross, that too was written off as coincidence, as one brother
pointed out that he had no idea how that might have gotten there; after
all, they would have to have gone to the black part of town to steal a sign
like that, and that would have been too dangerous! Yes, it was sure good
to know the KAs weren't racists.

Interestingly, a valuable lesson emerged from the community discussion that followed the KA incident. At the outset of the evening, one
young white man rose to ask a question, for which he apologized at the
outset, so certain was he that it would prove offensive. He noted that
he was a KA himself, and although he recognized why a burning cross
was offensive to him as a Christian, he honestly had no idea why it was
offensive to blacks. Could someone please explain it to him, he wanted
to know?

At first everyone gasped, taken aback by such lack of awareness, and
in a few cases, ready to pounce on the kid for his ignorance. But then
it hit us: he really didn't know. He wasn't trying to minimize the sever-
ity of what his fraternity brothers had done. He simply had never been
told anything about the history of that symbolism, its use by the Ku
Klux Klan going back over one-hundred-and-twenty-years, and the
way burning crosses had been utilized to terrorize black families in the
South and elsewhere for generations.

That he didn't know these things was hardly his fault. His schools
had never seen fit to teach them, probably concerned that such lessons
would detract from the far more palatable narrative of America's greatness, exceptionalism, openness, and commitment to liberty for all. He
had been lied to, as had the rest of us. The fact that a few of us had
gotten the truth from parents or mentors was hardly something over
which we had the right to be smug. It simply meant that we had an
obligation to struggle with him, as we would want others to struggle
with us in our own moments of ignorance. People like that young man
couldn't be written off, especially by other whites, content that our own

radicalism somehow made us superior. He was one of us, after all. And there are plenty of times the rest of us hadn't seen things clearly either, or wouldn't in the future. As I would soon learn.

* * *

WITH A NEW batch of activist students ready and fired up about the divestment struggle, those of us who had been leading the charge for two years tried to once again jumpstart the movement. In the fall of 1989, our alliance—now renamed Tulane Students Against Apartheid because of the University's threat to sue us if we continued to call ourselves the Tulane Alliance, thereby implying (supposedly) official university endorsement—once again took over a board meeting. Facing several hundred demonstrators, and with the divestment petition having grown to include the names of over 3,500 students, staff, and faculty, the trustees finally agreed to negotiations with the protestors.

At our first meeting to discuss divestment with the board, it became obvious that the university's wealthy white policymakers had no intention of taking the issue seriously. First, we noted that the university already had an ethical investment policy in place, passed in 1985, which prohibited it from investing in companies that contributed to human rights violations. It seemed apparent that continued investment in the twenty-five corporations in South Africa was a violation of the board's own policy. Upon being issued this challenge, one of the board members—either Sybil Favrot or Virginia Roddy (rich white women all look alike to me)—responded.

"Well, how do we know if those companies are actually contributing to human rights violations?"

Putting aside the argument that any corporate investment in South Africa would automatically bolster apartheid and thus contribute to human rights abuses, I posed a hypothetical.

"Imagine," I asked, "that we were invested in Shell Oil" (which given the powerful presence of the petroleum industry in and around New Orleans seemed reasonable, though we couldn't be certain given the school's refusal to open the portfolio). "Since Shell recently called in

South African security forces to shoot rubber bullets at striking workers, would that, in your mind, constitute a human rights violation sufficient to trigger the policy with regard to ethical investment?"

"Well," she began, before clarifying beyond any doubt that money and ethics bear no necessary relationship to one another, "I guess it would depend on why they were striking."

I am rarely at a loss for words, but this was to be such a time. Suffice it to say that the rest of the meeting didn't go much better.

Fast forward to winter break. I was home for the holidays when I stumbled upon a book detailing the connections between university investments and political and economic repression in South Africa and Central America. In the book's index, the author provided a summary of several companies involved in human rights abuses, and the names of some of the schools that held stock in those companies, along with the number of shares held at the time of the book's writing. Tulane was listed several times, and was invested in about a dozen companies that had contributed everything from oil-refining technology to the South Africans, to military helicopters to the dictatorships in Guatemala and El Salvador. It was the material we'd been looking for.

Upon returning to campus in January, we called a press conference to release the list of Tulane's "dirty dozen" corporations, and to demand that the school follow its own policy with regard to ethical investment by divesting itself of stock in those firms and any others about which we were unaware. The board, in response, announced they were breaking off negotiations with the anti-apartheid group, because the release of the information indicated we were acting in bad faith—this, coming from people who needed to know why workers were on strike before they could say, definitively, that shooting them might be objectionable.

In the third week of March, we again built shanties, but this time on the lawn in front of the administration building (Gibson Hall), facing the streetcar line on St. Charles Avenue. By bringing the protest to the exterior of the campus, in front of its most visible structure, we hoped to heighten the public's awareness of the school's practices, and to force divestment, or at least the opening of the portfolio to full scrutiny. A week into the protest, when Jesse Jackson came to campus (for an unrelated speech) and called for the university to heed the protesters' demands, we figured we were on our way to victory. That evening I announced that several of the group's members, including myself, would begin a hunger strike the following Monday if our key demands, short of divestment itself, were not met by that time. Needless to say they wouldn't be, and so the hunger strike started on schedule.

On the fourth day of the strike we received word that the university had agreed to five of the ten demands, including those we had insisted upon in order for the action to end and for negotiations to resume. These included the opening of the portfolio and a commitment to bring in ethical investment experts to help plan future directions for the management of the school's general fund.

Though we celebrated this outcome as a victory for the movement, deep down everyone knew there was something unsatisfying about it. Apartheid was, thankfully, in its waning days, as signaled by the release of Nelson Mandela in February. As a result, the board had recognized that before it would really have to make any changes, the situation in South Africa would probably change, and with it, there would be no more need to clean out its portfolio. Tulane was going to hold out longer than the racists in Pretoria, which was saying a lot.

But what the divestment effort taught me about the moral compasses of the Tulane Board of Administrators would prove to be among the more unimportant lessons of the campaign. Far more intriguing would be the lesson I would learn about myself and even the best-intended of activist efforts; specifically, the lesson I would learn about how even in our resistance to racist structures we can reinforce racism and collaborate with the very forces we claim to be opposing.

Though I saw none of this for most of my time at Tulane, the closest I ever came to having one of those "lightbulb moments" that people always ask about was during that period, on the second night of the hunger strike. That evening, with only a month or so left in my academic career, we had a public debate on campus against representatives of the New Orleans Libertarian Party. The Libertarians would argue that investment in South Africa was a good thing for blacks because it provided them with jobs, however unequal those jobs might be, and that if companies pulled out, black South Africans would suffer most. It was an argument with which we had been contending from the outset and which all of us knew how to pick apart. By the time the debate was over, virtually everyone in the crowd of three hundred or so was on our side. Confident that we had made our point, Eldann Chandler and I leaned back during the question-and-answer period, expecting to further drive home the moral imperative of divestment to the audience. Most of the questions were pretty routine and were directed at our opponents, rather than us.

And then it happened. The moderator for the evening called on a young woman in the dead center of the small but packed auditorium, who would get the last question of the night. Because she was black, I assumed that she would be on the side of divestment. She was, of course, but she hadn't come that evening to praise the movement. After identifying herself as a first-year student at Xavier University—the nation's only historically black Catholic college, located about two miles away—and prefacing her question by noting that as a New Orleanian she was embarrassed that Tulane was still invested in these companies, she got to what was on her mind. In the process, she dropped the bomb that would, more than anything, alter the way I understood my own relationship to privilege.

"Tim," she asked. "How long have you lived in New Orleans?"

"Four years," I replied.

"Okay," she continued. "Then tell me, in that four years, what one thing have you done to address apartheid in this city, since, after all, you benefit from that apartheid?"

She crossed her arms in front of her, and stood, and waited.

One Mississippi, two Mississippi. . . . The seconds crept by, each one pounding like a drill into my skull. By now, the air had been sucked out of the room, she having asked the one question for which I had been unprepared, the only one I had never anticipated, and the only one that, at the end of the day, really mattered.

Three Mississippi, four Mississippi. . . . It seemed like hours since she had asked her question, and I briefly considered the possibility that we had been sitting there overnight waiting for my answer. I'm sure no more than a few seconds had passed, but in those seconds, enough truth was revealed to last a lifetime.

I began to have the sensation that I was in my car, speeding away from town, and suddenly saw the blue lights flashing in my rear view mirror—the lights that say, "Gotcha!" But unlike the last time I got a ticket, I wasn't going to have thirty seconds to come up with some story that could get me out of whatever trouble I was in. This time the officer was at my window, badge out, gun drawn, and it was now or never that I would offer an answer. So I did.

"Well," I said, clearing my throat before the silent audience, "I mean, um, ya know, um, we all pick our battles."

Oh.

Shit.

No. He. Didn't.

Yes, I had, and as soon as the words tumbled from my lips, I knew something significant had happened. More to the point, so did just about everyone else.

The young lady uncrossed her arms and smiled a knowing smile, her expression betraying a mix of satisfaction and disgust at how easy it had been to expose me.

A buzzing started behind my ears, coupled with a strange warmth that made me fear my head might explode like that guy on the stage in that sci-fi flick *Scanners*. I started having flashbacks to all those dreams—I'm sure you've had them too—where you suddenly find yourself naked in front of your third-grade class or at prom or something.

An earthquake could have hit at that moment—thinking back to it, I probably wished that one would have—and had it done so, I likely wouldn't have noticed. I don't remember another thing from that night, so shaken was I by her question and my answer, not because I had been in possession of a better answer that I had simply forgotten to offer, but because I had had no answer at all. That had been it. I had told the truth, and now had to confront what such disturbing honesty suggested.

Over the next few days, the administration would partially cave to our demands, the shanties would come down, and the hunger strike would end. But even after I began to replenish my body with the nourishment I had been denying it, the pit in my stomach remained, because it had nothing to do with food. I tried to put the whole thing behind me but couldn't. I kept coming back to the fact that I had been doing all this work against racism half-a-world away, but frankly had done nothing to speak of in opposition to the racism in the town where I had been living. I had done nothing in answer to the *de facto* apartheid conditions that existed in New Orleans—conditions that, as the young woman that night had pointed out, had benefited me as a white man who could count on my privilege to insulate me from their impact.

I began to remember all the things I had ignored or downplayed as I focused on the racial oppression that was occurring on another continent: Harry Lee and racial profiling in Jefferson Parish, or Tulane's lack of recruiting in New Orleans schools, being two of the most obvious.

And there was one more, even worse, which had just transpired under our noses and about which we had said and done nothing. Three days after our shanty siege had begun, New Orleans police killed a black man named Adolph Archie, suspected of killing a white police officer. When police caught him, beat him, and took him to the hospital, a lynch mob of additional officers had gathered, after broadcasting open death threats over their police scanners. Instead of entering the hospital with Archie, they drove him to a precinct station and over several hours beat him so badly that every bone in his face would be broken. He would die at the hospital after police got tired of brutalizing him, and although his death would be ruled a homicide "by police intervention," no officers involved in his killing would ever be punished.

As Adolph Archie was being pulverized by New Orleans cops, my comrades and I had been sleeping the sleep of the just (or at least the self-righteous) uptown, in shacks of our own construction, protected by Tulane police around the clock for the entire two-week period of the protest. We had never even discussed the killing of Archie, never connected the all-too-obvious dots, never supposed that perhaps there might be something similar about the way police operated in New Orleans and the way they operated in Soweto. Remember, *we all pick our battles.*

I had been completely oblivious to the way in which my own privilege and the privilege of whites generally had obscured our understanding of such issues as accountability, the need to link up struggles (like the connection between racism in New Orleans and that in South Africa), and the need to always have leadership of color in any antiracist struggle. It's the same lesson still not learned by white activists in most cases, whether in the anti-sweatshop movement, the justice for Darfur movement, or the anti-war movement. Too often the same mistakes are made: mostly white radicals, who have the luxury of picking and choosing issues on which to get active (unlike people of color who also care about different issues but have to deal with racism as a matter of survival), refuse to connect the dots between the oppression taking place in another country, and the oppression going on down the block.

Although we have to forgive ourselves for the mistakes we make, we must first acknowledge them. We must first face up to the fact that in our resistance we too often reinforce the hierarchical arrangements we strive to oppose. Only by being called out, as I was, can we learn this in most cases. Only by being exposed to our flaws, forced to deal with them and learn from them, can we move forward and strengthen our resistance in the future. If there is one thing I've learned, it's that we who are white (and specifically white antiracists) will screw up more times than we care to count, more times than we expected, and just about as often as people of color already figured we would. Saying this does not diminish us, and it doesn't mean that we have no important role to play in the destruction of white supremacy. It just means that privilege sometimes costs us the clarity of vision needed to see what we're doing, and how even in our resistance, we sometimes play the collaborator.

LOUISIANA *GODDAM**
*(WITH APOLOGIES TO NINA SIMONE)

IT WAS ONLY during the waning days of the shanty siege that I firmly decided to return to New Orleans in the fall. I had been thrown for a loop by the young woman at the divestment debate, her question, and my miserable answer, bouncing around in my brain for days afterward. Although I had toyed with the idea of moving out West after taking time off that summer—to do what, I wasn't sure—it was obvious that having done little to address racism in New Orleans, I had some work to do before I could move on.

For several years a group of about a dozen of us had been publishing an alternative paper called the *AVANT*, and during the two weeks we'd been camped in front of the administration building, we'd begun to discuss creating a press collective so that those of us interested in continuing it could live together and work on its production. With five people (initially) in the house—which was already being rented beginning in August by one of the *AVANT* principals, Don Morgan—rent would be cheap, and we'd all be able to get by with monies generated from ad sales, hopefully, plus whatever odd jobs we might pick up. Having no better plan and feeling as though I needed to return to the city to work on issues related to racism, I cast my lot with the press co-op and took claim to one of the rooms in the large house on Robert Street.

I spent the summer in Nashville at the old apartment, living on what little graduation money I had managed to get from my parents and grandparents. I also took the better part of a week in late June to travel to Kansas City and Louisville with Debbie, my girlfriend at the time, to see Grateful Dead concerts, which were a potpourri of white privilege if ever the word had meaning. Needless to say, if black concertgoers ever did as many drugs openly as Deadheads did, we'd need a lot more prisons to hold them all. But so long as you didn't do anything violent or disruptive, you could pretty well get as high as you liked at a Dead show, confident that nothing would happen to you.

The trip was a fun diversion, but ultimately I was disenchanted with the largely apolitical and disconnected vibe of the whole Dead scene. Traveling the country selling tempeh and falafel in the parking lot of some stadium is not only *not* going to produce positive social change, it's terribly self-indulgent. The people who spent years of their lives following the Dead around—though they might have thought they were doing something important and "alternative," by dropping out of the rat race—were really only substituting a new kind of conformity, in which tie-dye took the place of slacks or business suits, but ultimately participants were no more truly individual than anywhere else in America. In many ways, this had long been the problem with hippies: most of them had always been more focused on living in countercultural ways rather than in organizing for social transformation. It had always been very ascetic, very self-referential, very much about "doing your own thing," but not as often about liberation in the larger institutional sense. As for the Deadheads, it's one thing to like the music, but to turn vagabondism into a lifestyle while the world is burning is simply an exercise in privilege and social irresponsibility.

Around mid-July, a few weeks before I was due to return to New Orleans, some disturbing news from Louisiana began to circulate, which called into even starker relief the difference between the real world and the world I'd left behind after the last Dead show in Louisville. According to polling data from around the state, ex-Klansman and lifelong white supremacist David Duke was gaining ground in his campaign for the U.S. Senate, having picked up a few points on the incumbent Democrat, J. Bennett Johnston. Because the conventional wisdom was that Duke "flew below radar"—since many who intended to vote for him might be hesitant to admit their plans to pollsters—even a poll showing him with one-quarter of the likely vote was disturbing. By now, he was pulling numbers close to a third.

When Duke had announced he was running for the Senate, few had taken him seriously. Although he had won a state legislative seat the year before, by 227 votes, most had seen that victory as a fluke, the result of a lackluster effort by media to expose his ongoing ties to extremists and his neo-Nazi philosophies.

Frankly, even I hadn't fully appreciated the threat Duke posed. Back during the legislative race, in early 1989, I had gone to Duke's campaign headquarters with the woman I was dating at the time to check out his operation. Georgia called his office and asked if we could come pick up some campaign materials. She told them we were Tulane students and were interested in getting some information to counter the liberalism on campus. They were all to happy to oblige, and said to come right away, as they'd be closing up soon.

David's office was in the basement of his house, so when we arrived, we walked into his home and saw the volunteers—all female, and all blonde, except for one older woman who looked like someone's grandma—answering phones, preparing mailers, and excited to see us. "We don't get many inquiries from Jew-lane," one said, thinking herself quite clever for having voiced a common anti-Semitic slur on the university, seeing as how it included a large Jewish student population.

As I looked around, trying to take in the scope of his operation, David burst through a curtain separating the main campaign office from what seemed like a smaller room—perhaps an alcove or a walk-in closet—to the right of where we stood. I hadn't expected him to be there (indeed, I had hoped he wouldn't be), and was alarmed when he bounded towards us, hand extended, ever the campaigner. Though I had received some media attention for the anti-apartheid work the previous spring, most of it had been in the paper, rather than on television, so I wasn't particularly worried about him recognizing me. Still, having to shake his hand—the hand of the nation's most prominent Nazi—so as not to blow my cover was nauseating.

As we prepared to leave, loaded up with campaign materials, I looked over to a bookshelf in the office and saw five or six copies of the book "The Hitler We Loved and Why," as well as copies of "The Hoax of the Twentieth Century," which argues that the Holocaust of European Jewry never happened. The sightings confirmed everything I knew about Duke going into the headquarters, yet, for reasons I still can't understand, I didn't think to go public with what I'd seen (which would have made for a great story, and might have even derailed his legislative campaign). Later that year, when his Nazi book-selling operation would be exposed by Beth Rickey, a longtime Republican activist and committed Duke foe, I realized how stupid I'd been for not having gone public earlier. But at least the truth would eventually come out.

Among those who took Duke very seriously were Lance Hill and Larry Powell, the first of whom was a friend and a grad student at Tulane, and the latter of whom had been a history professor of mine. Lance had been on Duke's case since before the state House race and had compiled an impressive array of research on David's ongoing white supremacist activity, most notably, his leadership at the time of an outfit known as the National Association for the Advancement of White People (NAAWP). The group, which Duke had founded after leaving the Klan in 1980, fashioned itself the equivalent of the NAACP, but took all kinds of overtly racist positions, such as calling for eugenics programs to produce a master race of superior whites, advocating the creation of separate racial nations within the borders of the United States, and claiming that Jews were controlling the media so as to destroy the white race. Additionally, Duke sold merchandise from the back of the *NAAWP News*, including the books I'd seen on his office bookshelf, praising Adolf Hitler and suggesting that the Holocaust of European Jewry was a hoax.

All throughout the spring semester of my senior year, Larry had asked if I might be interested in coming back to town and working for the newly-formed Louisiana Coalition Against Racism and Nazism, the group he, Lance, Beth Rickey, and a few others had formed as a PAC, specifically to defeat Duke in the fall. Initially not planning to return to town, and really not expecting Duke to do that well in the election, I had always passed. But now, sitting in my bedroom in Nashville, hearing the news about David's building momentum, I began to think that I'd made a terrible mistake, just like the one I'd made after seeing the inside of his campaign headquarters and not taking him seriously enough to have called the press.

I got back to New Orleans in August, moving into the big yellow house at 1805 Robert Street, which (as I would later learn) was next door to the home to which Truman Capote had been brought from the hospital after his birth, and in which he had lived for a few years as a child. Truman's old abode was in far better shape than ours. The house in which we would be living had been divided into two sides, each rented out separately, and each in equal states of disrepair. It was, simply put, a hovel. Many years later, after Hurricane Katrina, I would go back to see how it had held up and could discern very little difference between its condition after the flooding and that fifteen years before.

Within a few months the number of people living in the house would reach probably illegal (and surely unsanitary) levels, growing from five to ten, as several of us began moving in our significant others, or, in another case, taking in two high school seniors from the Catholic girls' school down the road whose parents didn't mind them living on their own. The only positive thing about this arrangement was how it kept costs down. With rent coming to five hundred and twenty-five a month, and all of us broke, we were willing to make it work. Fifty-two dollars and fifty cents per person was awfully good, even in 1990.

But as the people in the house changed, its mission as a press collective did too. We would only put out two more issues of the *AVANT* before closing it down for good in March 1991. By the time we had moved in, it seemed as though we all had different ideas about what we wanted to do, and the paper wasn't high on anyone's priority list. Most of the roommates were still in school, and by then, I was spending the bulk of my time at the Louisiana Coalition offices, doing what I could in the anti-Duke campaign.

The job that Larry had offered me before graduation was no longer available, it having been filled by Hari Osotsky, a Yale undergraduate who was home for the summer. Her task was to coordinate the anti-Duke network on Louisiana college campuses, which in places like New Orleans wasn't all that complicated, but in northern Louisiana or at some of the smaller-town schools could prove daunting, given Duke's support in such communities. I'd known Hari for a few years, so when I started volunteering at the Coalition offices, we worked well together. I knew that the more I ingratiated myself to Lance, and the harder I worked to assist the campaign, the better the chances were that once Hari returned to Yale (which would still be six weeks before election day), I would likely be picked as her replacement.

I basically lived at the Coalition headquarters, volunteering all day every day. Within a few weeks, even before Hari had left, Lance brought me onto the paid staff to work with her, and then ultimately to take over her position once she went back to New Haven. My salary was five dollars and fifty cents per hour, but Lance didn't put me on a fixed number of hours; as such, since I was coming in early and staying late, finding plenty to do, I was able to rack up sixty to seventy hours weekly with no problem, which meant I was making over three hundred dollars a week—way more than I needed to live in the Robert Street house.

To be working in the campaign against Duke was exhilarating and occasionally scary. We would constantly have to monitor our mail, worried as we were that some of Duke's supporters might send something other than a love letter or donation our way. As it turned out, we got plenty of angry diatribes, death threats, and envelopes filled with dead cockroaches and human feces (at least I *think* it was human), but thankfully, no bombs. Listening to the answering machine each morning was always entertaining. Who knew there were so many ways to call people "Jew bastards" and "nigger lovers?"

I had known of David Duke since I was nine. That was when I had first seen him on the *Phil Donahue Show*, at which point he was still the Grand Wizard of the Knights of the Ku Klux Klan, the largest of the various Klan groups in the U.S. People had always commented on how attractive and well-spoken he was, but in retrospect, back in his Klan days, the only reason people could have felt that way is because they were comparing him to the toothless, semi-illiterate folks who had long been the image of the typical Klansman. The bar had been set pretty low. Frankly, his high-pitched nasally whine and his slickeddown mop of hair—along with a squirrelly moustache that looked like a ferret perched on his upper lip—had always made him appear as an underfed Adolf Hitler, which, come to think of it, is probably what he'd been going for.

By 1990, David had undergone numerous plastic surgeries to Aryanize his look, trading in the flattened down 'do and moustache for a neatly coiffed and lightened blonde head of hair—all the better to represent the interests of the white race. It was a white race, he insisted, that needed him to stand up for it, to repel the attack from "reverse discrimination," busing in schools, "parasitic" welfare recipients, immigration, and any other evil under the sun onto which he could cast a brown face.

Much of Duke's rhetoric was classic right-wing boilerplate, mirroring mainstream conservative discourse on such subjects as affirmative action, anti-poverty programs, and education, and sounding quite a bit like previous narratives spun by politicians like Ronald Reagan, Richard Nixon, and George Wallace for the previous twenty years. Because Duke steered clear of his more blatantly racist positions—those he'd advocated in the Klan or the NAAWP for instance, like racial separation—he was able to convince some right from the beginning that he had truly changed. The Klan was in his past, he would insist, and after all, hadn't Senator Robert Byrd of West Virginia, a Democrat, also been a Klansman in his youth?

Of course, there were some differences between Byrd and Duke that the latter conveniently ignored. To begin, Byrd's youth had been fifty years prior, whereas Duke had only been out of the KKK for a decade. Additionally, Byrd had never joined another white supremacist group after leaving the Klan, while Duke had actually *started* another one, in the form of the NAAWP (of which he would remain the head until a few days before the Senate election). More to the point, Byrd had apologized for his Klan membership and called it a mistake, while Duke had never repudiated the organization. In fact, Duke said he was proud of the work he had done in the Klan, and in 1985—just two years before he turned to electoral politics and began running for public office—admitted that his ideology had "not fundamentally changed" since his Klan days.

Obviously, despite Duke's attempts to convince voters of his turn from racism, the only thing that had really changed about David was his face.

* * *

YOU MIGHT EXPECT that organizing a campaign against a neo-Nazi would be easy, especially in the sense of settling on the proper strategy for doing so. You might think that since Nazis are pretty well reviled, pointing out Duke's ongoing affiliations with Hitlerian types would be an easy call and a winning plan about which all could agree. And if you did think that, you would be terribly wrong, as I would learn.

Within the Coalition ranks, there was an ongoing battle about how to respond to Duke and how to combat his candidacy. On one side were those of us who came from a more progressive tradition—and in this group one could include Larry and Lance—and on the other were several of the Board members from more conservative and Republican backgrounds, who were nervous about challenging Duke on the matter of racism at all. As one would put it, "we need racists to vote against Duke too," so, presumably, we shouldn't make a big deal out of the fact that he didn't like black people much. They preferred that we talk about Duke having "dodged the draft" during Vietnam, or failing to pay taxes on time, or the fact that he once wrote a sex manual under a female pseudonym.

For the most part, Lance, as Director, was able to sidestep these unprincipled positions coming from board members, aided in that process by Beth Rickey, who despite being a relatively conservative Republican, was motivated by an intense dislike for racism and a recognition that indeed that *was* the issue. Lance would placate the more conservative board members as best he could, but from his perspective—and all of us on staff agreed—the only ethically acceptable approach was to focus on Duke's ties to racial hatred and neo-Nazi extremism. Yes, we might need people who were far from enlightened to vote against Duke in order to beat him, but that didn't mean we had to ignore racism, or pretend that draft-dodging or late tax payments were equivalent to calling for the creation of a master race or separating people into their own sub-nations based on color.

There were, of course, those who thought even this approach was too conservative. I had several friends, for instance, who believed we shouldn't call Duke a Nazi, not because he wasn't one, but because to do so was no better, ostensibly, than for right-wingers to call those of us on the left "communists." It was, to their way of thinking, no better than red-baiting. They preferred that we simply rebut Duke on the issues: explain why his claims about welfare recipients were wrong, why his stance on affirmative action was mistaken, why his perspective on immigration flawed. One friend and colleague even said that the answer was to just go into the union halls and tell working class white guys that black workers were their brothers and sisters, and they should recognize that all of them were being manipulated by the ruling class. Sure. Simple. Just like that.

Fact is, we did try to rebut Duke's public policy narrative, but with a limited amount of time in which to mount an effective campaign, changing white folks' minds about subjects like affirmative action and welfare spending was pretty unlikely to work; their views on these matters had taken many years to ossify, and would take time to dislodge. Rather, we tried to remain focused on Duke's extremism—his connections to assorted white supremacists, as well as his overtly racist ideology, spelled out in his own writings—and occasionally (and unfortunately) threw a bone to the conservatives who wanted to talk about taxes, the draft, and sex manuals, by mentioning those as well.

Because Louisiana's elections were open—meaning there were no party primaries, so all the candidates ran in a big pack and the top two vote-getters would face one another in a runoff—we were all nervous about the outcome. With the official Republican candidate, Ben Bagert, pulling six to ten percent in polls, the concern was that Duke might win the most votes in a three-way race, or at least get into a runoff with Johnston, where the outcome would be uncertain. Afraid of the same, Bagert dropped out in the waning days of the campaign.

Having traveled the state in the weeks leading up to the election, I knew to be worried. I had organized students in Lafayette, Lake Charles, Alexandria, Monroe, Shreveport, and all places between, and knew that Duke had a strong underbelly of support from scores of disaffected whites who were convinced that all their problems could be laid at the feet of black people. Although Duke's personal obsession had always been Jews and the role of the Jewish community in undermining the white race, because the Jewish population of Louisiana was small, he rarely discussed the matter; but it wasn't because he hadn't wanted to. As one of his campaign managers would explain, they had had to beg him not to talk about Jews too much because it didn't resonate with people in Louisiana the way going after blacks did, so he had stuck to the script and built his support base by doing so.

Sadly, it wasn't just the racist white folks—or the desperate whites, convinced by Duke's racial siren song to vote their resentments—who posed a threat. There were also more than a few relatively liberal and even far-left folks I knew and considered friends who genuinely mused about their desire to abstain from the election and not vote at all. To them, both candidates were unacceptable, and in keeping with their purity-of-arms leftism, they would refuse to vote for Johnston—the "lesser of the two evils." That J. Bennett Johnston was indeed a conservative Democrat whose record on everything from foreign affairs to the environment was rightly offensive was inarguable. That anyone claiming to believe in justice could think a bad environmental record was morally equivalent to being a Nazi, however, suggested an intellectual and ethical miscalibration so profound as to boggle the mind—but in any event, there it was.

On election day, the Coalition and our supporters gathered downtown at the Sheraton on Canal Street to watch returns and celebrate Duke's defeat—which despite our fears, we fully anticipated would yet be the outcome. And although Duke did lose, the celebration quickly turned into something more closely resembling a funeral procession or a wake. Unmoved by the evidence of David's racism and his connections to the neo-Nazi movement, a whopping 60 percent of white Louisianans had voted for Duke: in some northern Louisiana parishes, and even next door to New Orleans, in St. Bernard Parish, the numbers climbed closer to 70 percent. Only a high black voter turnout had prevented him from winning, but even then, his final tally of 43.5 percent of the overall vote sent shockwaves through the state and nation. As Lance explained that evening to the media, the election had been a referendum on hate, and hate had won.

* * *

HAVING MANAGED TO score such a great job right out of school, I was unprepared for the professional insecurity that would follow in the wake of the anti-Duke campaign. Not that I had expected to find jobs as easily as I'd wrangled the one at the Coalition, but still, what would transpire over the next several years was the very definition of an occupational roller-coaster.

For at least four weeks after the election I would still have work, acting essentially as a gopher on the Congressional campaign of Marc Morial, who was running against William Jefferson for the House seat vacated by longtime Congresswoman Lindy Boggs. I had known Marc for two years, having met him during the anti-apartheid movement; he was a local civil rights attorney and son of the city's first black Mayor, Ernest "Dutch" Morial, and would become Mayor himself in 1994. In this race, however, and despite the clout of his late father's political machine, Marc would lose to Jefferson, the latter of whom would go on to serve nearly twenty years in Congress before being indicted on corruption charges a few years ago, another in a long line of not-quite-honest Louisiana politicians.

My responsibilities in the campaign were essentially banal. I answered phones, went to the post office to mail campaign fliers and other materials, ran errands for supplies, and did whatever else was needed around the office. It was boring but it was a paycheck, and I'm grateful for the experience, if only because it taught me how much I despised the game of electoral politics. Any thought of working on campaigns for traditional candidates—even those I respected, like Marc—went out the proverbial window by November 1990. There was no aspect of it that appealed to me: not the glad-handing for money, not the ass-kissing for votes, not the pandering to people you didn't even like just to seem "electable," and certainly not the gamesmanship, which turns such efforts into mere competitions between high-priced consultants, who, if they weren't selling politicians, would be hawking get-rich-quick schemes on late-night infomercials, or perhaps Extenze tablets.

At the same time that I was trying to figure out the direction in which I wanted to go professionally, I had just begun a new relationship with a woman I'd met during the anti-Duke campaign, but who was, to be sure, not the typical activist type. Nicol Breaux was a local, born and reared in the mostly-white suburbs of Jefferson Parish: in other words, David Duke country. Though she didn't live in the district from which Duke had been elected to the statehouse in 1989, she spent a lot of time there, including at her—and soon to be our—favorite dive bar, Mick's: a pub run by a young Irish American kid named Rusty, and frequented by more than a few Duke supporters.

Nicol was a student at Tulane, a year behind me, and although her social circle included a lot of whites with less-than-enlightened racial views, she was militantly opposed to Duke—she would, in fact, throw a beer on him during a St. Patrick's Day parade a few years later—and was committed to challenging those friends of hers to see what she saw in the Klansman who was so covetous of, and had likely received, their votes. Indeed, among the things that attracted me to Nicol had been her fearlessness in standing up to the kinds of white people who, frankly, I had never spent any significant time around. Coming from a liberal-left background, where I had been able to construct a life that allowed me to avoid too many overtly racist white people—and even working class white folks, period, racist or not—her bravado at telling her most-ly male social circle where to step off was fascinating to me. Although we couldn't have been more different—at the time I was wearing tie-dyed T-shirts and a woven bracelet in the colors of the African National Congress, while she coveted Chanel bags and DKNY—there was some-thing about her that I found alluring.

Nicol would move in with me at the house on Robert Street, despite how its hippie vibe and unhygienic condition no doubt offended her fashionista sensibilities. While there, she would put her own mark on the place, lining up a house party performance by an old friend of hers, Jeff Roberson, whose drag alter ego, Varla Merman—though now famous—was just beginning her career. Varla would perform at a party we all threw for Dayna Leaumont's eighteenth birthday, she being one of the two high school seniors who had moved in earlier that year. I feel certain that Varla, who came festooned in a Pucci cat suit and per-formed for an hour, has never since played in such a truly dreary envi-ronment as that provided for her at 1805 Robert. Given her now regular appearances in Provincetown, not to mention a stint on Broadway, let it suffice to say, she's come a long way.

For the next several months, after the Morial campaign flamed out, I worked off-and-on for Lance at the Coalition offices. Money was still trickling in from contributors, and so occasionally he would have enough cash on hand to hire me back as a research assistant or handle some leftover media interviews about Duke and what we thought he might be up to next. It wouldn't take long to be able to answer that question, as Duke announced that he intended to run for

Governor of Louisiana in the fall of 1991, the very next year. Round two was about to begin.

* * *

BUT FOR ME, it may have well been over before it even started, had it not been for Lance's willingness to stand up to at least one Coalition board member who sought to have me fired.

In November 1990, I penned an article for what would prove to be the next-to-last edition of the *AVANT*. Therein, I discussed my personal outrage at the way in which the state of Israel had consistently supported the racist South African regime, all throughout the decades-long struggle against apartheid. As an American, I was offended by U.S. support of the white minority regime there, and as a Jew, I was horrified that this government to which we Jews were expected to have some fond regard—if not outright religious loyalty—would support the oppression of black South Africans by way of technology transfers, economic investment, and even military involvement with the government there.

The essay was scripted in response to an article I had read the previous summer in the Nashville Jewish Federation newsletter, written by Bertram Korn Jr., a spokesperson for a militantly anti-Arab organization called CAMERA (Committee for Accuracy in Middle East Reporting), the primary purpose of which was to insulate Israel from even the mildest of criticism. To Korn and the hyper-Zionists who think like him, nothing Israel does in defense of the Jewish state is ever objectionable. Jews are always innocent, always victims, never victimizers—and to suggest otherwise is to make one an anti-Semite. In Korn's view, Israel shouldn't be criticized for trade and investment with South Africa, since several Arab states also engaged in such activity—a geopolitical equivalent of the old, "Billy threw the rocks too, Mom" defense, and about as unconvincing.

In the piece, I detailed the various entanglements between the Jewish state and the white racist government in South Africa, and noted the special irony of such linkages given the way in which the first four apartheid governments had been led by men who were Nazi collaborators during World War Two. What self-respecting Jew would tacitly support connections of this sort, by way of their silence, just so their precious Israel could avoid well-deserved rebuke?

Apparently, the answer was Jane Buchsbaum, the treasurer of the
Louisiana Coalition (and head of the local Jewish Federation), who
decided that my apostasy with regard to Israel was grounds for ter-
mination. Upon learning of the article—thanks to the frenetic call of
Harley Karz-Wagman, the Rabbi at the Tulane Hillel House, who fashioned himself quite the liberal, and who had seen it within hours of
its release—Buchsbaum called Lance and said that in her opinion, I
should have no further role in the Coalition. Blurring the lines between
actual anti-Jewish bigots like Duke, and anti-Zionist Jews like myself
(or merely Jews who didn't think it right to support anti-black racism
in South Africa), Buchsbaum and Karz-Wagman suggested that I was
hardly better than the man whom I'd been working to defeat the past
several months.

I learned of Rabbi Harley's outrage while having dinner at Nicol's
mom's house. I was there when Shiloh Dewease, one of the roommates
at Robert Street and a longtime *AVANT* collective member, called to
inform me of his present temper-tantrum. Harley had called the house,
incensed by the essay and demanding a retraction. Shiloh had asked him
what, if anything, about the piece was factually inaccurate, to which he
had replied, *nothing*. There was nothing inaccurate about the claims I
had made—Israel indeed had supported South African apartheid—but
according to the Rabbi, Jews shouldn't write such truths, no matter how
accurate. We should not, in Harley's words, "air other Jews' dirty laundry."
That such lunacy confirmed my decision nine years before to leave the
Temple seemed apparent. If this was the orthodoxy required to remain
a Jew in good standing, by all means, I thought, let me be a Jew in exile.

Lance would have none of it of course. My views on Israel (which he
largely shared, unbeknownst to Jane and Rabbi Harley), were irrelevant
to my work at the Coalition, he explained. Not to mention, all of three
hundred people (if we were lucky) might have read the article, and I
hadn't identified myself in the byline as working for the Coalition, so
what difference did it make? Though I received several hostile calls at
the *AVANT* house from right-wing Jews who lectured me on my insuf-
ficient devotion to our supposed spiritual homeland, the controversy
blew over rather quickly. That said, it had demonstrated to me the ten-
dentious nature of antiracist allyship.

All of my life I had heard that we as Jews were almost inherently predisposed to oppose injustice—the result of our religious teachings and our experiences as targets for oppression and even extermination. But as it turned out, we were just as motivated by naked power and self-interest as anyone. Liberal and left Jews could turn into apologists for murder and discrimination just as soon as Israel was in the picture, whether regarding South Africa or the Palestinians. Jane and Harley had taught me a lesson alright, but it hadn't been the one they'd set out to impart. What I'd learned was that, politically speaking, we Jews were really just a slightly different brand of white folks.

* * *

HOWEVER, IT WASN'T only the organized Jewish community that could prove inconsistent on the ally front. In late spring 1991, funding for the Coalition hadn't picked up sufficiently to allow for my full-time re-hiring to work on the Gubernatorial campaign against Duke. So, worried about finances, but wanting to remain involved in progressive activism, I took a job as a statewide coordinator for Students Organizing Students (SOS): a New York-based group working to secure reproductive freedom for women, especially in states like Louisiana, where abortion access was constantly being threatened by lawmakers.

Although the job was supposed to be for one person, Anneliese Singh (who had just graduated from Tulane and with whom I'd been friends for several years) approached me about sharing the responsibilities with her. It was too much for her to do alone, she said, and since I still had occasional work at the Coalition, a part-time gig would work well for me, so I jumped at the chance. I knew Anneliese to be a first-rate organizer, and being a staunch supporter of abortion rights and the full-range of women's reproductive choices, I saw it as an opportunity to make a difference on an important issue, while gaining critical organizing experience in the process.

The timing of my work with SOS couldn't have been more propitious, as it dovetailed with David Duke's authorship of a bill in the state house that would pay poor women on income support to be temporarily sterilized with NORPLANT contraceptive inserts. As if the legislature's annual attempts to prohibit or severely curtail abortion access weren't bad enough, now Duke was offering to limit reproductive freedom in the other direction, by all but bribing desperate mothers to undergo sterilization so as to limit childbirth. Anneliese and I both thought it would be an excellent opportunity to demonstrate the intersectionality of three oppressions: racism, classism, and sexism, since anti-welfare sentiment was obviously aimed at women, and poor women in particular, and poor women of color even more directly; so, in addition to organizing against proposed abortion restrictions, we began working against House Bill 1584 as well: the Duke sterilization plan.

During this time I co-authored, along with Lance, a report critiquing the NORPLANT bill for the Coalition, which we distributed to lawmakers and the media. Therein, we explained the connections between Duke's plan and his longstanding support for Nazi-like eugenics programs. House Bill 1584, we explained, was a throwback to Hitlerian population control efforts. Not to mention, it was based on flawed policy premises regarding women on welfare, including any number of false assumptions about the link between income support and out-of-wedlock childbirths, which studies indicate is no real link at all. States with the most generous income support programs have lower rates of out-of-wedlock childbirth, while those with the highest rates of out-of-wedlock childbirth invariably have the weakest social safety net programs.

Seeing the sterilization bill as an obvious organizing opportunity for pro-choice forces, Anneliese and I approached Louisiana Choice, the state affiliate of the National Abortion Rights Action League (NARAL), and the largest abortion rights group in the state, hoping to work together to defeat Duke's assault on the reproductive freedom of poor women. Despite several attempts to gain their interest, or involve them in public events to discuss restrictions on abortion access *and* restrictions on the right to have children if so desired, the only reply from the NARAL folks was silence. They showed no interest in fighting the Duke bill. Though their lack of apparent concern may have been due to overwork at trying to beat back the restrictions on abortion that were pending in the legislature, it's hard to avoid the thought that they were also making a decision influenced by their own race and class biases. To the white and middle-class led group, the reproductive freedom of poor women, especially of color, to *have* children in the face of a society that despises them, took a back seat to securing the rights of mostly middle class and white women who could afford abortions, to terminate their pregnancies.

In the end, House Bill 1584 was defeated, no thanks to the mainstream women's rights groups who ignored it. Sadly, the underlying logic of the proposal—that poor women are too fertile and need to have their reproduction restricted either by force or bribe—remains with us. Indeed, another state lawmaker in Louisiana proposed similar legislation in 2008, suggesting that while Duke may have been defeated in his attempts to shape the law, Dukism remains a force to be reckoned with, even two decades later.

* * *

ALL THROUGHOUT THE early-to-mid-1990s, New Orleans was known nationwide for its crime problem, and by then it had already been notorious for years for its overzealous police force. The combination of these two facts made it difficult sometimes to know who the good guys were. For people of color, calling on the police for help was a dicey proposition, mostly because they could never know whether help is what they'd receive as opposed to brutality and mistreatment.

One night while we were living on Robert Street, one of the roommates, Darryl Barthé, got to experience the brutality of the NOPD up close and personal. Darryl, who remains to this day one of the most no-bullshit people I've ever met—he says what's on his mind and could give a rat's ass if you like him or not—was and is a character, possessing an almost encyclopedic knowledge about the city of New Orleans, and especially its color divide, not only between black and white but between Creoles, which he is, and everyone else. Darryl also is imbued with a classic punk-rock mentality, not only because it's among the many styles of music he enjoys, but because it fits perfectly with his political sensibilities. He has always struck me as a combination of Jello Biafra (founding member of the iconic punk band Dead Kennedys) and Dr. Madd Vibe (lead singer of the ska/punk/funk group Fishbone), along with a little Bakunin and Huey Newton thrown in for good measure.

On his way back from a party near the Riverbend area (close to the top of Uptown), Darryl had the misfortune of walking while black, on an evening when apparently someone else, also black, had mugged some white folks. Turning from Freret Street onto Robert, and by this point only a few blocks from our house, Darryl found his path impeded by a police cruiser whose occupants hopped out and demanded that he tell them about "jumping the white people." He replied that he had no idea what they were talking about and was just walking home. When Darryl proceeded to mumble something about the absurdity of the encounter, one of the officers grabbed him, prompting Darryl—who was fully aware of the reputation of the city's police and rightly concerned about being manhandled—to attempt to push the cop off of him. Enraged by the act of defiance, the officer then fulfilled his expected and typecast role by slugging Darryl in the mouth, splitting his lip in the process.

The police then proceeded to shove Darryl into the car and drive to the corner of Freret and Calhoun streets, where another officer was speaking with a white female college student who had just been mugged. When the officers pulled Darryl from the car and asked if he was the one who had jumped her, the young woman insisted he was not. Unbowed, the police asked her three more times if she were sure, clearly disappointed by their bad collar and hoping to nail Darryl for the crime. She stood firm however and repeated that Darryl had not assaulted her. In truth, it would have been pretty hard for her to have forgotten Darryl had he been the one; after all, he was wearing a T-shirt that said "Fuck You" in bright red letters.

Rather than release him, though, the police proceeded to throw him back in the car and begin the drive downtown, where, they explained, he would be booked, presumably for the shove he'd administered to the cop who had sought to detain him for a crime he didn't commit. On the way downtown, as the officers lectured Darryl about how his family clearly hadn't raised him right, as evidenced by his lack of obeisance to the police, he proceeded to mention that his family included police officers and that his uncle had been Deputy Superintendent at one point and Chief Detective. Unconvinced, they asked for his uncle's name, which he gladly provided, prompting the police to pull over, let Darryl know how lucky he was, and then put him out on the curb to walk back home.

Such treatment would not be that which I would receive at the hands of the New Orleans police, however, and the difference is worth commenting upon.

Around the same time, I too had encountered one of the city's finest. It had been early on a Tuesday afternoon. Nicol was in class at Tulane, and I had kept the car that morning while she was on campus so I could run errands. After returning home for lunch, I headed back out onto the street to get in the car and drive to Newcomb Hall to pick her up, at which point I saw that I had locked my keys in the car.

Pissed but not panicked—I had, after all, learned how to get into locked cars with a coat hanger when I was sixteen, sacking groceries at a Nashville market where I'd often been called upon to help elderly ladies who'd made the same mistake—I ran up the stairs, grabbed a wire hanger, and headed back to the car to break in. Unfortunately, the 1988 Toyota Tercel is among the hardest cars on earth into which one may break, which is ironic, considering how few people could possibly want to steal one. No matter my truly veteran efforts to open the door, I was having no luck even after ten minutes.

It was then, as I was furiously bending the hanger back and forth, trying desperately to jam it between the metal door frame and the rubber insulation around the window, that a police car pulled up. The officer hopped out and approached me.

"What's going on here?" he asked, more curious than accusatory.

"I locked myself out of my car and I've got to pick up my girlfriend in like five minutes," I replied, exasperated with my shitty luck.

I fully expected the officer to ask me for identification or some kind of proof that this was my car, which only goes to show how little I understood about the value of white skin in the eyes of law enforcement.

"Well, I can tell you right now," he interjected. "The problem is, you're doing that all wrong."

"Excuse me?" I replied, not having expected to be told by a police officer that I lacked the necessary acumen to break into a car the *right* way.

"Yeah, that's no way to break into a car," he insisted. "Here, let me show you how it's done."

And with that he went to his trunk and pulled out a slim jim, which is a long piece of flat metal that can pop a car door open by being shoved down behind the rubber seal around the bottom of the window until it meets an interior rod that controls the door function. Once it connects with the rod, a small hook on the end of the slim jim can pull up on the rod, thereby opening the door. The officer proceeded to demonstrate the proper method for breaking into a car, and seemed to take great glee at the opportunity to demonstrate his own technique for the maneuver. Sadly, he too would be unsuccessful, stymied as I had been by the superior workmanship of the Tercel.

Still unconcerned about my identity or legitimate claim on the vehicle, he suggested that I should throw a rock through the window. When I told him my girlfriend would be pretty pissed at me for doing that, he said I could always tell her someone had broken into the car. Breaking the glass might even be fun, he insisted, making me think that perhaps he was wanting to do the honors himself.

It is, of course, incomprehensible that had it been Darryl (or any black person in his twenties) who had locked himself out of his car and was trying to break in with a coat hanger, that anything about the encounter would have been the same. To think that an officer would have simply taken for granted that the vehicle belonged to the would-be black or brown break-in artist requires a level of naiveté almost too stunning to fully comprehend. For whites, innocence was presumed until proven otherwise, while for blacks, the presumption of guilt was the default position.

* * *

BY APRIL, NICOL and I had moved, along with two other roommates, from our overcrowded house on Robert, into a smaller but much cleaner place on Dante Street. It was so clean, in fact, that Darryl took to derisively calling it the "aqua fresh condo." Between SOS and the increasing volume of work with the Coalition as the Governor's race began to heat up, I was staying plenty busy.

Duke picked up where he'd left off in the Senate race, rallying angry whites around such themes as welfare reform, affirmative action, and taxes, promising that if he were elected he would stand up for whites, whom he proclaimed to be the victims of "massive reverse discrimination." Likewise, we at the Coalition swung into high gear, coordinating our second "campaign without a candidate" in two years. This go-around, the choice was going to be between Duke, incumbent Governor (Democrat-turned-Republican) Buddy Roemer, and former three-time Governor, Edwin Edwards. Once again, as Duke came on strong, the more moderate Republican faded. In the primary, Duke won a third of the vote, knocking off Roemer and setting up a runoff with Edwards.

Edwin Edwards had been a fixture on the state political scene for thirty years by 1991. A freewheeling Cajun from Southwestern Louisiana, Edwards had built a reputation as a man of the people, but also as a flamboyant womanizer, gambler, and occasional practitioner of good-old-fashioned corruption. Once famous for saying that when it came to unlawful campaign contributions, it was "illegal for them to give but not for me to receive," he quipped now that the only way he would lose to David Duke was if he were found in bed with a "dead woman or a live boy."

Knowing that there was no way to skirt Edwards' checkered past, we decided to use it as part of the campaign strategy, developing bumper stickers that would become known around the country to people who were watching the race. They said simply, "Vote for the Crook. It's Important." Soon, it became a battle on the roadways to see which side would claim the allegiance of the most automobiles. On the one side there were the Duke supporters with their blue and white DUKE stickers, and on the other, those of us with our red and white NO DUKES stickers (a play on the 'No Nukes' slogan of the '70s and '80s), or the black and white one liners about the importance of choosing corruption over its opponent, Nazism.

During the Governor's race, Lance and I discussed the importance, ethically if not strategically, of more directly confronting Duke's public policy narrative than we had in the previous campaign. Having already released the report on HB 1584 in June, in which we had sought to confront the widespread misperceptions about so-called welfare and the people who received it, it seemed like an important addition to the existing campaign narrative. And seeing how the unprincipled discussions of Duke's taxes, draft dodging, and other minor matters had failed to move voters in the Senate race, those sideline distractions would not be making a comeback this time. Although much was made—especially by the Edwards campaign—about the likely economic disaster that would follow a Duke victory (thanks to corporate and tourist boycotts of the state), even that argument rested upon the notion that Duke's racist extremism is what made him so eminently boycott-able. So even the economic argument rested, indirectly, on an antiracist foundation. It was still about the unacceptability of bigotry.

We took out full page ads in newspapers across the state challenging Duke's politics of racial scapegoating, pushing back directly against his tendency to blame poor blacks for everything from high taxes to crime to white unemployment, and looking instead at the real sources of working- and middle-class insecurity: corporate tax giveaways, downsizing, deindustrialization, and budget cuts for education. Though it wasn't to be the key element of our campaign, it was nice to be inserting a clearly progressive critique of mainstream conservatism into the mix, in ways we hadn't before. For the sake of movement building, it's critical to develop a counter-narrative, and not merely to rebut the narrative with which you find fault. This time around, we would do that in a much more concerted fashion.

Still, the focus was, as it needed to be, on Duke's neo-Nazism. And shortly before the open primary in October, we would come across the kind of bombshell we'd been looking for the previous year, which would tie Duke, beyond any doubt, to a politics of Hitlerian ideology. It came in the form of a series of interviews with British researcher Evelyn Rich, who had met with Duke on several occasions in the mid-1980s while doing dissertation research on the white supremacist movement. Rich (who ironically would later marry one of the nation's leading white nationalists, Jared Taylor) turned out to have done some of the best work for the Coalition, without even knowing she had done so.

Lance had found the recordings of Duke's interviews with Rich, as well as some transcripts, and had me go through them piece by piece, over eight hours of recordings in all. There were gaps in the transcripts, often at key points of the dialogue, which Lance wanted me to fill. He hoped that we'd be able to pull enough extremist content from the tapes to use in the campaign. Sure enough, the recordings were filled with open admissions by Duke that his views had really never changed after leaving the Klan, as well as long, manic rants about Jews and their pernicious, conspiratorial designs on world domination. Listening to his hours-long rambling was like listening to the ravings of a woefully under-medicated psychotic, peppered as it was with references to Jewish responsibility for pornography, obscene poetry, race-mixing, drugs, suicide, and incest. And of course, Duke expounded at length in the interviews about his belief that the Nazi Holocaust had been entirely fabricated by a "Jewish writer in Hollywood."

But best of all was a recording from February 1986, in which Duke had discussed strategy with an open Nazi by the name of Joe Fields. While Fields had no problem proclaiming his devotion to Hitler, to whom he referred as the "ultimate" role model for whites, Duke cautioned him to be careful, because "if they can call you a Nazi and make it stick . . . it's going to hurt." Although Duke noted it was "unfortunate it's like that" (in other words, it's a shame people can't just openly embrace Nazism), he counseled Fields to "leave his options open" when it came to being so brazen about his views. Finally, when Fields exclaimed that "Hitler started with seven men," Duke chimed in, excitedly noting, "And don't you think it can happen right now, if we put the right package together?" When Fields again insisted that he would never deny he was a Nazi, Duke ended by saying, "I wheedle out of it because I'm a pragmatist."

Although the audio quality on the recordings wasn't spectacular— they had been made on cassette tapes, which by then were four to five-years-old—I took them to a recording studio at Xavier University, where the background noise was taken out and the audio quality boosted, thereby leaving us with a clear articulation, not only of Duke's extrem-ism in his own words, but also his *admission* that he was conning every-one into believing he had changed. We turned the recordings into radio commercials which ran on hundreds of stations across the state, and planted the story in virtually every print outlet in Louisiana. The state Democratic Party picked up on the recordings too, running TV ads fea-turing Duke's comments in the final weeks of the campaign.

There was no question by election night that Duke would lose. The only real issue was, as with the Senate race, how resounding a defeat could be handed to him. Although the result was better than that from the previous year—Edwards prevailed by a 61–39 margin—the victory for the saner forces in our state was dampened once again by the vote tally among whites. Although we had managed to help pare off a few percentage points of Duke's white support, he had still managed to capture nearly 55 percent of all white votes cast. In other words, most whites in Louisiana had been perfectly prepared to elect a Nazi as Governor of the state. As had been true in the previous election, black folks had saved us from ourselves, turning out to the polls in record numbers to defeat Duke, and to defeat white racism.

The two anti-Duke campaigns had been eye-openers. On the one hand, I knew that most whites in Louisiana were not Nazis, or overt racists who believed in the creation of a master race or the carving up of the United States into distinct racial sub-nations. But what I also knew, given the election results, was that most whites were willing to vote for someone who was all of those things. Sitting alone with my thoughts in the days following the election, I was forced to contemplate what that fact meant, not only about white people generally, but for *me*, specifically. After all, as easy as it would have been to become smug in the face of such a thing—to pride oneself on having been enlightened enough and perhaps even evolved enough to know better than to vote for the Nazi—the truth was, there was very little separating me from those six hundred thousand-plus whites who had voted for Duke. I had had one set of experiences growing up that delivered me down a particular path, and they had had a different set of experiences that delivered them down another one. It could easily have gone the other way. I could no more congratulate myself for my insights than I could bash them for their decided lack of the same. These were my people, after all, and if we who aspire to be white allies cannot or will not struggle with our people—as we would hope others would struggle with us (and often have)—then who is going to do it?

One thing I knew at that moment was that it wasn't the job of people of color to fix us; it was *our* job. It was on us to practice that "personal responsibility" about which we so readily preach to people of color. It was time for self-help.

* * *

AFTER THE GOVERNOR'S race, the Coalition went through another financial implosion, as contributions dried up, the job of defeating Duke seemingly accomplished. That the name of our organization was the Louisiana Coalition Against Racism and Nazism, and not David

Duke *per se*, always seemed to escape some people. Getting folks to see racism as a broader matter was often a struggle, so much easier as it was to remain fixated on the blatantly obvious example of bigotry dominating the news cycle. As contributions flatlined I was laid off again, but would be brought back within a few weeks as Duke, unbowed by his two defeats, announced he was going to run for President and would enter the Super Tuesday primaries in the South, in March 1992.

We went back to work, making sure that media across the region understood what the Louisiana media had come to realize; namely, that Duke was a white supremacist not merely in his past but also in his present. The effort was hardly needed. Not only did most everyone know by now, but any concerted anti-Duke effort was superfluous by the spring of '92. Duke's luster was gone, less because his brand of politics was passé—far from it—but because his thunder was being actively stolen by Pat Buchanan, who became the voice and embodiment of white resentment for the presidential race: a political commentator without the Klan baggage, and a member in good standing of the conservative cognitariat. Buchanan pushed all the same buttons as Duke—the anger over affirmative action, crime, immigration, and welfare moms—but he did it without the obvious ties to extremist groups that had characterized Duke's entire adult life. By Super Tuesday, Duke was relegated to pulling double digits in only one state, Mississippi. Meanwhile, Buchanan had already stormed forward in places like New Hampshire, stealing from what the columnist himself described as Duke's "winning playbook" of issues. David had been out-Duked, beaten at his own game.

In the larger social sense, Duke's electoral demise was a huge victory for antiracist forces, and never has anyone been so grateful for having worked himself out of a job as I was in that moment. That said, I *had* indeed worked myself out of a job. Little did I know that it would be a while before I really had another one.

Unemployed and uncertain as to what I might do next, I could hardly put up much of a fight when Nicol got offered a job in Houston and decided to take it. Though I couldn't imagine living in Texas, I was in no position to argue the point, and so in April of 1992 we packed our things into a large U-Haul truck and headed off to the only place capable of making New Orleans look temperate.

PROFESSIONAL DEVELOPMENT

WE HAD ONLY been in Houston for a little over two weeks when Los Angeles went up in flames. On April 29, 1992, a jury in Simi Valley, California, acquitted the four white officers who had beaten Rodney King in the aftermath of the now-infamous high-speed chase the previous year. As word spread of their acquittal, South Central Los Angeles exploded. With no job, I sat and watched the drama unfold on television by the hour, the story being one of the first to receive virtually twenty-four-hour news coverage for days on end. Images of neighborhoods engulfed in smoke and fire sent shock waves through the nation. Folks who had enjoyed the luxury of ignoring the rage of the dispossessed were now having to stare it dead in the face, and they were none too happy with what they were seeing. The black and Latino communities of L.A. had reached their boiling point, having seen far too much police corruption and brutality go unpunished over the years (and by the mid-90s even more evidence would emerge about police illegality on an epic scale in the city's Ramparts division). Though most of white America couldn't understand the anger, it was only privilege that allowed such obliviousness.

Much was made by commentators and the public of the horrific attack on Reginald Denny, a white truck driver, by four black men at the corner of Florence and Normandie avenues. Denny was pulled from his truck and beaten—a cinder block smashed onto his head—in full sight of helicopter cameras, the scene playing out for millions to witness during the live coverage. The viciousness of the attackers was, to some, evidence of black barbarity and criminality—this would be the take of

Pat Buchanan, for instance, who would use the riots as a political chit during his presidential bid. Interestingly, and in keeping with the way in which people are so quick to find evidence to suit their pre-existing biases (and ignore that which contradicts them), few seemed to notice the decency and heroism of the two African American men (Bobby Green, Jr. and Rev. Bennie Newton) who came to the defense of Denny and another of the mob's victims, Fidel Lopez. While the negative acts of four black men were somehow evidence of a larger group flaw, the positive acts of the other two black men were taken to mean nothing in the opposite direction.

By the time our first month in Houston was done, I was sure I was going to lose my mind. I still couldn't find work, and except for excellent food and a decent nightlife—we would go to the city's gay dance clubs, mostly because Nicol didn't have to worry about getting hit on, and I could gauge my fashion sense by the extent to which I *did*—it was tough to find much to like about Harris County. Furthermore, as national events unfolded in which race was clearly implicated, I realized how much I missed working on matters of racial equity, and how important the subject matter had become to my understanding not only of the nation, but also of myself.

Then one day in mid-May, I answered a phone call that would, in a number of ways, change my life. On the other end was a producer for a new syndicated television show based in Boston, who had been told to contact me about appearing on an upcoming broadcast. She had gotten my number from Lance, who thought I might be perfect for an episode in which the host, Jane Whitney, would have a former Klan family on as guests, as well as a husband and wife who were still active members of the group. I would serve as the expert on the white supremacist movement. Initially, she had contacted the Southern Poverty Law Center, in Montgomery, Alabama, to see if someone from the group would appear on the show, but SPLC's policy is never to appear opposite racists and thereby give them more credibility than they deserve. Though I understood that logic, I also knew the show was going to proceed, with or without an antiracist analyst on the panel. Rather than leave it up to the host to know how to respond to the Klan members, I figured it was better to have someone do it who knew something about them.

Though I was skittish about the way talk shows typically dealt with these subjects—with good reason, since it had only been four years earlier that the infamous skinhead fight on *Geraldo* had broken out, during which the host had suffered a broken nose—I decided to do the show. Earlier in the year, while still in New Orleans, I had turned down an offer to appear on *Jerry Springer*, fearing the circus atmosphere that was already by that point his hallmark. But this time, something about the way in which Laura, the producer, described the episode, convinced me it could be a legitimate discussion.

I knew something of the ex-Klan family's story already, having seen the wife and mother, Jan Ralston, the year before on the *Sally Jesse Raphael Show*. She had first appeared as a proud member of one of the most militant and terroristic Klan factions in the country—the Southern White Knights. Rather than the white hoods associated for years with the KKK, the Knights preferred battle fatigues and black berets. But after spewing viciously racist diatribes from the stage, and then seeing the tape of the program provided her by the producers, Jan had experienced something of an epiphany. Shocked by her own demeanor, she had called up Sally's producers and asked to return to the program, this time to denounce the Klan and announce her decision to leave the organization.

By the time of the *Jane Whitney* appearance, Jan had convinced her husband Gary and two of their children to leave the Klan as well. They would be the primary focus of the show, opposite Ken and Carol Peterson, a Klan couple from Wisconsin. When Laura explained that the Petersons would appear by satellite, rather than live in the studio (because Ken was afraid to fly), I was convinced that my role in the program could be constructive. There was no chance that the show would descend into chair-throwing chaos with the unrepentant racists thousands of miles away.

The studio was outside of Boston, so about an hour and a half before the taping, I came downstairs to the lobby of the Bostonian Hotel, only to find myself face to face with the Ralstons, with whom I would be sharing the limo ride to the network affiliate. Despite knowing that they had left behind the white supremacist movement, I couldn't help but feel a momentary twinge of anxiety. These were, after all, people who just a year earlier would have wanted me dead.

I nervously introduced myself and was immediately heartened by the warmth of the Ralston family. Jan was as sweet and kind as she could be, and Gary, though gruff, was also polite and probably just as nervous as I was—in his case, wondering to what extent I was judging him and his family. With Jan and Gary were their two sons: Steven, who had been forced to join the Klan by his dad, and Allan, who had refused to join and had been initially disowned by his parents after telling them he was gay.

On the ride to the studio we talked about their story, which, as it turns out, was far deeper than I had known. Not only had the family disowned Allan, but Gary had actually been plotting with some of his Klan brothers to murder his son after learning of his sexuality. In part, it was Jan's horror at realizing that her husband was planning to kill her flesh and blood that had begun to snap her out of the white supremacist coma into which she and the family had fallen three years earlier. At one point, as Allan was planning on coming home to Stone Mountain, Georgia, for a visit, Jan had pleaded with him to stay in Texas for fear that had he returned home, Gary and other Klansmen would have murdered him.

The show went well, as the Ralstons and I effectively dismantled the incoherent ramblings of Ken and Carol Peterson (or really just Ken, since he rarely allowed his wife to speak). After returning to the Bostonian, we sat in the hotel bar for two hours, discussing how they had come to join the Klan, how they had come to realize the error of their ways, and how they were committed to making it right by speaking out against racism. I told them about my life as well, after which point Jan said I was one of the first Jewish people she had ever really talked to at length, and how she was so sorry about all the things she had said and felt about Jews in the past. I quickly forgave her of course, thanked them for their courage, and as night became early morning, we all said our goodbyes and went off to bed.

I didn't sleep. Putting aside the exhilaration at having been on my first national television show and having solidly represented the antiracist perspective, I was more excited by what I had come to realize, sitting in that limo with the Ralstons, or later having beers with them and discussing race. What I had learned was the fundamental redeemability of even the most distorted human soul. Staring at these folks, looking deeply into their eyes and witnessing the pain only barely concealed behind them, I had come to know that although David Duke had not changed, those who thought as he did were capable of transformation; that even the most vicious of racists is damaged, before ever joining such a movement, and even more once there. And if people such as that can be redeemed, then perhaps anything is possible—even justice and the end of white supremacy altogether.

* * *

THOUGH IT HAD been nice to be on TV, the appearance still hadn't opened up the floodgates when it came to job offers. To make ends meet I started working in the stockroom of the Bombay Company, the furniture store where Nicol was manager. Then in August, Nicol somehow managed to wrangle a decorator's contract to design the VIP suites at the Republican National Convention, which was being held in Houston that year, as well as the official "Bush family residence." The residence, as it happens, was just a hollowed out game room at the Houstonian Hotel: the Bush family's permanent Houston address so they could avoid paying state income taxes in Maine, where they actually lived when not at the White House.

Not having other work, I was immediately drafted into Nicol's decorator's army for the GOP shindig. Though I dreaded being that close to so many Republicans—especially so many of Pat Buchanan's supporters—I thought it might be a good opportunity to do some enemy reconnaissance, and to peek behind the curtains of the right-wing machine that was gearing up to take on Bill Clinton in November.

To a large extent, it wouldn't be necessary to peek behind any curtains, as much of the extremist lunacy present at the convention would receive ample coverage in the press. On opening night, Pat Buchanan delivered his infamous "culture war" speech, in which he raised the specter of the L.A. riots, repeating an utter fabrication that the rioters had been prepared to attack an old folks' home until brave soldiers stopped them, and then noting that just as the soldiers had reclaimed Los Angeles, block by block, so too must conservative Christians "take back their country" block by block from the un-American pornographers, feminists, and homosexuals who were seeking to hijack it.

Referring to Democrats as "cross-dressers," Buchanan suggested that if elected, Bill and Hillary Clinton would usher in an era where children would be encouraged to sue their parents, and the institution of marriage would be utterly eviscerated by militant lesbians and Hillary herself. I was in the convention hall that night, bringing furniture to the VIP rooms in the Astrodome, and was reminded of nothing so much as old footage of rallies at Nuremberg, sixty years prior, led by a certain German Chancellor to whom Buchanan had once referred as "an individual of great courage."

Although the convention's hostility seemed mostly focused on the LGBT community, there was always room for a little racial anxiety too. So early on the first day of the convention, as delegates were beginning to arrive (and as Nicol and I were hauling boxes of furniture from the car to the VIP lounges), I happened to look out at the mostly-empty floor of the convention space, to the Jumbotrons overhead that would soon show up-close coverage of the event to attendees in the nosebleed seats. There, in full-screen color, snarling out over the hall, as if to remind those entering who the enemy was, was a freeze-frame image of the rapper Ice-T.

The previous month, Ice had come under fire from law enforcement (and groups like Tipper Gore's Parent's Music Resource Center) for the song "Cop Killer," which appeared on the first album of his speed metal band, Body Count. The song, which told a story of revenge being taken on law enforcement because of police brutality, was seen by some as a call for murdering officers. Although no one really believed Johnny Cash had wanted to "kill a man in Reno, just to watch him die," when violence fantasies are spun by black men, naturally, they are never just fictionalized accounts intended as art, but are to be viewed as ruminations on the inherent nature of the person singing them. And there he was, the big, bad rapper (though "Cop Killer" was not a rap song), scaring the Republican faithful as they entered the Astrodome. Let it suffice to say, subtlety was not their strong suit.

* * *

BUT THE WILLINGNESS of conservatives to exploit racial fears for the purpose of revving up the troops was hardly a revelation. It wasn't even remotely surprising. What *was* instructive, however, was coming to understand more viscerally than I ever had before, just how much my white skin insulated me from the harsh judgments or suspicions of others.

After we were done with the rooms at the convention hall, Nicol and I headed over to the Houstonian, where we were to meet two of her Bombay Company colleagues, so as to begin setting up Barbara and George H.W. Bush's "living room," from which place they would be interviewed throughout the convention by the networks. It was an interminably hot and humid day, and we made the drive from one side of town to the next (which, in Houston, routinely takes over an hour) without air conditioning, in the Tercel, the back seat and hatch area filled to the brim with boxes of cheap imitation antique tables, chairs, and accessories. By the time we arrived at the checkpoint for the hotel—which was set up near the road, just inside the driveway to the main building—we were more than a little ragged around the edges, covered in sweat, and desperate to get out of the heat.

Despite the way we looked, and despite the way in which the car was stuffed with closed boxes (in which, frankly, could have been anything—weapons as easily as furniture), when security asked us why we were there, and we told them, they did nothing more than briefly glance through the back window and then wave us on. They did not ask for identification or a contact number for the persons with whom Nicol had contracted for the job in the first place—nothing.

We proceeded to spend the next four hours setting up the room in which the President of the United States and First Lady would be staying throughout prime time convention hours. We rearranged furniture from the hotel, brought in new furniture from outside, and did all of this with no oversight or security whatsoever. There were no cameras in the room and we finished a mere five minutes before the Bushes were to enter, which is to say, there was no time for any security sweep once we had exited.

Simply put, no one considered that perhaps they might want to check out who we were and what we were doing. Had we been black, security would never have been so sanguine. Had we appeared to be Arab, it is highly unlikely that our car and furniture boxes would have gone unchecked. But white twenty-three-year-olds? What could there possibly be to worry about? The fact that I had been told four years before that I couldn't even ride in a campaign motorcade with Michael Dukakis because I couldn't pass a background check—the result of my already-extant FBI file—didn't matter. They simply hadn't thought to ask or do their homework. Fact is, had I been the least bit inclined to kill the president, he would have been dead, and Dan Quayle would have inherited the office. We could have planted a bomb in that room or climbed one of the trees that sat not thirty feet from the room's large floor-to-ceiling windows and shot him. Of course we never would have done such a thing (and not only because Dan Quayle would have inherited the office), but the sickening fact is, we *could* have, because we're white, and therefore, presumed not to be dangerous.

*　*　*

THOUGH THE *JANE* WHITNEY SHOW had only been seen in about thirty-five markets, and thus, my television debut had been witnessed by a pitifully small number of people, there was one person watching that evening upon whom I had made a significant impression.

I received a call at our Houston apartment a week after the show aired from a man in South Haven, Connecticut, who told me his name was "Coach Jimmy Jackson." Coach Jimmy, as I would come to know him, had quite a story to tell, and felt that I was just the person with whom he could share it. Normally, this would have been the kind of thing I would likely have blown off—merely humoring him until he got tired of talking and then politely saying 'goodbye,' never to speak again—but there was something about Jimmy that struck me as genuine, and kind. Furthermore, his story of discrimination rang true for me, such that I offered to take a closer look and do whatever I could to help.

Jimmy Jackson had been everything from a cop to a recording artist with Buddha Records back in the late 1960s. He had also joined the New York Jets in 1966, only to suffer an injury in training camp, thereby ending his football career before it had started. But mostly, and what he wanted me to know, was that he was a football coach, and a damned good one, having won two national semi-pro championships, been in three semi-pro Super Bowls, compiled an overall winning percentage of 73 percent, and having been voted General Manager of the Year and

three-time coach-of-the-year in the minor leagues. Why all of this mattered was that Coach Jimmy was in the process of suing the National
Football League and the fledgling World League of American Football
for racial discrimination. The World League had formed a few years
prior as an experimental operation, with teams in the U.S., Canada,
and Europe, but despite his impressive accomplishments and the rec-
ommendations he had received from persons like Jack Pardee, head
coach of the NFL Houston Oilers; Gene Burrough, former GM of the
New Jersey Generals (of the United States Football League); legendary
quarterback Johnny Unitas; and Tim Rooney, Director of Personnel for
the NFL Giants, Jackson had been passed over for a coaching gig with
the league. Not only had Jackson not been hired for a job in the World
League, no black coach had been, despite the claims of the league director that a diverse coaching pool was among their top priorities. Jimmy
promised to send me the supporting materials for his lawsuit, and I
promised I would look them over.

When the first packet of information came, I have to say, I wasn't
immediately sold on the strength of Jimmy's case. He had representation—a pretty established law firm in downtown Manhattan—but all he
had for me at the time were some clippings regarding his prior coaching experience, and some publicity materials he had put together, as
well as various articles about discrimination in the NFL, including one
piece from *Sports Illustrated*, which detailed the difficulties that African
Americans were having obtaining jobs on the sidelines. Still, and despite
the paucity of hard evidence up to that point, I enjoyed talking with
Jimmy and felt there might be more to the case. So I insisted that he stay
in touch as his attorneys proceeded through the discovery phase of the
lawsuit, and to let me know what they came up with. I would be glad to
serve as an expert consultant of sorts if his lawyers thought I might be
of some assistance.

Of course, I reminded Jimmy on numerous occasions that I was only
twenty-three, the mere possessor of a Bachelor's Degree, and could in
no way be presumed an expert on discrimination the way many others
could. So, I explained, he might want to get someone with more formal
credentials to serve as an actual expert witness come time for trial. But
Jimmy would have none of it. He had seen me on *Jane Whitney* and felt

that I was the right person for the job. I thanked him for his confidence and promised to do all I could.

Though there would be no pay for any of the work I did over the next two years on Jimmy's behalf, ultimately, that work would become some of the most important I've ever done, if not for Jimmy, then certainly for myself. Indeed, my involvement with Jimmy would ultimately serve as the best education I could have received about how racism works, specifically at the institutional level. In fact, my work on Jimmy's case was one of the few high points during a period of my life in which most everything else was going wrong.

From mid-1992 until late 1994, my professional life would remain in constant crisis mode. We would leave Houston in September to return to New Orleans, but although I had more connections there than in Texas, I still had no luck finding activist work upon getting back. Broke, unemployed, and unable to contribute anything to the household that Nicol and I shared, I found myself desperate enough at one point to sell off my treasured baseball card collection, which I had cultivated as a youth. Although the cards were worth about thirty thousand dollars then (and, sickeningly would be worth nearly half a million dollars today), I felt as though I had no choice, ultimately letting them go for only about 15 percent of their value at the time. I also took a job in early 1993 as a stock boy at a local wine store, until finally landing a research position with economics writer and author Walter Russell Mead in June. But even during the work with Mead (for which those of us hired to assist him were paid two hundred dollars a week, and even then never on time), I was far more interested in Jimmy's case than anything Walter had us looking up on international trade and development policy.

By mid-'93, the lawsuit was in full swing, and over the next several months, as Jimmy's attorneys would depose the principals from the other side, they would load me up with deposition transcripts to look over, as well as internal NFL and World League documents uncovered during discovery. Whereas the initial materials Jimmy had sent me had left quite a bit to be desired, the new documents seemed a treasure trove of useful evidence. Though WLAF officials claimed to be concerned about the lack of black coaches in professional football, they had passed up several opportunities to hire African Americans for the league.

Jimmy was only one of the black coaches ultimately ignored by team GMs and the league itself, which had hiring authority over the clubs in Barcelona and London.

Rather than hire any blacks who applied for head coaching jobs with the World League—several of whom were assistant coaches in the NFL by that point—teams ultimately stocked up on white has-beens, most of whom had failed in previous positions. So, for instance, Sacramento hired Kay Stephenson, formerly the head coach of the Buffalo Bills, but whose record had been so bad that he'd failed to land another job after being fired several years earlier, and who was selling real estate in Florida at the time of his hiring. Likewise, Montreal hired Jacques Dussault, who had previously served as an assistant for two failed Canadian Football League teams, and Raleigh-Durham hired Roman Gabriel, a former star quarterback with the Los Angeles Rams, but who had been working as the GM of a minor league baseball franchise at the time of his hire, and who had only coached briefly at Cal Poly-Pomona, a school whose football program was so bad it had been disbanded after Gabriel's tenure there.

Although the league claimed in its defense that it *had* made offers to black coaches, a careful examination of those claims suggested the offers had been in bad faith, and were more to keep up appearances of fairness than to truly bring diversity to the professional coaching ranks. Offers were made to three coaches in particular: Dennis Green (at that time the head coach at Stanford), Tony Dungy (at that time an assistant coach with the Kansas City Chiefs), and Milt Jackson, a veteran wide receivers coach in the NFL. But Green and Dungy were already being groomed for NFL coaching jobs and were known to be within a few years of securing such positions; as such, there was very little chance that either of them would have taken the risk of joining an experimental league, for less pay and prestige, and potentially derailing their professional trajectories. In fact, Green had told League president Jerome Vainisi that he had no interest in coaching in the WLAF. As for Milt Jackson, he had made it clear that he would only accept an offer for the Sacramento franchise because it would allow him to live close to his family. But rather than even interview him for the Sacramento job, the League offered him the position in Barcelona, knowing there was no way he would accept it.

To see how the League and its team GMs continually "moved the goalposts," jiggling the job qualification requirements and relying on old boy's networks in a way that worked to the benefit of whites and detriment of blacks, was an incredible lesson in the way institutional racism operates. Far from the bigotry of a David Duke, this was slick and systemic racism, the kind that had worked to marginalize not only Jimmy Jackson and other black coaches, but millions of black job applicants across the nation in any number of professions for decades, ever since the passage of civil rights laws.

Even more instructive was the way in which the League had employed a hiring criteria that, while facially race-neutral, was guaranteed to produce a racially-exclusionary impact on black coaching aspirants. So according to Jerome Vainisi, the League had been looking for coaches with experience in one of three prior arenas: either as head coach of a pro team, head coach of a "top fifty" college program, or as an offensive or defensive coordinator in either the National Football League or the short-lived United States Football League (USFL). Of course, as I would explain to Jimmy's attorneys, such a criteria—even assuming the WLAF had been using it, rather than just going with the personal preferences of the white GMs—could not *but* produce an all-white outcome. At that point, there had never been a black head coach or offensive or defensive coordinator in a professional league, and the only African American college coach in a top program was Dennis Green, whose success in the college game ensured he would be holding out for a much more prestigious NFL gig. The World League certainly knew that the criteria would have that effect, so it seemed reasonable to conclude that their intent in using it had been to produce the disparate impact that was predictable from the start. But with or without intent, the exclusion of black coaches would be the result of such a criteria.

It was a perfect example of institutional racism, which allows racial disparity to be produced and maintained with or without the deliberate and bigoted intent of those producing the disparity, but merely as the product of normal operating procedures so common to employers. So often, the way in which qualification requirements are used favor those who have been in the pipeline for the best opportunities previously. Because of historic white privilege, relying on so-called experience indicators or seniority—as is normative on the part of most companies—will almost always screen out people of color who, through no fault of their own, haven't been afforded the same opportunities to accumulate credentials over time. It's not unlike having an eight-leg relay race, in which one runner has had a five lap head start, and then when the runner who started out behind fails to catch up and surpass the one with the unfair advantage, blaming that second runner for not being as good as the first.

Though the case seemed strong to me, sometimes circumstances work against the desired outcome in ways that can't easily be avoided. As it turns out, American jurisprudence on racial discrimination law makes it very difficult to prove a case without clear evidence of intent to injure. Although it is possible to sustain a case of disparate impact without proving intent, typically courts require such cases to involve huge classes of plaintiffs, statistically large enough to demonstrate a clear disparity over a long period of time. In the case of the NFL and World League, the potential numbers of injured black coaches would have been only in the dozens—and the case before the court was not on behalf of even that many, but rather, only Jimmy—so the Judge classified the action as a disparate treatment case, meaning that the burden would be on Jimmy's attorneys to prove that the League had deliberately excluded him from consideration because of race.

Although I felt there was still strong enough evidence to suggest disparate treatment, ultimately the jury would disagree. By the time the trial was held, Jimmy had ballooned to over four hundred pounds, his health suffering from the emotional impact of the mistreatment to which he'd been subjected, striking a visual that no doubt would make it difficult for any jurors to see him actively coaching a team from the sidelines. That, and the evidentiary limits imposed by the court, created long odds for Jimmy that he ultimately couldn't overcome. I felt terrible, having taken this ride with him for so long, only to see it end in defeat. I was especially upset that his attorneys hadn't warned me about the evidentiary rules for expert witnesses—rules that make it quite clear such witnesses are not allowed to testify to the ultimate issue (in this case whether or not the defendants had engaged in unlawful discrimination). Having not been advised as to what I could and couldn't say,

I had prepared an expert report in which I said, in no uncertain terms, that I thought the defendants had discriminated—a position I would repeat without hesitation at my deposition, much to the delight of the opposing attorneys (from the prestigious Covington and Burling law firm in D.C.), who were then able to successfully have me struck from the case for having overstepped the boundaries of expert testimony. Whatever I knew about racism and discrimination didn't matter. It was what I didn't know about the evidentiary standards of the American legal system that would make the biggest difference. It was the only time I would ever regret not having gone to law school. Still, what I'd learned about the way racism operates at the institutional level had been worth the experience, whatever the outcome.

* * *

OTHER LESSONS WOULD be forthcoming during this time too, specifically, lessons about whiteness and its consequences even for white people, which were nearly as disturbing as the ones I had just learned about its effect on folks of color, thanks to the Jimmy Jackson case.

Back in late 1991, amid the generally heightened racial consciousness that had emerged thanks to the David Duke campaigns, New Orleans councilwoman Dorothy Mae Taylor had proposed a citywide anti-discrimination ordinance aimed at the prestigious private clubs that paraded during Mardi Gras. The parade krewes were targeted by Taylor because the clubs did far more than just throw parties every Lenten season—they were also the location of substantial business dealings and high-powered connections, ultimately linked to the opportunity structure in the city. Among the old-line elite krewes, it was also known that they had never had black or Jewish members. Because the connections made in the krewes often led to contracts with the city, and because the city subsidized the krewes' activities (by providing clean up and security related to their parades), Taylor and other African Americans on the council believed it was only proper to insist that they be non-discriminatory in their operations. Ultimately, Taylor proposed that unless the krewes could prove they weren't discriminating by the end of 1993, the organizations would be prohibited from parading in the following year's festivities.

Almost as soon as the ordinance had been proposed, white New Orleanians had begun with the gnashing of teeth and the rattling of political sabers. How dare anyone tinker with the city's care-free celebration of debauchery by turning it into a political football, they would say. How dare Dorothy Mae Taylor spoil our fun. Taylor became, almost immediately, the "Grinch who stole Carnival," with whites across the political spectrum condemning her proposal and all who supported it as racial bomb throwers and troublemakers. One white gay civic organization actually compared her to David Duke and suggested the two should be married, given their presumably equivalent racial bigotries. Others would crow that people should be able to pick their own friends and club associates, no matter how racist they may be—an argument that was never the point, of course. Taylor was not seeking to restrict the krewes' freedom of association; rather, she was suggesting that if one wants to do business with the city, or exploit private connections to do such business, or have the city clean up after one's mess, one can and should be expected to play by the public's rules.

By the time Nicol and I had moved to Houston, the ordinance had passed (though it had been altered a bit, placing the burden of proof on those who would claim they had been discriminated against), and four old-line krewes had decided to take their toys and go home like children, announcing they would no longer parade, rather than abide by the new law. While we were gone, I hadn't kept up very much with public reaction to the ordinance, but by the time Mardi Gras season arrived in early 1993—the last year before the law was due to go into effect—the anger on the part of whites was still palpable.

On the one hand, it was never surprising that the uptown blue bloods would be upset about the rule. The sense of entitlement and untouchability that has long animated them all but ensured that outrage would meet any attempt to regulate their activities, or even to criticize their private practices as being bigoted in the first place. Rich people rarely take well to being told by the rabble that occasionally, their shit does indeed stink.

But what was disconcerting about white hostility to the anti-discrimination ordinance was how quickly and completely it emerged among the kind of white people who would never in a million years be invited to join an elite Mardi Gras krewe. When working class whites without a pot to piss in begin defending the prerogatives of wealthy folks who *hate them too*, you know instantly that something troubling is going on. And that was what we were witnessing—low-income whites in Metairie, holding signs on parade routes that read, "Hands Off Mardi Gras," and which pictured Dorothy Mae Taylor in grotesque caricature, with exaggerated lips and bulging white eyes against a coal black face (despite Taylor's far lighter complexion).

This is what Marx had no doubt been thinking of when he talked about "false consciousness" on the part of working people, ultimately causing them to identify more with their bosses and the owners of capital than with others in their own class, with whom they had far more in common. And surely it was what black scholar and socialist, W.E.B. DuBois had meant many decades later when he discussed the "psychological wage of whiteness," which allowed struggling white folks to accept their miserable lot in life, so long as they were doing better than blacks. To the white masses in Duke country, they had more in common with the multi-millionaires along St. Charles Avenue and on Audubon Place (the wealthiest street in the city) than with African Americans, struggling for opportunities much as they were. Racial bonding took priority over class unity, or in this case, common sense.

Of course, it probably shouldn't have been surprising. The same thing had animated white voting behavior during the Duke campaigns. It had been lower-income and working class whites who had made up the bulk of Duke's support base, despite the fact that none of his policy proposals would have helped them. He had promised to hold the line on taxes for wealthy homeowners and corporations, and had no plan for job creation, except for forcing welfare recipients to work off their checks, which actually would have displaced currently employed low-skilled labor (including a lot of his white supporters), to make way for those persons being required to work off their measly $168 per month average income support.

Rich whites, on the other hand, had overwhelmingly rejected Duke, not so much because they disagreed with his views about black people— they were likely every bit as privately racist as anyone else—but because a Duke victory would have reflected badly on the Republican Party. A Duke victory would have made it more difficult to distance the party from the racism that had animated so much of its previous thirty years of political activity—from Goldwater's opposition to civil rights legislation to Nixon's exploitation of "law and order" themes so as to scare whites about big city crime to Reagan's deft use of stories concerning mythical black "welfare queens" driving Cadillacs to the food stamp office. Conservatives, especially rich ones, placed a premium on keeping up appearances, and Duke would have ripped away the veil making the subterfuge even remotely believable.

So for the past several years, struggling white folks had cast their lot with racism—all so as to make themselves feel superior to somebody, *anybody*—even as the wealthy had remembered how the game was played. In the process, Louisiana had served as something of a metaphor for the history of race relations in the United States. This, after all, had been exactly how racism and white supremacy had taken root in the colonies to begin with: with the elite passing laws to divide and conquer workers, and convince indentured servants from Europe (who were only one level above slaves) that they had more in common with the rich who abused them than with the African slaves next to whom they often worked. It would be the same process that southern elites would use to convince poor whites to support the Confederacy despite the open admission by the aristocracy that the purpose of secession had been to preserve the institution of African slavery, which institution actually *harmed* the wages of lower-income whites, by forcing them to compete with no-cost labor. It would be the same process that would animate the attempt by labor unions to exclude blacks from membership, even though doing so weakened organized labor relative to the bosses from whom they often sought to force better wages and working conditions. However pathetic, by 1993, the process had become entirely predictable.

As a side note, a few years later, I'd really come to understand the impact of the psychological wages of whiteness during an online exchange with a young white college student from South Carolina. He would be agitated by an article I'd write, criticizing the continued flying of the Confederate flag. We would go back and forth over the course of two days, he insisting that the flag was an honorable symbol of the

South, and I trying to explain why it wasn't. After I pointed out to him the way the South had been harmed by racist thinking, and how our economic vitality had long been sapped by white supremacy, with wages being held down due to opposition to unions—opposition predicated on a fear of racial wage equality—he replied that although I was probably right, it didn't matter. As he put it, "I'd be willing to work for one dollar an hour if we could just go back to segregation."

The exchange would teach me something else about white people; namely, that some of us are just too damned stupid to save.

* * *

1994 WAS AN all-around terrible year. The Republicans took over Congress, catapulting Newt Gingrich to the position of Speaker of the House, Charles Murray and Richard Herrnstein released *The Bell Curve*—five hundred plus pages of nonsense proclaiming white-black differences in measured IQ to be the result of inferior black genetics—and I couldn't find steady work to save my life. Nicol and I also broke up in May, although because we would continue to live together until January of 1995, the full emotional weight of the split wouldn't hit me for several more months.

At the outset of the year, I was still working with Walter on the trade and development stuff, sponsored by the New School for Social Research, in New York. However, I was growing steadily frustrated. First, there was the tedium of the subject matter. I simply wasn't excited by data tables about the differences between the Asian model of development (or AMOD, as the ever-original Walter liked to call it) and the European model of development (predictably, EMOD, in Walter's terms). Apparently, my lack of excitement was shared by others, as none of the work we were doing for Walter was ever published or taken seriously by anyone, an outcome that can't be blamed on our efforts, but rather and only on the uselessness of his own theories. Then, there was the larger matter of Walter's personal ambitions to become accepted into the nation's foreign policy establishment, which required, by definition, accepting that the U.S. was an unquestioned force for good in the world, and in his case pontificating about the fundamental oxymoron known as "Jacksonian Democracy," and that mythical creature so worshipped by Sarah Palin, known as American "exceptionalism." Finally, there was the shitty and inconsistent pay, about which Walter seemed utterly unconcerned. Living in his phat Royal Street apartment, paid for either by the same New School that refused to pay his research staff on time, or perhaps by his parents, Walter had a way of making us all feel guilty for expecting something approaching a living wage for the work he was asking us to do. I began to drift away from the project by February, ultimately resigning, preferring the uncertainty of unemployment to the sure drudgery of the previous seven months. Although I would be brought on to conduct research for a progressive tax policy organization in Baton Rouge in May, the next three months would see me bounce around in a number of jobs that were decidedly non-political.

By then Nicol had taken a position with a management firm that operated one of the city's malls on the west bank of the river. Needing help with various things from time to time, she hired me to set up displays, co-plan and DJ a fashion show, and even to dress up as the Easter Bunny and hand out candy to about three hundred children during the weekend before the celebration of Christ's proclaimed resurrection. Needless to say, later that year when I would be deposed in the Jimmy Jackson case as an expert witness on racial discrimination, I would neglect to mention my professional stint as the beloved holiday mascot. Of course, I *had* told Jimmy that he should probably call Cornel West, who likely wasn't having to moonlight in this fashion, so it's not as if he hadn't been warned.

After two months with the Louisiana Coalition for Tax Justice, I was let go, in part because the Board didn't see the value of a position that involved only research and no direct community organizing, and in part because some of the Board members thought I was having an inappropriate romantic relationship with the boss. Neither she nor I had any idea what they were talking about, but in any event, the deed was done, and I was once again out of work.

Three more months of unemployment were followed by my being hired to write grants for the Louisiana Injured Worker's Union: a wonderful bunch of mostly oil and chemical workers—as well as poultry plant processors and former employees of a local sugar refinery—who were fighting for a more fair and just worker's comp system in the state. Sadly, I was horrible at writing grants, procuring only about ten thousand dollars for the group over the next eight months. As a result, I did very little good for them, and even less for myself. In my continuing downward financial spiral, I was now earning only $150 weekly, which was my draw against the 15 percent commission I was being paid for any grant monies I brought in. By the time I secured the one grant, I was into my draw well beyond the fifteen hundred I was owed, so I would receive no payout. Now earning even less than I had made eight years earlier bagging groceries in Nashville, and seeing very little prospect that things would get better any time soon, I sank into a deep emotional funk.

As 1995 began, I felt certain that things could only get better, and although they would, within a few days I came to understand what people meant when they say that sometimes things have to get worse first. On January 4, Nicol and I had a huge blow-up, which ultimately made it impossible for us to live together for even another day. Because the fight had been my fault, she demanded that I vacate the premises while she arranged to move her things out over the next two days. I agreed. I had no money for a hotel, so the first night I crashed on a friend's sofa; but the second night, self-conscious about intruding on anyone else's space, I opted to sleep in my car, despite the fact that the weather was going to dip down below thirty degrees. Aware of how often cars got broken into in the city when parked on poorly-lit side streets, I parked on St. Charles, right in front of Tulane (about thirty feet from where I had spent two weeks camped out during the anti-apartheid struggle five years earlier). Afraid of being rousted by police, I slept no more than forty-five minutes all night on January 5, 1995, my mother's forty-eighth birthday.

The next day I went back to the house, Nicol having finished moving out, and was confronted by how bad things had really gotten. As I climbed up the back stairs and opened the door to the apartment, I was met by an almost entirely empty eighteen hundred square feet of living space. Other than a sole mattress on the floor in the bedroom, all that remained was my desk, a side table on which sat a phone in the hallway, a sofa that we had previously put in storage because it was so stained, intending to ultimately throw it away, a steamer trunk, a stereo, a portable seven-inch black-and-white television, a tennis ball, and my dog. When I entered the house, Bijoux looked at me like he was afraid he had been totally abandoned. Realizing this wasn't the case he became instantly excited, went and grabbed the tennis ball, and brought it to me, apparently presuming that with all this open space, we'd now have the perfect abode for playing catch. As I sank down onto the floor and grabbed the ball from his mouth, I couldn't help but laugh out loud. The absurdity of it all—and the recognition of what emotional rock bottom looked like—left me with no alternative but to engage in a bit of self-mockery. I laughed until I cried, and then fell asleep on the filthy sofa, hoping that when I woke up, things would be better.

* * *

THEY WOULDN'T BE, at least not right away. For the next month I had no money for anything, including food. Rent was paid through the end of January, but I had to buy groceries using a gas station credit card, meaning that for several weeks I subsisted on bean burritos, frozen meals, and assorted junk food from the Citgo market. But mostly, I bought beer, hoping that if I drank a six-pack every night, I might be able to forget how bad things looked. Worst of all, the brakes on my car were totally shot and the Citgo was five miles away in Metairie. To get there, I had to drive on the interstate and hope that I wouldn't need to stop too often. If I did, I would have to use the hand brake and time the stop just right so as to avoid running into another car.

In February, things started to look up. I got hired by Agenda for Children, a child advocacy group with an explicitly antiracist philosophy, to work as a researcher and community organizer. Back in the fall of the previous year I had penned an essay for Agenda's newsletter in response to the persistent attacks on income support programs (so-called "welfare") that were bubbling up again in Congress. Knowing that the attempt to roll back various social safety net programs would accelerate now that the GOP was in charge of the legislative agenda, Judy Watts, the group's director, felt it might be good to bring me on to do some research and writing on the subject, and also to work with residents in the city's poor communities to organize against the pending assaults.

The cornerstone of the Republican plan for welfare was to turn cash assistance into a state-level block grant, with a fixed amount of funds each year, regardless of the strength or weakness of the economy, the poverty level, or the volume of need. Knowing what that could mean in a place like Louisiana, we focused special attention on educating state lawmakers and crafting an alternative welfare reform proposal that would encourage employment for those on assistance, but which would have been less punitive.

I had only done limited community organizing before, but being brought around and introduced to the leaders in the city's public housing developments by Donna Johnigan (herself a resident of the Guste Homes) made the learning curve far less steep than it otherwise would have been. Rather than just turn the white Tulane grad loose on the community, which would have been a disaster, Agenda had me serve essentially as an apprentice to Donna, whose full-time job was as the office manager for the organization.

That Donna had any confidence in me was an honor, as her nose for bullshit was pretty fine-tuned. Despite my naiveté, she took me around, showed me the ropes, and taught me the fine art of listening, as the residents in the communities told me their stories, described their hopes and fears, and discussed—in a way far more instructive than any college professor had—the topics of racism and economic oppression.

Seeing the depth of poverty that characterized New Orleans' public housing was breathtaking. It's one thing to understand such matters in the abstract, from reading books or discussing destitution in a classroom; it is quite another, however, to see it up close. And the contrast between economic immiseration on the one hand, and the abundant *wealth* of knowledge and wisdom possessed by the people there, on the other, was even more difficult to fully take in. In short, people in this kind of economic condition were not supposed to be this *smart*. That they are lacking in fundamental intelligence and ability is what we are told, daily, by politicians and most everyone with an opinion. Although I was ashamed to admit it, I guess I had come to believe some of that too. Though I was paternalistically prepared to acknowledge that the system had produced whatever personal dysfunctions the poor in public housing might manifest, I was not at all prepared for the competence, insight, and utter *normalcy* of the residents there.

Once I realized the wisdom of the folks in public housing, I became downright belligerent when talking to others about the folks with whom I was working. Invariably they would start talking badly about public housing residents, having never met a single one of the folks about whom they felt entitled to rant, and they would start handing out unsolicited advice about what "those people" should do to improve their lives.

Sitting at a bar one night having a drink, I found myself in a conversation with a guy who thought he had the perfect solution to the problems of the poor; namely, they all needed to be required to take a class on "money management," which could be taught by local C.E.O.s, who would be paid for their insights by the state. If they could learn how to be responsible with money, the cycle of poverty could be broken, he insisted.

"Are you fucking kidding me?" I exploded. "Have millionaires go into the projects and tell *poor people* how to manage money? Jesus, they don't even manage money on their own. They pay investment experts to do that shit for them! If anything, we should be sending these poor women I meet every day out to the suburbs, or to Tulane, so they can teach spoiled motherfuckers like the ones I went to school with how to get by on three hundred motherfucking dollars a month: Now *that* takes fucking skill!"

I was asked to leave the bar, and was all too happy to go.

* * *

WHAT I LEARNED about poor folks from my time as an organizer was how little I understood them and what their lives were like. Contrary to popular perceptions, many if not most of the poor folks I met worked hard every day, whether in the paid labor force, where their wages were still too low to allow them to afford rent in the private market, or at home, trying to raise children into productive citizens. Interestingly, when cash welfare had first been created back in the 1930s (and when access had been restricted to white women), allowing mothers to stay home and raise kids, and not have to work in the labor force, had been articulated as the *very purpose* of the program. Only when women of color began to gain access to the same benefits did the nation suddenly decide that welfare was bad for you, made you lazy, and needed to be replaced with compulsory employment.

In a few of the projects where I was organizing, residents averaged twenty to thirty hours of work each week, but still couldn't afford private market rent. Instead, they paid one-third of their pay (whatever it was) to the Housing Authority of New Orleans, so as to remain in subsidized housing. They were not living for free, as most to whom I spoke about my job assumed. And as for the work ethic of such folks, Donna herself provided perhaps the best example in this regard. A few months after I started working with her, her son was murdered, becoming one of about three hundred and fifty black folks killed that year in the city. While it would have been understandable for her to have taken a few days off, she was at work the next day, insisting that she had a job to do and intended to do it. I had called out of work plenty of times because of a headache, or because I just hadn't felt like going in; yet here was Donna, whose son had just been killed, keeping it together and working through the pain. But in America, we are to believe that *she* is the one with the bad values. Go figure.

People with whom I'd discuss my job also wondered, constantly, if I was scared working in the communities where the projects were located. Although I was quick to tell them that I'd felt out of place when first arriving in a new location—and especially being the only white person around—I also would point out that, if anything, I was probably the *safest* person in the community on the days I was there. Indeed, precisely because I was white, most residents would view me as one of two things: either a cop or a social worker, neither of which they were too likely to want to mess with. If I were the former, I might arrest them, and if I were the latter, I might have the power to take their children away. So unlike other black folks, who might be mistaken for rival gang members (since the gangs in New Orleans were pretty much all black at that time), I was relatively protected in that space, despite the generally higher crime rates that existed in the communities where public housing was to be found.

Over the fifteen months that I worked as an organizer, I learned more about race and class subordination than I had ever learned in a classroom up to that point, and far more than I have learned since from having read hundreds of books on the subjects. What I also came to understand was how critical it is to *follow* the lead of the community where you're working, and its leadership, rather than assume you know the agenda around which to organize.

This last point came into view for me one day while sitting around talking with a community leader about some of the things they were working on in the neighborhood. I was there to build support for blocking punitive welfare cutbacks and the ill-advised Balanced Budget Amendment, which invariably would result in the slashing of any number of vital safety net programs as well as education spending. But what the local leader explained to me was that as important as those things were, they were not and could never be the first order of business. Yes, fighting racism and classism, which we agreed were inherent to these legislative items, was important. But to be an effective organizer, you had to start small.

I asked him to explain, and was surprised by just how small he'd meant.

"Well, for instance," he said. "See that corner right there?" He was gesturing to an intersection about fifty feet from where we stood.

"Yeah, sure, what about it?" I replied.

"Well, we've been trying to get a stop light there," he noted, causing me to realize for the first time that, indeed, despite it being a natural place for a light, there was none. The lack of the light intrigued me, but I didn't really get the importance of it all.

"Why a stop light?" I asked, puzzled, and wondering how such an item fit in with the larger struggle against institutional injustice.

"Well," he continued, "for a couple of reasons. First, three kids have been hit there on their bikes because folks just barrel on through without looking. And second, because we can get the stop light. It's a winnable fight. See, people who've been getting their asses kicked for years need to know they can make a difference. They need to know that they can fight and occasionally *win*."

He went on to explain the strategic value of small victories. Yes, the goal was social justice, the eradication of poverty and racism, and all the rest that went with it. But good organizers couldn't make those things the front-burner agenda items. Even a slightly smaller goal, like blocking federal legislation you didn't like, was too big for starters. The odds were against winning those battles in the short run. So if you started there, you'd accomplish little, except helping folks to burn out when, as so often happened, defeat was in the cards. But if you could "help the community gain a sense of it's own potential," he would say, "*now* you were on to something."

It wasn't the way I'd been taught how history was made. But then again, the folks who had taught most of us history hadn't exactly been committed to radical change, so little details like this were easily overlooked.

*   *   *

BY NOW, THE lessons were coming fast and furious: lessons about systemic injustice and how to fight it, lessons about how easy it was to fall prey to some of the stereotypes so common to the larger culture, and lessons about privilege.

In the latter case, I was starting to realize how my job insecurity and shaky financial situation for the past few years had said very little about my larger access to opportunity and advantage. Yes, I had struggled, and those struggles had been real. But the fact had remained that I was a college graduate, educated at one of the nation's finest universities, which I had only been able to access because my mother could take out that loan using my grandmother's house as collateral—a house that had only been accessible to our family because we were white. What's more, I had built up a solid work history beginning with the anti-Duke effort, which ultimately was going to pay off (a work history that had been made possible because I had known the two guys who started the anti-Duke organization, whom I'd met at Tulane, which place I had only been able to access because of the loan and the collateral and the white thing mentioned above); and, if things hadn't worked out, I could always have moved home for a while. I had options, in other words. They were options that almost no one I would meet in public housing had, and options that had far more to do with privilege than with my own hard work.

As bad as 1994 had been for me—and even as bad as the first six weeks of '95 had gone—by the middle of the year things were headed in the opposite direction. The work with Agenda was the most rewarding

in which I had ever been involved. Especially important was the antiracist analysis that animated their efforts on behalf of families and children. While many groups that work on matters of poverty give short
shrift to racism, preferring to discuss class issues in a colorblind vacuum, Agenda rejected that approach. In large part, this was due to their
affiliation with the People's Institute for Survival and Beyond, a New
Orleans–based group founded in 1980 by Ron Chisom and the late Jim
Dunn, which by the mid-1990s had become one of the premier groups
in the nation working to undo racism. As a condition of working at
Agenda, all staff had to attend an Undoing Racism workshop, put on by
the Institute, within the first year of becoming employed there. A few
months after joining the team, it would be my turn to go.

As excited as I was to attend the Institute training, I was also a bit
nervous. I had met some of the key players in the Institute and had great
respect for them all, but I also had heard horror stories from others
about what their trainings were like. "Oh, they're gonna make you feel
guilty for being white," some had warned. "Oh, they're gonna try and
make all the white people cry," added others. Though I had a hard time
reconciling those warnings with the people I was meeting thanks to my
connections with Agenda—not only Ron, but also Barbara Major, and
certain key white trainers with the Institute like David Billings, Marjorie
Freeman, or Diana Dunn—I couldn't help but wonder. The people giving me these warnings were friends, after all, and people whose political
sensibilities I trusted.

Several years earlier, I had been so convinced that the Institute's
modus operandi was the provocation of white guilt that I'd refused to sit
through a discussion on white privilege and antiracist accountability led
by Bay Area organizer (and now good friend) Sharon Martinas. Sharon
had been brought to Loyola University by the Institute, and although I
had attended, along with a local activist from Pax Christi—the Catholic
Peace and Justice organization—we ended up leaving early, so incred-
ulous were we about the supposed guilt-tripping that we saw as the
root of the group's analysis. I can recall walking to John's car, imitating
Wayne and Garth from the recurring SNL skit, "Wayne's World," saying, "We're not worthy, we're not worthy," as if somehow that had been
the message of Sharon and the Institute—that somehow white people

were inherently bad and unable to be antiracist allies. Fact is, we hadn't wanted to look at our privilege; so much so, in fact, that rather than process it, we drove over to the back of Audubon Park, parked in a dark gravel lot, and proceeded to smoke a joint, entirely missing the irony.

But once the first day of the training began, it was obvious that it was to be nothing like the warnings I'd received. The trainers engaged us in discussions and exercises that calmly but clearly allowed all the participants to see how institutional racism operated (often in spite of the people in certain institutional spaces being perfectly lovely and caring folks), and how the flipside of oppression—namely, privilege—adhered to members of the dominant racial group, irrespective of our own personal "goodness." Although there was certainly discussion about the way that all whites had internalized certain biases, having been raised in a culture that so readily teaches them, there was also a discussion of how people of color had inculcated those biases against themselves, and often acted from a place of internalized oppression. In other words, the Institute was clear that we were all damaged by this system. It wasn't just white folks who'd been messed up. There was nothing about the training that was intended to produce guilt. A sense of responsibility, both individual and collective? Yes. But guilt? Absolutely not.

Most impactful was how clear the trainers were about the damage done to whites in the process of internalizing white supremacy and accepting privilege. One of the most telling moments came when Ron asked the participants what we liked about being whatever it is that we were, racially speaking. What did black folks like about being black? And what did whites like about being white?

For most whites, it was a question to which we had never given much thought. Looks of confusion spread across most of our faces as we struggled to find an answer. Meanwhile, people of color came up with a formidable list almost immediately. They liked the strength of their families, the camaraderie, the music, the culture, the rhythms, the customs, their color, and they mentioned most prominently, the perseverance of their ancestors in the face of great odds.

When it was our turn, we finally came up with a list, and it was the same one offered pretty much every time I ask the question to white folks around the country. We like not being followed around in stores on suspicion of being shoplifters. We like the fact that we're not presumed out of place on a college campus or in a high-ranking job. We like the fact that we don't have to constantly overcome negative stereotypes about intelligence, morality, honesty, or work ethic, the way people of color so often do.

Once finished, we began to examine the lists offered by both sides. The contrast was striking. Looking at the items mentioned by people of color, one couldn't miss the fact that all of the attributes listed were actually about personal strength or qualities possessed by the participants, and in which they took real pride. The list was tangible and meaningful. The white list was quite different. Staring at the entries, it was impossible to miss that *none* of what we liked about being white had anything to do with us. None of it had to do with internal qualities of character or fortitude. Rather, every response had to do less with what we liked about being white than what we liked about *not* being a person of color. We were defining ourselves by a negative, providing ourselves with an identity rooted in the relative oppression of others, without which we would have had *nothing* to say. Without a system of racial domination and subordination, we would have been able to offer no meaningful response to the question.

As became clear in that moment, inequality and privilege were the only real components of whiteness. Without racial privilege there is no whiteness, and without whiteness, there is no racial privilege. Being white means to be advantaged relative to people of color, and pretty much *only* that. Our answers had laid bare the truth about white privilege: in order to access it, one first had to give up all the meaningful cultural, personal, and communal attributes that had once kept our peoples alive in Europe and during our journeys here. After all, we had come from families that once had the kinds of qualities we now were seeing listed before us by people of color. We had had customs, traditions, music, culture, and style—things to be celebrated and passed down to future generations. Even more, we had come from resistance cultures—most Europeans who came had been the losers of their respective societies, since the winners rarely felt the need to hop on a boat and leave where they were—and these resistance cultures had been steeped in the notion of resisting injustice, and of achieving solidarity. But to become white required that those things be sublimated to a new social reality in which resistance was not the point. To become the power structure was to view the tradition of resistance with suspicion and contempt.

So while the folks of color in the room would have dearly loved to be able to claim for themselves the privileges filling the white folks' pages on the flipchart, we would have just as dearly loved to be able to claim for ourselves even *one* of the meaningful qualities mentioned by people of color. But we couldn't.

To define yourself by what you're not is a pathetic and heartbreaking thing. It is to stand bare before a culture that has stolen your birthright, or rather, convinced you to give it up; and the costs are formidable, beginning with the emptiness whites often feel when confronted by multiculturalism and the connectedness of people of color to their heritages. That emptiness gets filled up by privilege and ultimately forces us to become dependent on it, forcing me to wonder just how healthy the arrangement is in the long run, despite the advantages it provides.

* * *

IN ADDITION TO Agenda for Children, the spring of 1995 brought with it yet another professional opportunity. In the summer of the previous year, one of the only good things to happen had been that a progressive speaker's bureau in California, Speak Out, had called to let me know that they'd like to add me to their roster of speakers, educators, and artists. Though they couldn't promise me that I'd get any speaking engagements, they were going to add me to their catalog, which they sent each year to thousands of colleges and other organizations.

I had actually sent them a packet of material back in 1993, thinking that perhaps the lessons of the anti-Duke campaigns would be of interest to folks across the nation, but they had turned me down. Undaunted, I had applied again the next year and this time they had found a place for me. "Don't quit your day job," they had counseled (which was no problem, seeing as how I didn't have one at the time), but hopefully they'd be able to get me out on the road, where I could share my own insights and meet with organizers and activists around the country.

In March of 1995, I got my first speaking engagements, at the Chicago Teacher's Center and Northeastern Illinois University, respectively. It was bitter cold and I was running a fever by the time I got to Midway airport. But I did the best I could under the circumstances.

At Northeastern I spoke to a number of sociology classes about every-thing from affirmative action to hate crime activity to media-generated racial stereotypes. After one of my talks, a young white woman in the front row raised her hand somewhat tentatively and asked how I was received doing this work, as a white man, by black people. I asked why she was curious about this, trying to figure out the motivation for her question.

"Well," she said, "I would love to do the kind of work you do, but I'm afraid black people won't trust me, won't accept my contribution, and so I'm just wondering how you think blacks feel about you. Do you think they like you, or that they still don't really trust you?"

Although I was brand new to nationwide lecturing, I had been doing antiracism work in some capacity for several years (and was working in several black communities in New Orleans), so I explained that based on my experience, I had never personally felt any hatred or resentment on the part of black folks. Of course there is going to be some mis-trust up front, and in fact, I'd be worried about any person of color who *didn't* look at whites who choose to fight racism a bit suspiciously. They've been burned too many times to take it for granted that we're serious and in it for the long haul.

It was then that I noticed a young black woman in the back row who had her hand up and wanted desperately to talk. I had observed her facial expressions all throughout my speech, and could read her body language well enough to know that she simply wasn't buying anything I was selling. Thinking this might make for an interesting interaction given the white woman's fears and concerns—not to mention, the African American woman clearly wanted to be called on—I pointed to her and asked her for her input. Her response was classic, and perfect for the situation.

"Make *no* mistake," she insisted, "We *do* hate you and we *don't* trust you, not for one minute!"

I thought the white woman in the front row was going to come unglued, as if her classmate's comment had only confirmed her worst fears.

"Well, I'm sorry to hear that," I said to the black woman who had made the statement, "since after all, you don't know me. But that's fine, because I'm sure you haven't got much reason to trust me, and anyway, ultimately I'm not doing this for you."

The room was deathly silent at that point, no one knowing quite what to make of a proclamation such as that.

"I mean no disrespect," I explained. "It's just that I'm not fighting racism so as to save you from it. That would be paternalistic. It would be like saying that black folks aren't capable of liberating yourselves from white supremacy. I think you are, though it might be easier with some internal resistance from whites. But regardless, I fight racism because racism is a sickness in *my* community, and it damages me."

I explained to the young white woman that if she wanted to do this work for black people, then of course they wouldn't trust her. White missionaries have rarely brought things of lasting value to peoples of color. If, on the other hand, she wanted to do it because it was the right thing to do, and because she no longer wanted to collaborate by way of her silence, then what the woman in the back thought of her sincerity shouldn't matter. And if she really did the work and proved herself, black and brown folks—including the woman who had made her so nervous that day—would likely recognize her seriousness and work with her. Or not. Either way, why should it matter?

People of color don't owe us gratitude when we speak out against racism. They don't owe us a pat on the back. And if all they do is respond to our efforts with a terse "about time," that's fine. Challenging racism and white supremacy is what we *should* be doing. Resistance is what we need to do for *us*. Although people of color have often thanked me for the work I do, it's a thanks that I am not owed, and whenever it's offered I make sure to repay the compliment. Accountability demands it.

While much discussion had recently been about whether or not America should apologize for slavery—and I happen to think apologies are pretty empty absent substantive reparations and recompense—perhaps before we focus on apologies, we could simply say thank you to people of color for pointing the way when it comes to resistance. People of color owe us nothing, but we owe them at least that much, and a lot more. Being able to teach that to another white person, and on my first day out, suggested that perhaps there was something to this traveling educator thing after all. Perhaps the potential impact of such work was far greater than I'd imagined.

* * *

BY LATE 1995, I was really starting to grow fond of the road. Though there was part of me that intuitively recognized the dangers of going down that path—it was eerily similar to what my father had done for all those years as a comic and actor—there was another part of me that thrived on it. And it wasn't because I was speaking to overflowing auditoriums or reaping the standing ovations of adoring crowds, because in neither case was that true. Fact is, almost nobody knew who I was. I was only twenty-seven by the fall of that year, and hardly a common name within the antiracism community. Far from receiving rock star treatment, that first few months of the circuit had been more like some struggling band riding around in a grimy van than anything else, but I still loved it. Maybe it was because as an only child (and the child of an alcoholic), I had grown up having to be self-directed and find ways to engage my brain with no one else around. It was one of the reasons I never really proved to be very good working in organizational settings, no matter how much I loved the organizations for which I was working. My wiring, going all the way back to childhood, was set to solo mode. I liked being alone with my thoughts, having to represent no one's views but my own; not to mention, I also loved getting to meet activists, especially young activists, all over the United States.

There would be high points that first year, like being picketed by anti-gay bigot Fred Phelps and his family during an event at Kansas University, and also several low points. Among the latter, my two favorites were speaking at the University of West Alabama to five people in the basement of the student center, two of whom were playing pool; and then speaking in Rennselear, Indiana at St. Joseph's, and staying in a hotel room infested with flies, from which the only relief would be a fly swatter, handed to me by the clerk when I asked if there was any way I could change rooms. Glamorous it wasn't, but it was what I felt I needed to be doing.

Of course this posed a bit of a dilemma. I was still at Agenda, and dearly loved the people there. But by early 1996, I knew I would need to make a choice. Though I wasn't traveling much, even the little bit I was doing was becoming a problem for my job. This would be especially obvious after I went to New York to appear on a television show only to get stuck in the city for three extra days by the worst blizzard New York had seen in a century. Returning finally to New Orleans, it was pretty apparent that my work was suffering for my other commitments.

Additionally, I was coming to realize that as much as I loved the organizing work, I wasn't actually that good at it. I never had been, though I'd hoped that I might grow into it over time. But feeling that the work was too important to be done halfway, or halfway well, I decided to move on. In fact, not only did I leave Agenda for Children in February, I decided to leave New Orleans altogether by summer. As much as I loved the city, it was time for a change. Being untethered to any particular organizational structure, I was free to go wherever I might feel like living. Since I wasn't sure where I might want to live next, I decided to start by moving home to Nashville. Although my mom had moved from our old apartment, she was still there, living with my grandmother for the previous two years at that point, and my best friend Albert and his wife Dana were too. If one had to start anew, what better place than from home? As the middle of August rolled around—and as the life-deadening heat that came with it rolled in too—it was easy to walk away from New Orleans. So I did.

* * *

BEFORE GETTING HOME, however, there would be one more lesson about white privilege to learn. But first, a little backstory.

Each morning, until shortly after 9:00, it was common for those of us at Agenda for Children to have the office television on, just to stay up on the day's early events. But on April 19, 1995, before we would have a chance to turn off the set, breaking news came over the networks, followed by some of the most shocking footage any of us had seen up to that point, or would ever see, at least until a little more than six years later.

As we stood slack-jawed before the small screen, video from Oklahoma City was coming in, where the Murrah Federal Building had just had its front end blown off by a five-thousand-pound bomb that had been planted in a truck outside. Speculation immediately focused on one or another "Muslim terrorist." Perhaps it was Saddam Hussein, some said, or Hezbollah, said others. Within hours, mosques around Oklahoma City would be raided in hopes of finding evidence to implicate those whom most assumed were responsible.

Of course the perpetrators would be none of those. As we would learn within the next two days, the terrorists were white men named Timothy McVeigh and Terry Nichols, who had no compunction about killing innocent people (including children in the building's day care center) just to make some twisted political point. Ultimately, 168 would die and hundreds more would be injured thanks to the fulfillment of Tim McVeigh's bloodlust, fueled by right-wing anti-government hysteria and his admiration for racist fantasy novels like *The Turner Diaries*, parts of which were found in his car and the details of which he copied almost perfectly in the Oklahoma City bombing. That the Army had trained this lunatic to kill (and to view enemies as utterly expendable) only added pathetic and maddening context to a crime that was already bad enough.

Fast forward now to August 1996. McVeigh is awaiting trial, and I'm moving home to Nashville. To make that move, in spite of the fact that Nicol had virtually cleaned me out eighteen months earlier, I had by then accumulated enough stuff to require the renting of a truck to complete the task. The closest moving truck company to my home happened to be a Ryder Truck franchise (the same company that had been used by McVeigh), so when I was ready to load boxes and furniture, I headed down to the Ryder location and asked for a truck. It would be the same size and model as the one Tim McVeigh had used to bring down the Murrah building.

I walked in, put my license and credit card on the counter, and within fifteen minutes was headed to my house to load up. I am white. I am male. I have short hair. At the time I was clean shaven. My name is Tim. All of which is to say that I fit the profile of the nation's deadliest terrorist five different ways. Yet no one at Ryder thought to ask for an additional security deposit, just in case I decided to fill their truck with explosives and take out a city block. No one looked at me funny, ran a background check, or said anything at all, other than, "Mr. Wise, will you be needing a map?" That was it. They could tell the difference, or thought they could, between *that* Timothy and *this* Timothy.

   That's what it means to be white: the murderous actions of one white person do not cause every other white person to be viewed in the same light, just as the incompetence or criminality of a white person in a corporation (or on Wall Street, most recently) does not result in other whites being viewed with suspicion as probable incompetents or crooks. Whites can take it for granted that we'll likely be viewed as individuals, representing nothing greater than our solitary selves. Would that persons of color could say the same, even before September 11, 2001, let alone after.

HOME AND AWAY

AS MUCH AS I loved New Orleans, Nashville was a welcome sight that evening of August 15, 1996, when I pulled up to the home of my mom and grandmother, just outside the city. As we would learn later, it was an interesting night to have been getting into town. At roughly the same time as I had turned from Old Hickory Boulevard onto Hillsboro Road so as to head the final four miles or so to the house in Franklin, a local attorney by the name of Perry March had been disposing of the body of his wife, Janet, at a construction site only two miles from that same intersection. He had killed her earlier that evening, and although he would later dig up her bones and re-bury them with the help of his father in a culvert off the side of the interstate in Kentucky, no one could have known any of this at the time. Odd that I had left the murder capital of the nation only to enter a place where there might not be as many murders, numerically, but where the ones that happened were of a particularly salacious and high-profile nature.

The evening didn't start out well. I backed the Ryder truck into the basketball goal on which I had played since I was a kid, and my grandmother wasn't the least bit happy that I had Bijoux with me. As a matter of fact, the *day* hadn't started out well. I had been meaning to leave town quite a bit earlier, even before the sun had come up, with the goal of getting to Nashville by mid-afternoon; however, upon packing up and placing the keys on the driver's seat while I went to make sure the back door to the truck was closed tightly, I watched as Bijoux, already riding shotgun and ready to go, bounded over to the driver's side window, jumped up to greet me as I approached the door, and managed, with a precision unheard of in the history of his breed, to bring his paws down upon the lock. I ran around to the passenger's side door, hoping to get in that way, only to watch him follow me, excited and thinking that we were playing some kind of game, and do it again to the lock on *that* door. Though I could probably have gotten into the Ryder with a coat hanger (unlike the Tercel, which I was leaving in the street to be towed), the sad fact was that I didn't have any coat hangers. As I cleaned out the house, I had thrown them all away and they had been hauled off the day before I left by the garbage collectors. It was too early to wake my neighbors to ask for one, and the Ryder facility wouldn't be open for several more hours. I would have to wait, and so would Bijoux.

In any event, after a long and tedious trip, involving multiple bathroom breaks for my weak-bladdered dog, we were home. Well, at least I was. Bijoux had no idea what was going on, having always lived in New Orleans, and he likely didn't think too highly of Nashville at first, seeing as how the very next day my grandmother made me take him to the vet for boarding. He would stay there for four days while I looked for a place to live and until I went to stay with my dad's mom, who didn't mind the dog being there, for the final week or so before finding an apartment.

In early September I moved into a house in the Hillsboro Village area of Nashville, exactly where I had wanted to be. It was in the middle of pretty much everything in the city, and since I didn't have a car, that was a major plus. My roommates were two women, my age, who had been looking for someone to rent the third bedroom in their place. As one of the women would explain to me on the day I was offered the room, I had gotten it mostly because, out of all the potential roommates they had interviewed, I was the one that seemed least likely to be a serial killer. Quite an endorsement, that.

Bijoux and I moved into the house on 19th Avenue and more or less kept to ourselves for the first month. I was on the road for speeches, and for that first several weeks, didn't do much interacting with Liz, Shelly, or their social circle. But eventually, though I determined Shelly was a bit of a flake—and her Army boyfriend Mike a bit of an asshole—Liz and I became friends.

In November, having decided that I was a pretty good guy, Liz resolved that I should meet one of her co-workers. I had never been much for blind dates, but in this case it wasn't really a date, but rather just a meet up with a bunch of people at a bar in our neighborhood. It sounded good to me, having just returned from a particularly horrendous trip to Washington State, in which most of my events had been canceled due to snow and ice, and during which I'd been trapped for fourteen hours in the Yakima airport—a nightmare from which I still had not fully recovered. So I went to the bar with Liz, looking to make friends if nothing else. In the process, I met the beautiful, funny, intelligent, and incredible woman who would two years later become my wife.

Kristy Cason was everything I had never found in any woman with whom I'd been in a relationship. She wasn't an activist—wasn't even particularly political—but she shared my values, supported my work, and yet made it clear from the beginning that she was not a fan. She was no groupie. She had her own life, every bit as interesting as mine, and I'd best be as in to her as she was in to me, or we'd not last long. Turns out, our parents had known each other for more than twenty-five-years. At one point, in fact, I had been in her home and we'd played together at the age of perhaps three, my parents unable to find a babysitter on a night when her folks had been throwing a party. Some things, it seemed, really were fated, and like I said before, I've never much believed in coincidences.

* * *

HAVING LEFT NEW ORLEANS, I had all kinds of folks giving me advice on where I should go next: New England, some would say, while others insisted that I simply had to move to the Bay Area, or the Pacific Northwest. Fact is though, I was a born and bred southerner, and as much as I liked those places, was having a hard time seeing myself in any of them.

Having grown up in the South, I had long been familiar with the ways in which my people, regionally speaking, had long wished to bury the issue of racism, to remove it from the public consciousness, the history books, and certainly from our understanding of the land we loved. But I hadn't been prepared for the same kind of denial and hostility elsewhere, in those parts of the country that so prided themselves on their racial ecumenism, if only by comparison to the part of the nation from which I hailed.

At least southerners know the language; at least we know that race is an issue, however incredibly deformed our understanding of that issue may be. The problem is, white folks in the Northeast or the West Coast—oh God, *especially* the West Coast—find it hard to imagine that racism is an issue there too. And when you tell them it is, prepare for the backlash because it's surely coming.

Over the next several years I would learn this with a vengeance. In April 1997, I received a call at home from the organizers of an upcoming event at Cal State–San Marcos, informing me that there had been what they perceived as a legitimate bomb threat made against me and a professor at the college. The threat, sent electronically by someone identifying himself as a member of White Aryan Resistance (WAR) came from the campus, and indicated that if the event went ahead as planned, we would both be killed. After giving me the news, they asked, very plainly, if I was still willing to come. Having had my life threatened plenty of times over the past decade, it wasn't especially frightening to have it happen again, so I said of course. They promised they would have security, I said that was great, and within a few days I headed off to California.

Nothing ended up happening in San Marcos, but frankly, had anyone really wanted to hurt me it wouldn't have been difficult. The campus had contacted law enforcement about the threat, which prompted them to secure an FBI agent as my bodyguard for the day; the problem being, he *looked* like an FBI agent. In fact, he was so directly out of central casting that had anyone wanted to hide out on the hill overlooking the campus and splatter my brains all over the stage as I spoke at the big outside rally that day, they could have pulled it off. Just shoot the big guy with the dark suit, flattop, sunglasses, and fucking *earpiece* first. While they took bomb-sniffing dogs through every room into which I would enter, and while the FBI guy shadowed me everywhere I went, including to the bathroom or when I went to call Kristy, the outdoor rally was completely unsecured, which scared the hell out of me. Had a car backfired in the parking lot, I probably would have had a heart attack.

A year later I would once again learn the limits of the much presumed liberality of white folks in the Golden State, when speaking in Lafayette, California—which is part of Alameda county, along with

Oakland, but likes to think of itself as part of Marin, the much wealthier and more prestigious county next door. I had been invited to speak at Acalanes High School, a well-resourced public school that was as different from the schools of East Oakland as day was to night. But naturally, there were parents who didn't like their children being reminded that they had privilege, despite how glaringly obvious it was by merely looking around, and so they picketed my speech. Not in Tennessee. Not in Alabama. Not in Mississippi. In California, and more to the point, in northern California.

When asked about their protest by the press they explained that I was "viciously anti-white and anti-American." Really? To criticize racism in the United States means that I hate white people and my country? Under what rational definition could either of these things be true? If this was the kind of logic to which these mostly white children were being subjected in their homes, I thought to myself, there was very little that even the best formal education could do for them. When I noted during the assembly that parents in East Oakland loved their children just as much as those students parents loved them (a point I was making so as to get them to think about why, other than parental values, they might have such better resources than the kids in East Oakland), I was accused by one student of saying that white parents didn't love their children. So much for the value of honors classes.

Sometimes, however, the protests would prove funny. In October of 1998, I would be met at Central Washington University, in Ellensburg, by two neo-Nazis, David Stennett and Justin something-or-other, who reminded me of nothing so much as George and Lennie from Steinbeck's *Of Mice and Men*, or even better, Lenny and Squiggy from Gary Marshall's *Laverne and Shirley*. David was the smarter of the two, and Justin the clear sidekick. If Hitler had needed a wingman, Justin would have been his guy. They were among the founders of something called the Euro-American Student Union, and dressed in jaunty black berets and T-shirts. Stylish fascism is important, after all.

Upon arriving to campus, I was handed a flier they had been passing around, in which David proceeded to "out" me as a Jew—a trick which would be tantamount to "outing" Perez Hilton as gay, or revealing for all the world to hear that that Captain guy from the 1970s supergroup,

The Captain and Tennille, had never *actually* piloted a boat. Being a Jew, he explained on the flier, I was unfit to discuss white privilege. Rather, he suggested, I should discuss my role as an agent of Jewish subversion, seeking to destroy the white race. I would have been happy to do that, I said at the outset of my talk, but unfortunately, I had left my "Agent of Jewish Subversion" speech notes sitting on my table at home. Maybe next time, I promised.

Undaunted, the Skipper and Gilligan stuck around for the Q&A, at which point, the little buddy said something about how awful the Yugo was as an automobile, and how, given its reputation, he would never buy one. Though I found his consumer advice fascinating, I had to inquire as to his point. Simple, he said: just as the reputation of the Yugo meant he would never want to buy that car, so too, the reputation of blacks as criminals meant he would never want blacks as neighbors. If one prejudice was rational, so was the other.

Actually, I pointed out, if there's a lesson to be learned from the automotive inadequacy of the Yugo, it wasn't that you don't want blacks as neighbors, but rather, that you don't ever want to buy cars made by white people from Central Europe—in other words, from *his kind* of people. Better to stick with the Japanese or the multiracial teams of assembly line workers in Detroit, because those fucking Slavs are a pathetic lot of craftsmen.

After the event, the school threw a reception for me, to which Justin and David came. Amid lemon squares and punch we proceeded to talk for about an hour. I have no idea why I indulged them, but I found them fascinating, much like the Ooompa-Loompas in *Charlie and the Chocolate Factory,* if only they had been racists. In any event, I was glad I did. Fact is, nothing is more amusing than to have a Nazi look you in the eye, mouth full of lemon square, and insist that whereas jazz music is really just a discordant fad, *polka* is a permanent art form that will never die, tied as it is to the inherently European diatonic scale, which scale serves as mathematical confirmation of the unity of the white soul. Uh huh, and good luck selling that last part in Mississippi.

A month or so after I left, I noticed that David had posted a personal ad on Stormfront—the leading white nationalist and neo-Nazi web board in the world—hoping to connect with a modern-day Eva Braun, or, short of that, some skinhead gal. Therein, he noted that he was look-ing for a "true lady" who could also "get down and dirty," preferably while whistling the *Horst-Wessel-Lied*, hopping on one foot, while the other foot, firmly inserted in a Doc Marten boot with red laces was hap-pily curbing some kid fresh from his Bar Mitzvah. That last part is a joke, but the "down and dirty" part was hilariously real. I told the stu-dents of color at CWU that they should immediately blow up the per-sonal ad on twenty-four by thirty-six paper and wheatpaste it all over campus, with a big bold headline reading, "Find This Nazi a Date: Even Assholes Need Love." I'm not sure if they did it, but David dropped out of Central shortly thereafter, bringing to three the number of colleges from which he had failed to graduate. So much for the master race.

* * *

OF COURSE, IT would be so much easier if all the racists were Nazis. Nazis, after all, are hard to miss. They tend to give themselves away, going all giggly before a finely-woven lederhosen, or adorning their chat room identities with bad-ass avatars (like pics of Edward Norton's skinhead character, Derek Vinyard, in *American History X*), intended to suggest a toughness that they typically lack, living in their parents' basements and all.

Most racists are less vicious than Nazis, and at the same time, they're considerably harder to deal with. It is precisely the way that garden-variety racists don't think of themselves as such that makes it tougher to address them, especially because, despite their lack of self-awareness when it comes to their biases, their willingness to deploy the same is legion.

Several years before I got on the road, I began to notice a disturbing tendency whenever issues of race would come up in a group of whites who really didn't know each other that well, but who happened to be together at a party or other social event, or for that matter, in a pub. In these situations it seemed almost inevitable that someone in the group would take the opportunity to make some kind of overtly racist com-ment, or tell a racist joke, as if it were perfectly acceptable to do so, and as if no one else in the group would mind. "White bonding" was what I called it for lack of a better term.

At first I thought I was the only one having this experience so I kept it to myself, but then when I began to mention it to others, they talked of having the same thing happen to them. In fact, I would later learn that others whom I had never met were actually using the same term I had chosen to describe it—white bonding. Given the frequency with which it seemed to be happening, it became apparent that I would need to develop some kind of interruption strategy.

This became even clearer to me when I began lecturing around the country and was asked how best to respond to racist jokes or comments. Although it seemed like a relatively minor matter—especially when compared to the larger issues of institutional injustice to which I was mostly speaking—I had to apply the logic of the organizer here too: after all, if we can't figure out how to respond to the "small stuff," so to speak, we'll never be able to deal with the bigger issues.

At first, I didn't have an answer. One thing I knew though, was that my own normal responses weren't sufficient. Sometimes, I wouldn't know how to respond any more so than the people asking me for advice had known. At other times, I might respond with a pissed-off reply like, "I'm really offended you just said that, and I'd appreciate it if you wouldn't say those kinds of things around me again." Though such a reply lets everyone know where you stand, it's almost guaranteed to make the offending party defensive, and to reply the only way a person in that situation can, which is to make *you* the problem—the one without a sense of humor, the one who needs to "loosen up," or to understand that "it's just a joke." Not to mention, telling someone not to engage in racist commentary in front of you isn't the same as getting them to stop practicing racism. It amounts to seeking protection for one's own ears rather than trying to truly challenge the offending individual and move them to a different place.

So I decided I would try an experiment. If it worked, I would have something to tell the people who asked me the question—something more productive than for them to simply shut the offending party down. I thought about it for a while, began to rehearse the approach in a mirror, and waited for the opportunity to try it out.

Then one night, while speaking at a college in Montana, I was out with a group of people, all of them white, including several students who had brought me in for the presentation at their school. As the evening went along, one young man who knew some of the other students at the table (but who was unaware of the purpose for my visit) joined us. At some point, and for reasons I can't recall, conversation turned to race, and I braced myself, knowing that things could turn bad, very quickly.

The young man asked if we wanted to hear a joke, and then, without waiting for a response, he simply launched into it. As expected, it was every bit as racist as I had feared it would be when he began.

When he was done, most everyone remained quiet or rolled their eyes. A few people laughed nervously and a few others said something to the effect that the joke had been terrible, and that he "really shouldn't tell jokes like that." I, on the other hand, laughed as though it had been the funniest joke I'd ever heard, which naturally confused my hosts who had just paid for me to come in and be an antiracist, not the kind of person who would likely appreciate racist humor. But I stayed in character because I needed to gain the young man's confidence for the set-up that was to come.

"Hey, I've got one. Wanna hear it?" I asked. Naturally, he did.

I continued: "Did you hear the one about the white guy who told this really racist joke because he assumed everyone he was hanging out with was also white?"

"No, I haven't heard that one," he replied, not seeing where this was headed, and apparently expecting a genuine punch line, all the while missing the fact that he was it.

"Actually there is no joke," I explained. "That was just my way of tell ing you that I'm black. My mom is black."

This is the part I had had to rehearse in the mirror, since it wasn't remotely true. But all that practice had paid off. I had sold him. Indeed, I could have been black. There are lots of African Americans lighter than myself, or folks with one black parent who may look white but who would certainly have been classified as black back in the day, and who identify themselves as such now.

His response was as immediate as it was revealing.

"Oh my God," he demurred. "I'm so sorry. I didn't know."

It was at that point that I confessed: I wasn't really black, but as white as he. Now his look of embarrassment turned to one of confusion. After all, whites don't normally claim to be black when we're not. There isn't much in it for us.

"I'm not black," I said, "but I find it interesting that when you thought I was, you apologized. In other words, you know that joke was messed up, so that if you'd been around a black person knowingly, you never would have said it. So why did you feel comfortable saying it in front of us? Why do you think so little of white people?"

Now he was really confused. It was one thing to have someone imply that he didn't much like black folks—which he no doubt already knew—but to be told that he must have some kind of bias against whites, against his own group? That was a new one.

"What do you mean?" he asked.

"Well," I explained, "You must think all whites are racists, and specifically, that we're all the kind of racists who enjoy racist jokes. Otherwise you wouldn't take a chance making that kind of comment around white folks you don't even know. So tell me, why do you think so little of white people?"

He stammered for a few seconds, but instead of getting angry, instead of telling me to get a sense of humor, he began to actually engage, and we proceeded to have a conversation about race. There is no way we'd have had that talk had I chastised him in the traditional manner. But by engaging him in a process, a reflective process that called into question how he knew what he knew—how he knew we were white, and how he knew we would all approve of racist jokes—I was able to stretch out the dialogue and contribute to making it more productive than it otherwise would have been.

For whites to resist racism this way sends a message to other whites: they can't take anything for granted; they can't presume to know our views; they can't be sure that we'll accept their efforts at white bonding. Far from merely providing a feel-good moment, planting those seeds of doubt is an important step in the process of resistance, because racism, especially of an institutional nature, requires the collusion of many persons; the lone bigot can't accomplish it. By throwing racists off balance, we increase the costs associated with putting their racism into practice. In the case of joke tellers, they can never be too sure that the next stranger they try that with isn't one of *those* whites—the "black white" people, or the kind of white person who won't appreciate the commentary—and as such, may dial back their tendency to act in racist ways.

If we can impose enough self-awareness and doubt into the minds of those who engage in racist behavior, we make it harder for such persons to blindly act on it. Racism, like anything, takes practice in order to be really effective.

* * *

YET RACISM ISN'T the only thing that takes practice—so too does antiracism. It takes practice, and a consciousness of mind, the truth of which statement came home to me in an especially glaring way during the last year of my paternal grandmother's life.

My dad's mom, Mabel (McKinney) Wise, was a central figure in my life. She was the person to whom I would often turn for emotional support when things got too chaotic at home. If life with my father turned especially volatile, it was to her and Leo's that I would flee, spending the night until things blew over.

When Leo had died in the summer of 1989, my grandmother had begun to disintegrate. When I arrived at the hospital shortly after he had passed and first saw her in the arms of one of his doctors, it was as if even then her system had started to shut down.

As it happened, she would live until 1998, though only a few of those years would be of much quality. A year after Paw Paw's death, while I had been at home following college graduation, she had a car accident. It was nothing serious, but when I got the call to head to the scene, just a half-mile or so from our apartment, it was obvious that the fender-bender had shaken her up. As the years went by, it became apparent that she was in the early stages of Alzheimer's, and had probably begun succumbing to the disease at the time of that accident.

We would watch as her grip on reality slowly slipped away. It was a process that, in its early years, is hard to categorize because a certain amount of mental slippage is inevitable as we get older. Since there are still moments of clarity, there are times when you're inclined to think that there really isn't anything all that serious going on. Then you see the person on one of their cloudy days and you're snapped back into reality, unable to ignore that your loved one is dying, and it's not going to be a pretty thing to watch.

By the mid-'90s, Mabel was still able to live on her own, in the house she and Leo had purchased four decades earlier, but she needed considerable help during the day. For the last two years of her life she relied on a couple of different nurses who would stay with her for several hours, make her lunches, clean up after her, and, near the end, bathe her as well. We always worried that after the nurses left she would burn the house down because she was a smoker, and in the depths of her growing dementia she could easily have fallen asleep, cigarette in hand, and that would have been the end of her.

In 1996, when I moved back to Nashville and was looking for a place to live, I had spent a week or so with her, sleeping in my father's old room, and witnessed the deterioration up close. At any given moment she would have as many as two-dozen open Diet Coke cans in the refrigerator, having started to drink one, then placing it back in the fridge after a few sips and opening another, forgetting about the first. She would repeat this process until she ran out of shelf space, or until someone—myself, a nurse, or another visiting relative—would pour them out. At night, she would forget that I was in the back room, and if she heard me moving around it would scare her, so she would come to investigate the source of the noise. I would have to remind her, several times a night, that it was just me. A few mornings, when I came into the den to see her, she would be startled, having forgotten that I was staying with her.

By 1998, her deterioration had rapidly accelerated. Seemingly at once she began to forget who people were, confusing me with my father or even calling me Leo on occasion. In July, she came down with an infection and had to be hospitalized. While there, it became obvious that she could never return to her house. Upon release, her mind barely functioning, she was placed in a nursing home, on the Alzheimer's ward. She would live a little less than a month, dying two weeks before Kristy and I were married.

That a story about a little old lady with Alzheimer's might somehow be related to the subject of race, or whiteness, may seem like a stretch. But once you know the rest of the story, the connections become pretty clear.

First, it's important to note that Mabel Wise was no ordinary white woman. Though not an activist, she very deliberately instilled in her children, and by extension in me (as her oldest grandchild and the one with whom she spent the most time), a deep and abiding contempt for bigotry or racism of any form. She was very proud of what I had chosen to do with my life, and although her antiracism was of a liberal sort that didn't involve an amazingly deep understanding of the way that institutional injustice operates—it was an interpersonal level at which she tended to think of these issues—it was nonetheless quite real.

That she saw racism and rebelling against it as a personal issue made sense, because it was at that level that she had learned to deal with it many years before. Her father had actually been in the Klan while working as a mechanic in Detroit in the 1920s, and after moving back to Tennessee shortly thereafter. It was an association that would become a problem for her several years later when, at the age of fifteen, she would meet and eventually fall in love with Leo Wise, a Jew.

Around the age of seventeen, she could no longer abide her father's racism, and that, combined with his anti-Semitism, which she now took very personally, led her to confront him, to tell him in no uncertain terms that either he was going to burn his Klan robes, or she was going to do it for him. I can't begin to imagine the kind of strength it would have taken to issue such a challenge in 1937, especially to a large man, given to anger, and hardly used to being accosted in such a way by a young girl, or any woman. But it worked. My great-grandfather, having been given an ultimatum, burned his robes, quit the Klan, changed his life, and would later accept the man who was to become my grandfather into his family.

From that experience, I suppose Mabel decided that standing up to racism wasn't so tough, and so she would do it again often. For instance, once when a real estate agent announced that the house he was showing to her and Leo was desirable because it was in a racially-restricted neighborhood, she informed him that he had best get in his car and leave, or else she would run him over in hers. That's who she was, and had always been, so long as anyone could recall.

Which brings us then to the rest of the story, the part that provides dramatic evidence of the way in which racism is capable of diminishing even the strongest of us, even the ones who have long made a point of resistance.

If you've ever had a loved one who was suffering with Alzheimer's, you know that the loss of memories is among the more benign symptoms of the disease. The others are far worse; namely, the paranoia, anger, and even rage that accompanies the slippage of one's mental faculties.

As she went through these stages of the illness that would ultimately contribute to her death, she began to work out the contours of her deepening crisis upon the black nurses whose job it had been to take care of her. And how might a white person treat a black person when they're angry, or frightened, or both? And what might they call those black persons in a moment of anger, or insecurity, or both?

Resisting socialization, you see, requires the ability to choose. But near the end of my grandmother's life, as her body and mind began to shut down, this consciousness—the soundness of mind that had led her to fight the pressures to accept racism—began to vanish. Her awareness of who she had been disappeared, such that in those moments of anger and fear, she would think nothing of referring to her nurses by the term Malcolm X said was the first word newcomers learned when they came to this country.

Though I'm not sure when white folks first learn the word, Maw Maw made clear a more important point: that having learned it, we will never, *ever* forget it. It was a word she would never have uttered from conscious thought, but which remained locked away in her subconscious despite her lifelong commitment to standing against racism. It was a word that would make her violent if she heard it said, and a word that for her to utter it herself would make her another person altogether; but there it was, as ugly, bitter, and no doubt fluently expressed as it had ever been by her father.

Here was a woman who no longer could recognize her children, had no idea who her husband had been, no clue where she was, what her name was, what year it was; yet she knew what she had been taught at an early age to call black people. Once she was no longer capable of resisting this demon, tucked away like a time bomb in the far recesses of her mind, it would reassert itself and explode with devastating intensity.

She could not remember how to feed herself. She could not go to the bathroom by herself. She could not recognize a glass of water for what it was. But she could recognize a *nigger*. America had seen to that, and no disease would strip her of that memory. It would be one of the last words I would hear her say, before she stopped talking at all.

Importantly, it wasn't just some free-floating word bouncing around in her diseased brain, which she was tossing about as if it had no larger meaning. She didn't call any of her family by that word, even though we were the recipients of plenty of her anger and fear as well. She knew exactly what she was saying, and to whom.

Given Mabel's entire life and the circumstances surrounding her demise, her utterance of a word even as hateful as this says little about her. But it speaks volumes about her country and the seeds planted in each of us by our culture; seeds that we can choose not to water, so long as we are of sound mind and commitment, but seeds that also show a remarkable propensity to sprout of their own accord. It speaks volumes about how even those whites committed to living in antiracist ways and passing down that commitment to their children have been infected with a deadly social pathogen that can fundamentally scar the antiracist who carries it, whether or not they are fully aware of the damage. Maybe this is why I tire of white folks who insist, "I don't have a racist bone in my body," or, "I never notice color." Maw Maw would have said that too, and she would have meant well, and she would have been wrong.

Watching all this unfold, it was especially interesting to observe how the rest of my family dealt with it. Whenever she would say the word in the presence of either of her two daughters, they would quickly reassure the nurses that she didn't mean anything by it (which was patently untrue), and that it was just the illness talking (which the nurses already understood, far better than my aunts). While apologizing for racial epithets is nice, I suppose, far nicer would be the ability to learn from this gift my grandmother was giving us—and it *was* a gift, her final way of saying *look* at this, see what is happening here, do something about this. What those women at my grandmother's nursing home need and deserve, much more than sincere but irrelevant apologies from embarrassed family members, is an end to this vicious system of racial caste and the conditioning it provides to us all.

Those nurses knew, and so do I, why my grandmother could no longer fight. For the rest of us, however, there is no similar excuse available.
We don't have Alzheimer's, and yet we all go through our moments of
fear, anger, and insecurity. It doesn't take a disease to usher us into those
states of mind from time to time. We are all at risk, all vulnerable to
acting on the basis of something we know is wrong, but which is there,
ready to be used if the chips are down, or if we simply aren't paying
enough attention to the details.

* * *

THE NEXT TWO years were defining ones for me, personally and professionally. I started writing in March 1999, for an online commentary
service operated by *Z Magazine*. It was the first regular writing I'd done
in about four years, and I quickly remembered how much I enjoyed
it. But at the same time, I was getting nervous about the financial sus-
tainability of the lecture circuit. Though I had never prioritized money,
the fact remained that having grown up under conditions of persistent
fiscal insecurity, I also knew better than to glamorize monetary struggle. There was nothing cool about it, nothing radical, nothing political. People who think starving for their art or their politics is somehow
tantamount to making a statement have almost never done without;
and they sure as hell never spent much time speaking to people who
had, not one of whom wants to be poor. No, living hand to mouth was
something I had had more than enough of. I wasn't about to continue
that cycle in a new family, whether it was just Kristy and me, or whether
the family would come to include children.

When summer came and I didn't have many speaking engagements
booked for the fall semester, I panicked. Thinking that perhaps it was
a sign from the universe that I should go in a different direction, I
applied for and was ultimately hired as the Director of the Tennessee
Coalition to Abolish State Killing (TCASK), the statewide anti–death
penalty organization. Unfortunately, almost as soon as I began working for TCASK, I started to think I'd made a terrible mistake. I cared
deeply about the issue, but as I tried to go about the task of running an
office, coordinating chapters around the state, and paying bills (even
simply remembering to pay myself on time), I started to realize how

incompetent I was at almost everything but that which I had been doing the past several years. Literally, writing and speaking *were* my only talents, and my time at TCASK would finally prove it.

The organization and I would part ways in April 2000, after just eight months. In part this was due to my incompetence as an organizational manager, and in part it was because my personal biography became a liability for the group. Working for TCASK meant that among the condemned for whom I'd be advocating would be Cecil Johnson, the man who had killed my friend, Bobby Bell, in 1980. I guess I should have figured that those who supported state murder would potentially seek to exploit that connection in the eyes of the public, and bash me to Bobby's dad. What kind of person, after all, would support the continued heartbeat of a man who had killed one of his good friends? When I managed to embarrass the associate D.A. in a debate at Vanderbilt Law School and again on the nationally-televised *Nancy Grace* show—along with Nancy herself, who I managed to fluster to such an extent I thought her head may explode—it was clear that the only way to get back at me would be to call Bob Bell Sr. and accuse me of "using" his son's memory to argue against capital punishment. This, all because I had mentioned having lost a friend to murder when I was a kid, and yet, still opposing the death penalty. I hadn't mentioned Bobby's name, but all the D.A. needed was an opening to discredit the far more informed side against which he was arrayed. Opening provided, he took it.

When word got out that pro-death penalty forces were planning on having Bobby's father make some kind of public statement against me and TCASK, I knew that it was time to go. I certainly didn't want to put Mr. Bell through any more pain, nor did I want the group's important work to be harmed by my continued presence as their director. I prepared to resign, but ultimately wouldn't need to. A few days before I was planning on leaving, Joe Ingle, a TCASK founder and board member, called me to his office and very graciously suggested that things weren't working out, on multiple levels. He was right, and I was relieved.

By then, fortunately, the speaking engagements were starting to roll in again, but even if the money was going to be tight, I knew that the road was where I belonged, and so back to the grind I went.

In October, we learned that Kristy was pregnant and we'd be having a child that coming summer. Though pregnancy becomes immediately real for the woman who's carrying the child-to-be, for the man (or non-gestating woman) in the relationship, it really doesn't register fully, in most cases, until that child is actually born. So although I was thrilled at the thought of being a dad—though scared, given my own lack of a real role model when it came to fathering—I had no idea how powerful the experience would be until our daughter, Ashton Grace, was pulled from her mother by C-section, early in the morning of July 2, 2001. At the first sight of her I was overcome by the emotion of it all, and literally dropped to my knees, my tears flowing like water through a city fire hydrant after being opened by children attempting to cool off on a hot summer day.

Trying to make the world a better place had suddenly taken on an even more immediate urgency. Little did I know how much more complicated creating that world would become, and how quickly.

* * *

KNOWING THAT THE baby was due in July, I had cleared my calendar for about two months after the due date, so I could be at home with Kris and Ashton. By late August though, it was time to head back out again. I far preferred being with my family, even though at that stage Ashton was mostly sleeping and eating. Just holding her, or getting up to do midnight feedings while Kris tried to squeeze in some badly needed sleep, was like heaven to me. I looked forward to going into her room early in the morning, warming up a bottle and feeding her while sitting in the glider, lights dim, the sounds of Meshell Ndegeocello's *Bitter* album coming from the CD player just behind my head.

By early September, I was to be out for the better part of two weeks. Beginning on September 10, I was scheduled to serve as a visiting scholar at the Poynter Institute, in St. Petersburg, Florida, where several such visiting faculty were to conduct five days worth of seminars on race and reporting. About twenty journalists from around the country would be attending the session, where we would examine everything from how to productively frame stories on racial inequality to how to avoid inadvertently replicating stereotypes in print and broadcast media. As fate would have it, the timing for such a series of discussions could not have been better.

The morning of Tuesday, September 11, was a beautiful day in St. Petersburg: blue skies, not too warm, a pleasant breeze meeting the seminar participants as we walked the five blocks or so from our hotel to Poynter. We began filing in to the main seminar room a little after 8:30, where we grabbed some coffee and started to plot the day's events. Each of the visiting scholars was to make a presentation over the next few days and then facilitate discussions with the visiting journalists when it was one of the other scholars' turns to present. Within a few minutes though, whatever schedule we'd intended to keep would be scrapped.

Shortly before 9:00, Keith Woods, a permanent faculty member at Poynter (who would later become Dean of the Institute and eventually V.P. for Diversity at National Public Radio) came into the room, a nervous look on his face, and headed for the television. As he turned it on, I heard him mutter something about a plane hitting the World Trade Center in New York. Already the cameras were covering the smoke billowing from the North Tower, which had been struck by an American Airlines jet about ten minutes earlier. As we sat, transfixed by the tragedy unfolding in front of us, hardly able to understand what was happening, CNN cut away to a local station's coverage, which began with a tight shot of the damage to the north tower, indicating a hit somewhere near the eighty-fifth floor of the giant structure.

After about a minute of commentary and speculation as to what had happened, the cameras pulled back, just in time for us to watch a new image come into view over on the right hand side of the screen. It came into the frame so quickly and proceeded to move to the left so rapidly that at least for me, it didn't immediately register as to what it had been. Was that a plane? Wait, what? *Another* plane?

As a huge fireball shot from the side of the south tower, we all recognized that not only had it been a plane that we'd seen, but more to the point, it was history we were witnessing, in all its horrific splendor. There was no question now what was happening. The odds of two planes accidentally smashing into the tallest buildings in New York were so ridiculously small as to be incalculable, although one of the New York–based commentators speculated about that possibility for a few more minutes, perhaps unwilling to face the terrible truth. This was no coincidence. These had been deliberate attacks. About a half hour later it became obvious how deliberate, when yet another plane was reported as having smashed into the Pentagon, and an hour after that, when a fourth plane crashed into a field in rural Pennsylvania after having been hijacked.

We all scrambled to call loved ones from the lower level of the Institute, as most people didn't have cell phones in 2001. Patient, but worried, we waited to place calls on the pay phones, many of us checking on people we knew in New York to make sure they were alright. Of course, it was almost impossible to reach anyone in the city in the midst of the chaos, as all the lines in and out were tied up. I reached Kristy, and asked if she had heard from Wendy, a friend who lived in the city and passed through the World Trade Center subway stop each morning about the time of the tower strikes, before heading on a train under the Hudson to New Jersey where she worked.

"Why would I have heard from Wendy?" she asked.

"Oh shit," I said, "are you not watching the news?"

"No, what happened?" she answered.

"Just turn it on," I said. "Two planes just hit the twin towers."

"Oh my God," she replied, placing the phone in the crook of her neck and grabbing the remote. As she did, I could hear our baby girl in the background making the sweet nonsense noises of a ten-week old, and it almost broke my heart, thinking about the kind of world into which she had just been born. She would not, I thought to myself, know even three months without war.

With Kris on the phone my mind flashed back to our honeymoon, three years prior, the first few days of which were spent in New York. We had looked out over the city from the observation spots at Windows on the World, and taken pictures of the rest of Manhattan and Wall Street below from that vantage point—a vantage point that no longer existed except in my mind. I imagined all that empty space below where we had stood, and below that, now lying stacked forty stories high, millions of tons of steel, plaster, and human remains. I felt instantly nauseous.

After getting back to the session, we all agreed that although events had altered the trajectory of the seminar, we'd continue. No one was going to be able to fly home anytime soon, so we might as well get back to work. Not to mention, as media began to speculate about the role that Arab and/or Muslim terrorism may have played in the attack, the need to examine the tragedy without fueling racial or religious bias became even more apparent. Several years earlier, after the bombing in Oklahoma City, Muslims in the area had been briefly targeted until the white, Christian identity of the perpetrators was announced a day or so later. That such targeting could happen again was something about which we were all aware, especially given the magnitude of the acts that were unfolding at that moment.

As a first order of business, we were all asked to write something, anything, about our feelings in the midst of the attacks. Whether faculty or "students," the assignment was the same. Yes, we needed to think about the professional implications of what had happened—how could we bring an anti-bias lens to reporting at such a critical time—but first, we needed to check in with how we were doing. Anger, fear, hopelessness—all that and more would spill out as we listened to each others' journal entries, poems, essays, and rants over the course of that initial day.

For some reason, I couldn't write anything at first. Perhaps it was my unwillingness to think about the implications of what had happened, given the newness of my daughter's life, or maybe I was just trying to think of how to say something in a way that hadn't been said already by someone else—ever the writer, looking for an angle. Whatever the case, I wouldn't write anything until late that night, after watching hours of news coverage and hearing the first inklings of war talk and massive retaliation against whomever was responsible, streaming from the mouths of enraged Senators, ready to use the attack as justification to drop bombs and demonstrate American military prowess.

What would ultimately emerge would be a letter to my little girl, not really meant for her consumption, but spoken as if to her at some later date, when she might understand. It would be the most emotionally exhausting piece of prose I've written to this day, and when I read it to the seminar participants, several cried, as did I. Five days later, I would read it at the University of North Carolina at Greensboro, to a crowd of about eight hundred people, fully expecting to be booed from the stage for its open challenge to U.S. militarism, bombastic retaliatory rhetoric, and talk of launching a "war on terror." Quite the opposite, the piece would receive a standing ovation from two-thirds of those assembled, signaling that the unanimity of support that some would proclaim for the nation's war plans was a lie. There were more people questioning the wisdom of that approach than many realized.

Back at Poynter, Heidi Beirich, who had recently been hired by the Southern Poverty Law Center as a researcher on the far-right, and who was attending the seminar, said she thought there was something I might find interesting being said on one of the neo-Nazi chat boards she regularly monitored. Curious as to the take of white supremacists on the day's events, she had logged in to one of the boards and started reading the posts. Almost immediately she had come across one racist who praised the attacks on the World Trade Center and Pentagon, and said he wished that whites had even half the "testicular fortitude" to carry out similar actions. Billy Roper, head of recruitment at the time for the Hitler-worshipping National Alliance (whose founder had been the author of *The Turner Diaries*, which McVeigh had found so inspiring) added that anyone who was willing to fly planes into buildings in order to kill Jews (whom Roper naturally assumed predominated in the buildings since it was in the New York financial district), was "alright" by him. Another chat room member said the attacks made him feel "excited and more alive than ever."

One after another, these white warriors expressed their glee, their unbridled exuberance for the mass killing that had just transpired, but there would be no news coverage of this *anywhere*. Rather, the media would show coverage from the Palestinian West Bank, in which residents were seen cheering and dancing as if to say they were happy about the death of thousands of Americans at the hands of the Saudi and Egyptian hijackers (whose identities we would come to know because the luggage of Mohammed Atta, the lead hijacker, had not made it onto the fatal flight he boarded and would be discovered within hours).

Of course, neither the Nazis nor the Palestinians had played any role in the attacks, but whereas the media thought the celebration by the latter was worth covering, that of the former was conveniently ignored. It was much like the L.A. riots in 1992, during which a news crew had taken footage of a white woman looting designer dresses from an expensive clothing store, piling them into a BMW, and justifying the actions by saying "everyone's doing it." When the footage came into the possession of reporters in Milwaukee who wanted to show it on their broadcast, they had been blocked from doing so by their producer, who told them the footage was irrelevant, since the story wasn't about rich white people looting, but rather, angry black and brown folks who did.

Soon, the journalists who were at Poynter for the seminar started getting requests from their home offices to go interview the local Arab or Muslim communities in and around St. Pete. Go ask people at the local mosque how they were feeling about what had happened, and if they condemned the attack. One reporter from Detroit was asked to get home as soon as possible so she could go to neighboring Dearborn (which has the largest concentration of Arabs of any city outside the so-called Arab world), and ask the same questions. Realizing the absurdity of such a request—after all, she would note, they never sent her there to ask Arabs or Muslims about anything but terrorism—she had declined the request, as did everyone else when asked to get local Arab and Muslim feedback. The seminar was becoming more than an educational experience. It had become a tool for resistance.

* * *

UNABLE TO RETURN home by plane, as flights remained grounded through the end of the week, Heidi rented a car and asked if I wanted to share the ride. Having no better plan as to how I might get home, I agreed. I would take her to her house in Montgomery and then drive the rest of the way to Nashville, dropping the rental off there. All the way home it was apparent that the nation was headed into full-froth revenge mode. Callers to one after another talk show (and not just on right-wing radio) demanded massive retaliation and even the use of nuclear weapons against Afghanistan, Iraq, Iran, whomever. Many callers weren't discriminating; they were prepared without hesitation to turn the Middle East, in their words, into a "parking lot." Of course, calls for racial and religious profiling were heard everywhere, with very few willing to challenge the position in those first weeks.

It was only rational to profile Arabs and Muslims, most folks insisted, since they were the ones who posed the greatest threat. That no similar calls for the racial profiling of whites had been issued after Tim McVeigh's crime, or those of the Unabomber (Ted Kaczynski), or the Olympic Park Bomber (Eric Rudolph), or the dozens of abortion clinic bombers and arsonists over the years (all of whom had been white and ostensibly Christian), went largely unmentioned. That al-Qaeda operated in more than fifty nations, and that the physical appearance of persons from those nations ran the gamut from the lily-white skin of the Chechen rebels to the olive color of most Indonesians and Filipinos to the blue-black of the Sudanese (and thus, profiling was an almost Sisyphean task, regardless of the ethics of the matter) was even less important, it seemed.

Immediately, I could notice the difference during my travels. Anyone who looked even remotely Arab, or just *brown,* was searched more intently than anyone else, like the family of five named Martinez, who were headed from Nashville to Guadalajara, Mexico, during the last week in September, and who were given the red alert treatment from security. I was about to say something to the officials when they finally let the family go, after contenting themselves that the infant's diaper bag was not an incendiary device and that the Spanish they were speaking was not some form of coded Arabic.

The only thing more maddening than the calls for profiling or apocalyptic violence was the way in which whites seemed so oblivious to why anyone might have attacked the United States in the first place. "Why do they hate us?" became a commonly heard question, asked by folks when they would be interviewed by news crews across the country. But not one of the persons who I saw issue this query—and I saw it hundreds of times if I saw it once—was of color. *Not one.* Yet no one seemed to notice the monochromatic nature of the naiveté, or if they did, they didn't think it interesting enough to remark upon.

The lack of inquisitiveness on the part of folks of color as to why anyone might hate America wasn't due to insensitivity, of course. It surely wasn't because they were any less horrified by the slaughter of three thousand innocent people, or any less scared about future attacks. But to be black or brown is to *know* that there are reasons to feel less than giddy about the United States; it is to have a love-hate relationship with the nation. Only whites have the luxury of thinking the world sees us as we see us, and that the U.S. has been a force for unparalleled and uninterrupted good, doing nothing around the globe that could possibly explain America-hatred the likes of which we discovered on that fateful day. But people of color know that things have been a bit more complicated, that terrorism isn't new, that innocent people have been targeted before, and by the very same empire that now seemed to believe it had been victimized in ways never before seen in human history. People of color have never had the luxury of believing the national fairy tales upon which white Americans have come to depend.

The events of September 11 would make quite apparent the glaring experiential divide between whites and folks of color in the United States. Over the next several months I would keep track of how many cars I saw with "United We Stand" bumper stickers, and the racial identity of the persons behind the wheels of those cars. Whereas I saw plenty of people of color driving cars with "support the troops" stickers (likely because they had a relative in the armed services, given the disproportionate number of people of color in uniform), I saw literally *zero* vehicles driven by black or brown folks that sported a sticker proclaiming national unity. I encountered over five hundred such cars driven by whites, by the time I stopped counting, but none driven by African Americans, Latinos, Asian Americans, or indigenous persons. People of color know that national unity is not something that we can make real by simply proclaiming it; nor are they likely to think war a sufficient basis upon which to rest a claim for togetherness. Unity requires a unity of opportunity, treatment, and experience in everyday settings: on the job, in the schools, or in the justice system. What people of color knew, but whites had the luxury of ignoring, was that being attacked by foreign forces had done nothing to bring unity in those areas. The bumper stickers, for them, would have to wait.

The extent to which whites and blacks have almost completely different lenses through which we see the country and the world was made glaringly apparent the night in 2002, when professor Michael Eric Dyson and I were on *Phil Donahue*. We were there to discuss comments made by Republican leader Trent Lott, in which he had praised archsegregationist Strom Thurmond, suggesting at Thurmond's one hundredth birthday party that the country would have been better off had we all listened to Strom back in the day. In attempting to make the point that whites and blacks remember our history differently, Mike noted, as an example, that although 9/11 had been a tragedy of great magnitude, black folks had known about terrorism for a long time. As he put it: "I know a lot of you here in New York were running for your lives on 9/11, and that was terrible, but my people have been running for four hundred years, so what else is new?"

Immediately, a young white woman in the third row blew up as if he had called her momma a name. Her agitation got Donahue's attention, prompting Phil to bound over to her seat, in his trademark fashion.

"How dare you compare the experience of black America with 9/11," she exclaimed, furious that he would have made such a comparison.

How dare *he*? "Oh no sister," Dyson retorted, "How dare *you* compare the events of 9/11 with four hundred years of oppression. Don't get it twisted."

The ability of whites to deny nonwhite reality, to not even comprehend that there *is* a nonwhite reality (or several different ones), indicates how pervasive white privilege is in this society. Whiteness determines the frame through which the nation will come to view itself and the events that take place within it. It allows the dominant perspective to become *perspectivism*: the elevation of the dominant viewpoint to the status of unquestioned and unquestionable truth.

White reaction to 9/11 reminded me of the white man in his mid-thirties, who I'd seen on national TV after the not-guilty verdict in the 1995 criminal trial of O. J. Simpson, who lamented, "I now realize that everything I was taught in the third grade about this nation having the most wonderful justice system imaginable was all a lie!"

Now he realized it! He had lived several decades believing the patriotic, pep rally propaganda of his teachers, preachers, and parents, but because of O. J., he had concluded that the system might not be fair. Had he grown up around people of color, they could have set him straight on how not-so-wonderful the American system of justice was by the time he was eleven. But he had had the luxury of believing the lie and then assuming that only the O. J. case demonstrated a crack in the system. Everything in his world had been fine until O. J. walked; then, and only then, was it as if the world was about to stop spinning on its axis.

With the attacks of September 11, the naiveté that had begun to crack for whites because of the O.J. verdict now lay shattered among the wreckage at the foot of Manhattan. Between the two events, not to mention a string of suburban school shootings that had transpired from the mid-'90s until early 2001—which were always met by cries of disbelief that such things could happen in places like that—it had been a tough few years for white denial. The only question was whether or not we'd be capable of learning anything from the truths being revealed.

*   *   *

SOMETIMES, THE TRUTHS that are revealed to us are difficult to accept, after all. Especially when they tell you something about yourself that you'd rather not face.

In April 2003, I boarded a plane bound for St. Louis. From there I would fly to Iowa for a conference. Prior to that day, I had flown on a thousand or so individual flights in my life, but as I walked down the jet bridge that morning, I glanced into the cockpit and saw something I had never seen before, in all my years of air travel: not one, but two black pilots at the controls of the plane—a rare sight for any air traveler, considering the small percentage of commercial pilots who are African American.

Given the paucity of pilots of color in the United States, and given what I had at that point been doing professionally for thirteen years, one might think that two black men in the cockpit that morning would have been a welcome sight to me. And upon sufficient reflection it would be. But upon a mere instantaneous reflection—which is to say, no reflection at all—this had not been my initial reaction. Sadly, my first thought upon seeing who would be in charge of delivering me safely to St. Louis was more along the lines of, "Oh God, can these two really fly this plane?"

Now don't get me wrong, almost as quickly as the thought came into my head, I was able to defeat it. I knew instantly that such a thing was absurd; after all, given the history of racism, I had every reason to think that these two men were probably among the very best pilots that the airline had—had they not been, they would never have made it this far. They would have been required to show not only that they could fly, but that they could do so over and above the prejudices and stereotypes that black folks have had to overcome in any job they do.

I also knew that in the months before this flight, several white pilots had been hauled off of planes because they had been too drunk to fly them, or because, in the case of two pilots for Southwest, they had decided to strip down to their underwear and invite the flight attendants into the cockpit as a practical joke: the kind of stupid human trick that no person of color would have imagined he or she could get away with. So, from a purely rational standpoint, I suppose I should have been glad to see anyone *but* a white pilot on my plane that day. But we don't always react to things on the basis of intellect, or on the basis of what we know to be true; rather, we sometimes operate from a place of long-term conditioning, which, having penetrated our subconscious, waits for just the right moment to be triggered, and invariably manages to find it.

In this case, no matter what I knew, I had been conditioned no less than anyone else to see people of color and immediately wonder if they're really qualified for the job—to automatically assume they aren't as good as a white person. The fact that I'd been working on my conditioning, and therefore was able to get a grip on my racist reaction is nice, but rather beside the point. All that really matters is that it happened, and could happen again. Maybe it wouldn't happen every time, and maybe it wouldn't happen to you (though don't be so sure; until it happened to me, I might have doubted it too), but the fact is it could. All it takes is a situation that calls forth the conditioning, prompts the stereotype, and cues the response.

When I first told this story publicly, about a year after it happened, other white folks and even people of color responded by sharing their own stories of internalized racial supremacy or internalized oppression—stories in which they too had reacted to people of color in leadership positions skeptically or nervously, despite their own conscious commitments to equity and fairness. The lesson was clear: advertising works, and not just for toothpaste, tennis shoes, and toilet paper, but also for the transmission of racial stereotypes.

As I had sat in my seat on the airplane that day, I found myself shaking, not so much because of what I'd learned about myself, as for what I'd learned, yet again, about the way society can distort us. And with Kristy expecting our second daughter in just three months, the realization was fraught with even more emotion than it might otherwise have carried. No matter what Kristy and I would teach our girls, no matter how we would raise them, Ashton, and very shortly, Rachel, would be exposed to the culture's presumptions and prejudices; and once exposed, they too would always be vulnerable, at risk for having those presumptions and prejudices transform them.

CHOCOLATE PAIN,
VANILLA INDIGNATION

ON AUGUST 29, 2005, the city I loved and had called home for ten years ceased to exist. Though there is still, today, something called New Orleans, whatever it is cannot compare to what once was. Its zombified transformation to a place neither truly dead nor really alive was accomplished not because of that thing to which we so often refer as "mother nature," not because of an act of God, however defined, and not directly because of the Hurricane known as Katrina. New Orleans as we knew it was destroyed by the acts of men: first and foremost, the men who constructed faulty levees for the Corps of Engineers, so that when Katrina came ashore in late August, though it did very little damage to the city itself, the storm surge overtopped and collapsed levee walls in dozens of places, leading to the inundation of roughly 80 percent of the town.

As the news began to filter out that the waters were rising, and as over fifty thousand people crowded into the Superdome and Convention Center, which were being used as evacuation facilities of last resort for those who hadn't fled the city (or couldn't, as there were one hundred thousand people in New Orleans without access to cars), I sat glued to my television, unable to look away. Most of my friends had been able to get out in the days leading up to the storm making landfall. But others had not been so lucky. And I knew that those persons with whom I'd worked in public housing were likely trapped.

The media broadcast images both enraging and heartbreaking: people stranded on rooftops waiting to be rescued by helicopters; the elderly and small children sitting outside the Convention Center in the scorching August heat, no food, water, or medicine to provide relief; people wading through waist-deep water to find dry land, their clothes drenched with the fetid fluid of Lake Ponchartrain, mixed with whatever street funk had joined it on its journey downtown. They also showed us endless footage of looters, though it was often the same five or six incidents shown from different angles, giving the impression to a public already inclined to think the worst of lower-income black folks (the disproportionate composition of those left behind) that theft was more common than it really was. And there were the reports of massive violence as well: murders, rapes, and even the killing of small babies, dumped in trashcans, according to one report. That these allegations would be investigated and found almost entirely false wouldn't matter. Most people probably never even heard that the violence claims had been debunked by five different national and international news outfits, so ready were most to believe the worst about those who had been left behind. Even fewer would probably learn of the *real* violence during those days; namely, the white vigilante terror squad that formed in the Algiers community on the city's west bank and shot at least a dozen African Americans for being in their neighborhood—a story that wouldn't break until 2007, and even then, would receive very little media attention.

On Tuesday and Wednesday, I spent hours browsing the comments sections of stories posted on NOLA.com, the main web-based news and information outlet for New Orleans, which remained operational throughout the crisis thanks to a server located outside of the city. There, one could read hundreds of hateful, even psychotically racist remarks about local area blacks. Commentators took an almost sadistic pleasure in referring to looters as "sub-human scum," "cockroaches," "vermin," "animals," "slime," and any number of other creative and dehumanizing slurs. Others openly called for the building of a separation wall between Orleans Parish and the much whiter Jefferson Parish, if and when the area was reconstructed, so as to "keep the animals out" of the areas with "decent people."

One poster, discussing those who were looting—even though most were taking necessities like food, water, medicine, or clothes to replace the rotting rags on their backs—wrote, in big, angry, unhinged capital letters: "TO ALL POLICE: PLEASE KILL THESE INCENSIVE (sic)

FOOLS! KILL THEM ALL! WE DON'T NEED THEM ON THIS PLANET ANYMORE . . . THEY DON'T DO US ANY GOOD . . . GOD BLESS AMERICA."

The individual who wrote those words was then outdone by another who said, "If I had my way, the National Guard would round these pieces of garbage up, make THEM clean up the mess Katrina left for us, and then machine gun the whole lot of them into the Gulf. The only good looter is a DEAD one. There are no exceptions."

And then, from a commenter who used his real name (Jim Hassenger), so I will too, there was this: "My city is destroyed and what is left the bastards are looting . . . I don't like living here with this disease anymore. I HATE YOU from the bottom of my heart. It's times like these I have to fight racist thoughts." Apparently, Jim was losing that fight.

While many refrained from comments of such a vicious nature, they nonetheless showed a disturbing insensitivity towards the suffering of those on the ground in New Orleans, calling them "unintelligent" for not evacuating. People seemed utterly oblivious to the real burdens of evacuation. If you didn't have a car, or money, or a place to go, how were you supposed to flee? Some argued that the city should have commandeered school buses to get folks out of town, but there weren't enough people to drive them, and they would have had no clear destination in any event. Unless the federal government mandated that hotels open their doors to the displaced and offered to pay for the rooms—which they never did— buses would have had no place to go, and few people would have agreed to just hop on them, drive into the night, and hope for the best.

Of course, sometimes when New Orleanians *did* try and flee the city, they were met with hostility and blocked from escaping. On the second day of the tragedy, a group of mostly black residents tried to walk out of the city by crossing the bridge to the west bank of the river, only to be shot at by sheriff's deputies from Gretna who wanted to keep blacks out of their city. And there were, of course, the African Americans on the west bank who tried to reach the pier in Algiers so as to get ferried out of the area, only to be shot by the white terror squad that presumed every black person in the neighborhood was a criminal.

Other voices suggested the city should never be rebuilt; its location, they would say, makes it too susceptible to a similar storm in the future, so it would be impractical to let people return. It's an argument that no one ever makes about small, white, Midwestern farm towns that get blown away each year by tornadoes, or to white retirees in Florida, just because they live in a hurricane zone, but which many felt was perfectly reasonable in the case of New Orleans and the folks who lived there. Whatever compassion and decency had animated the first few hours of the catastrophe on Monday was quickly vanishing by the middle of the week.

* * *

BY THURSDAY, SEPTEMBER 1, most who were stranded at the New Orleans Convention Center had no food or potable water, and what provisions existed at the Superdome had run out, yet to be replaced by FEMA. Indeed, President Bush's FEMA director would say later that day that he hadn't realized there were people trapped in such centers until that morning, despite the fact that the rest of us had been looking at them on national television for seventy two hours.

When desperate folks attempted to get into food pantries at the Convention Center, knowing that the supplies would spoil and never be used for their original purposes, National Guardsmen aimed guns at them and told them to "step away from the food or we'll blow your fucking heads off," according to reports from those among the crowd. Things were getting uglier by the minute.

Meanwhile, I wondered why there was no apparent presence of the Red Cross in the city, either to provide relief supplies or tend to the sick and injured. There were reports of their activities throughout the rest of the Gulf Coast, and in parts of Louisiana other than New Orleans, but nothing in the Crescent City itself, which seemed bizarre. Rather than a structured relief operation, the task was falling to private citizens, like Harry Connick Jr., who drove into the city to bring supplies to the stranded when no one else would do so, or like my former boss at the Louisiana Coalition, who did the same.

Lance and his family would never flee the city, and would make several relief runs downtown, seeing first-hand the orderly and largely peaceful way in which desperate folks were behaving and trying to survive. The need for private citizens to fill the relief gap had been intensified by the absence of the Red Cross, whose absence, Lance discovered, had been deliberate—the result of a relief blockade. Though he tried to get media to cover the blockade as a story of institutional injustice, few agreed to discuss it; this, despite the fact that the evidence for the embargo was right there on the organization's website, where one could read that, "The Department of Homeland Security continues to request that the American Red Cross not come back into New Orleans following the Hurricane. Our presence would keep people from evacuating and encourage others to come into the city." Government officials, more desirous of evacuating the city than helping the sick and dying, told the premier relief group on the planet to stand down and to do nothing within New Orleans. Nowhere else in the hurricane zone was this order given, but it was there. It was hard to avoid the conclusion that the demographic makeup of the effected might have had something to do with the different levels of concern.

That afternoon, I went with Kristy and the girls to a local Mexican restaurant, La Paz, for lunch. I had been riveted to the television for the better part of three days by that point, not even going out of the house, and needed a break from the coverage. As we waited for our food to arrive, I couldn't help but overhear the commentary emanating from the table to my left, filled with eight employees from a local call center, whose compassion for the suffering masses in New Orleans had clearly been exhausted.

The group prayed over their food—because, after all, God was responsible for the flakiness of their chimichanga—and then proceeded to heap scorn upon the people of New Orleans in ways that managed to only thinly veil the race and class bias at the heart of their critique. Between repeated "amens," the white men and women—the former appropriately preppy and the latter appropriately made-up with big blonde hair, bangs reaching for Jesus—wondered why the people of New Orleans hadn't left, or why they were looting, rather than helping one another, or shooting at relief helicopters (a story that turned out to be untrue—people on rooftops had been using guns as makeshift flares to gain the attention of helicopters, not to bring them down). One of the men attempted to draw a contrast between the decency of New Yorkers in the wake of 9/11 and the savagery of folks in New Orleans amid the current tragedy, and wondered why the difference? The neatly-coiffed female to his right quickly offered up an explanation.

"Well," Buffy explained, "It's probably because, in New Orleans, it's mostly poor people, and they don't have the same regard." (Regard for what? I wondered to myself. For life? For the sanctimonious and self-righteous consumption of chips and salsa?)

She then averred that police needed to shoot all looters. As I watched guacamole tumble from her mouth, she trying hard not to accidentally scrape off any of her lipstick with the side of her tortilla chip, her table-mates praised the Lord at her suggestion. That they were not struck down (I believe the Biblical term is *smote*), right then and there, may be the best evidence one can muster that there is no God—at least not one that actively intervenes in the affairs of mankind. Because I know that if I were God, there would have been a quickly available, albeit smoldering eight-top at the Nashville La Paz that afternoon.

Our food had come by now, but my appetite had vanished. I picked at the edges of my dish, unable to shut out the cacophony of contempt a few feet away. Kris asked what was wrong but I just grunted something about not being very hungry and that I was listening to the table next to us. The kids continued to eat. After a few more minutes I looked up, unable to bear any more and told them to hurry, that I really needed to go. I knew that if I stayed there any longer and had to listen to any more of the calumnies dripping from the lips of the call center lunch bunch, I was going to end up making a scene. Four days into the tragedy—a tragedy that was devastating the place and many of the people I loved—I was on edge, and I knew it wouldn't take much more to snap. Had I been alone or with only Kristy I might not have cared. Sometimes dumping queso on a person's head can be cathartic. But with the girls in tow, only four and two, I knew that such aggression and the inevitable expulsion from the restaurant that would have followed would only manage to scare them. I also knew that as a writer, I had better ways to get back at them than assault, be it verbal or physical.

I was starting to shake by the time my family finished their meal and we stood up to leave. I glared at the table as we passed by but to no effect. They never looked up from their bean burritos, and never stopped speaking of the people of New Orleans as animals unworthy of concern.

I told Kris that I needed her to drive. As we pulled away from the restaurant parking lot I broke down, tears cascading down my face as my sobs turned to the early stages of hyperventilation. Rachel asked what was wrong, having never seen me cry before, and certainly not like this. Kristy tried to explain it to her.

"You know those people we saw on TV in New Orleans, where daddy used to live, who were standing on their rooftops and stuck in the water?" she asked.

"Yes, that's so sad," she replied, the innocence of her words breaking my heart further.

"Well, daddy's just worried about them, and those people next to us in the restaurant were saying some mean things about the people there," she explained.

"Why would they say mean things about them?" Ashton wondered.

"Because some people just aren't kind," was all I could think to say. I knew the answer was more complicated than that, and one day I'd explain it to them in greater detail. But in that instant, it would have to suffice.

*　*　*

OVER THE NEXT few days, the narratives that began to develop from the Katrina tragedy showed how little most people understood either the city of New Orleans itself, its people, the political system under which we live, or the history of race and class subordination in America.

On the one hand, right-wing commentators holding forth on the nation's airwaves took the opportunity to bash the people of New Orleans for their "dependence on government." To the Rush Limbaughs of the world, the welfare state had sapped the individual initiative of the people there, and that was why they had remained behind, waiting on the government to save them. After all, he and others argued, they were living off the public dole anyway.

Having lived in the city for ten years and having worked with some of the poorest people there, I knew how incredibly and criminally inaccurate this meme was, but also realized that there would be very little chance of countering it, so ingrained were the race and class biases of the larger white public. Facts don't matter to the punditocracy or to those who hang on their every word like pliant sheep.

So for instance, no one mentioned that prior to Katrina, there were only forty-six hundred households in the entire city receiving cash welfare payments: this, out of one hundred and thirty thousand black households alone, which means that even if every welfare recipient in New Orleans had been black (and they weren't), still, less than four percent of such households would have qualified for the derision of the right. And of those few receiving such benefits, the average annual amount received was a mere twenty-eight hundred dollars *per household*, hardly enough to have managed to make anyone lazy.

In the Lower Ninth Ward, one of the hardest hit communities, and a place about which so much was said (and so much of it inaccurate), only 8 percent of the income received by persons living there came from government assistance, while 71 percent of it came from paid employment. In other words, folks in New Orleans were by and large poor in spite of their work ethic. Forty percent of employed folks in the Lower Ninth worked full-time and had average commutes to and from work of forty-five minutes a day. But the media didn't tell us that. I had to discover it by looking at the relevant Census Bureau data that investigative journalists were too busy or too uninterested to examine.

On the night of September 2, during the Concert for Hurricane Relief, broadcast across the nation, hip-hop artist, Kanye West, injected another narrative into the discussion, saying what had been on so many folks' minds, but which few had been willing to verbalize. Kristy and I were lying in bed, watching the concert when suddenly West, standing next to a stunned Mike Meyers (he of Austin Powers and SNL fame), went off script, discussing the media representation of looting and the way in which it stoked racial stereotypes. It wasn't what the cue cards in front of him said, but Meyers rolled with it, picking up at the end of West's soliloquy with another plea for financial contributions. Once Meyers finished reading his card, West blurted out the line for which he became instantly infamous in the eyes of many, including the president: "George Bush doesn't care about black people."

I have to admit that when we heard these words, both Kris and I roared. I, for one, laughed so hard I almost fell out of the bed. Although I knew the comment was simplistic—fact is, what was happening was less about any one individual's biases and more about a systemic and institutional neglect, by both major parties, that had jeopardized the lives of mostly black and poor folks in New Orleans—it provided a moment of almost comic relief. It was so unexpected, and the look on Meyers' face as he realized what had just happened was priceless. The comment would be edited out of later re-broadcasts, or even the first broadcast on the West Coast later that evening, but by then it was out there, for good or ill.

By the next week, other narratives would be launched, some of which were well-intended, but ultimately wrong. Filmmaker Spike Lee, for instance, who would go on to make a wonderfully poignant film about the tragedy, was quoted early on as saying that what had happened in New Orleans had been a "system failure of monumental proportions." Though I had always been a fan of Lee's films and most of his social commentary, I knew in this case that he had it wrong.

For the displacement of hundreds of thousands of poor, mostly black people in New Orleans to be considered a system failure would require that prior to the so-called failure, those individuals had been doing just fine by the system; it would suggest that the system had been working for them, and *not* failing, in the days, weeks, months, and years leading up to Katrina. But had that been the case? Of course not. In fact, it wasn't even the first time such folks had been displaced.

Although most Americans remain unaware of it, mass displacement of people of color, especially when poor, has been common, and not because of flooding or other so-called natural disasters, but as with New Orleans in 2005, because of man-made decisions. For example, from the 1950s to the 1970s, urban renewal and the interstate highway program had devastated black and brown communities in the name of progress, with hundreds of thousands of homes, apartments, and businesses knocked to the ground. In New Orleans itself, the I-10 had sliced through the city's largest black communities in the 1960s, the Tremé and the Seventh Ward.

The Tremé—the oldest free black community in the United States—is bordered on one side by Claiborne Avenue, above which the interstate would be constructed. The Claiborne corridor had been home to as many as two hundred black-owned businesses in its day, and included a wide median (known to locals as a "neutral ground") lined with huge oak trees and plenty of space for recreation, community picnics, family gatherings, and cultural events. Once completed, the I-10 had destroyed what was, for all intent and purposes, a public park sixty-one hundred feet long and one hundred feet wide, along with hundreds of business-es and homes. In the Seventh Ward, home to the city's old-line Creole community, residents saw the same kind of devastation, also from the construction of the I-10 along Claiborne, including the virtual elimi-nation of what was once the nation's most prosperous black business district.

No, there was nothing new about the current displacement, and it hadn't been the result of system failure. The people being affected had never been the priority of government officials. The system had let them down so many times before, and so consistently, that, indeed, one could even say that what happened in late August and early September 2005 was perfectly normative. If a system was never set up for you to begin with, and it then proceeds to let you down, even injure you, that's not failure; rather, it's a system operating exactly as expected, which is to say, it was a system *success*, as perverse as the implications of such a truth might seem.

Lee's comments about the system failing were only outdone for their historical lack of perspective by the remarks of columnist David Brooks, who opined in the *New York Times* that "the first rule of the social fab-ric—that in times of crisis you protect the vulnerable—was trampled." But what kind of fantasy world could allow one to believe something as pitifully quaint as that? For some, including poor black folks in New Orleans, every day had been a time of crisis, and they had never been protected from it. So whatever social fabric Brooks may have been refer-ring to, it clearly had never meant much to millions of people whom he appeared only after Katrina to have discovered.

Brooks went on to say that because of the government's "failure" in Katrina, "confidence in our civic institutions is plummeting." But con-fidence can only plummet when one has confidence to begin with. And who among us was saddled with such an affliction of naiveté? Surely not the black folks of New Orleans, and surely not the poor anywhere. Only middle class and above white folks have had the luxury of believing in the system and being amazed when it doesn't seem to work as they expected.

* * *

IT WOULDN'T TAKE long for the revisionists to begin whitewashing (pun very much intended), the racial element of the Katrina story. First, you'd hear rumblings that the real issue in New Orleans hadn't been race, but rather, class. Money, it was claimed, is what really determined whether or not you'd been likely to have suffered major property damage or displacement because of the flooding. And true enough, there was a definite economic element to the damage, with lower-lying and mostly working class communities bearing the brunt of the inundation. However, within a few months, research from Brown University would bear out that race was an even better predictor of property damage and displacement than economic status, with African Americans far more likely to suffer either, relative to whites.

In New Orleans, 75 percent of the people in damaged areas were black, compared to only 46 percent of the population in the undamaged areas. In Mid-City, 83 percent of the population was black, and 100 percent of the area sustained damage from the flood; in New Orleans East, 87 percent of the population was black and 99 percent of the community suffered damage; in the Lower Ninth Ward, 93 percent of the population was black, and 96 percent of the area was damaged. Likewise, in Tremé, Gentilly, and all of the communities with public housing, save one, significant damage tracked the blackness of the community.

Among white communities, only Lakeview sustained massive destruction: 90 percent of the area damaged, while being only 3 percent black. By comparison, the almost all-white Garden District sustained virtually no damage; the nearly two-thirds white Uptown area had damage in less than 30 percent of the community; most of the Audubon and University district remained untouched; the 80-plus percent white Marigny had damage in less than 20 percent of the area; and the almost entirely white French Quarter had virtually no damage at all. So much for class being the main issue, rather than race.

While in New Orleans for a conference in summer of 2006, I came across the second form of revisionism, spelled out in a letter to the editor of the *Times-Picayune*. Therein, the author put forth the newest meme going around the city, especially among conservatives; namely, that whites had actually been disproportionately victimized by Katrina and that blacks had been *underrepresented* among the fatalities, since, after all, blacks had been 68 percent of the city's pre-storm population, but comprised only 59 percent of those who had died. Whites, on the other hand, were merely 28 percent of the population before Katrina, but comprised 37 percent of the deceased.

Intrigued by the claim—and fascinated by the implicit racial animosity behind it (since it seemed to suggest blacks hadn't suffered *enough*)—I went in search of the statistics the author had used to make his argument. There appeared to be conflicting data, some from the Louisiana Department of Health and Hospitals, and other data reproduced on right-wing websites that had come from the Knight-Ridder news service. While both sets seemed to suggest that blacks had died at rates lower than their share of the New Orleans population, while whites had died at higher rates, more recent data from the state showed no real imbalance in the aggregate, with blacks comprising 65 percent of the dead and whites 31 percent—roughly equal to pre-storm population percentages.

But upon closer examination, which of course the revisionists saw no reason to perform, the problems with the conservative argument about disproportionate white suffering became clear. Fact is, the dead were overwhelmingly elderly, with three-fourths of all fatalities concentrated in the over-sixty age group. It was a statistic that made sense. Older folks are more likely to be in bad health to begin with, less able or willing to evacuate in a crisis, and are more susceptible to a major health event (like a stroke or heart attack) during a trauma. And since whites were far more likely than blacks in New Orleans to be elderly (more than twice as likely, in fact), that white fatalities might be slightly disproportionate should have been no surprise. Once mortality data was adjusted for age, so that only persons in the same age cohorts were being compared, blacks died at a much higher rate than whites, in every age category.

But the ultimate revisionism actually began just a few months after the catastrophe, when whites decided it was the city's black leadership that was racist, and especially Mayor Ray Nagin. The charge was leveled at Nagin for his off-the-cuff comment during an MLK day celebration that New Orleans should be and would be once again a "chocolate city," when displaced blacks were able to return. To whites, the remark was tantamount to saying that they weren't welcome, and to prove how racist the comment was, critics offered an analogy. What would we call it, they asked, if a white politician announced that their town should be a "vanilla" city, meaning that it was going to retain its white majority? Since we would most certainly call such a remark racist, consistency required that we call Nagin's remark racist as well, they maintained.

Of course, such reasoning was sloppy. For a white politician to demand that his or her city was going to remain white would be quite different, and far worse than what Nagin said. When cities, suburbs, or towns are overwhelmingly white, there are reasons (both historic and contemporary) having to do with discrimination and unequal access for people of color. Restrictive covenants, redlining by banks, racially-restrictive homesteading rights, and even policies prohibiting people of color from living in an area altogether—four things that whites have never experienced anywhere in this nation (as whites)—were commonly deployed against black and brown folks throughout our history. On the other hand, chocolate cities have not developed because whites have been barred or even discouraged from entry, but rather, because whites long ago fled in order to get away from black people, aided in this process by government subsidized loans. So, to call for a vanilla majority is to call for the perpetuation of obstacles to persons of color, while to call for a chocolate majority in a place such as New Orleans is to call merely for the continuation of access and the opportunity for black folks to live there.

It was especially interesting to note how Nagin's comments calling for the retention of a chocolate New Orleans brought down calls of racism, while the real and active planning of the city's white elite at the time—people like Joe Cannizaro and Jimmy Reiss—to change it to a majority white town, by razing black neighborhoods in the flood zone, elicited no attention or condemnation whatsoever from white folks.

That Nagin had actually been the candidate of white New Orleanians—receiving nearly 90 percent of their vote, but less than half the black vote—did nothing to assuage the anger over the Mayor's presumptive "reverse racism." He had promised to cater to white needs during the campaign, and had been amply rewarded for doing so. Now that he was stating a simple truth about the cultural and historic core of the city—and demanding that it be retained—his former supporters turned on him. As Nagin discovered his blackness, white New Orleanians did too, and it scared them. To hear many tell it, they were now the victims.

* * *

OVER THE COURSE of the next year, I would regularly run into youth groups—sometimes with churches and other times with schools—on their way to New Orleans to help with rebuilding efforts, or on their way home from the same. Whenever possible, I would try to strike up conversations with a few of the students or their chaperones, to find out what they'd be doing (or had already done) while there. If they were headed down, where would they be working and staying? With whom would they be meeting? What did they hope or expect to learn from the experience? If they had already completed their trek, I would wonder the same things, only in the past tense.

Occasionally, the answers I would receive suggested a very high level of critical engagement, which was heartening. By this I mean, the persons who had organized the trip had recognized the importance of preparing the students for the experience by having pre-arrival conversations regarding racism, classism, the history of the city, and the political and cultural context within which the tragedy had occurred. In those cases, the volunteers were not simply going to New Orleans to "get their help on," or perform some version of perceived Christian duty; rather, they were going to bear witness to inequality, learn from local leaders about their experiences, and work in real solidarity with the people struggling to rebuild the city—working *with*, not for.

I was especially impressed by the students from Northfield Mt. Hermon—a prep school in Massachusetts—whose preparation for their New Orleans service trip included an intensive class on the city, the storm, and the role of race and economics in understanding the tragedy, taught by veteran English teacher Bob Cooley. In the case of Northfield, the school had enrolled a few students from New Orleans who had been displaced, and not just the kids from the private schools, but public schools as well. One who I met while there was serving as something of a mentor and co-teacher to his classmates, and had clearly gained the respect of everyone on the campus for his wisdom and insights, despite the fact that he was basically their same age.

But sadly, this kind of preparation was rare for the people I met either going to, or coming from, service trips to the city. In most cases, when I would ask about their plans or experiences, the answers I got from the volunteers and their adult mentors indicated very little critical thinking or understanding of race, class, and the role of both in the disaster.

Most of the groups I met said they were going to be working, or had worked, not in New Orleans itself, but rather, in neighboring St. Bernard Parish, and specifically the community of Chalmette. Of those headed to New Orleans, most said they'd be working in Lakeview: the only wealthy and almost entirely white community hit hard by the flooding. I found this interesting and would always inquire as to how they got matched up with those communities, as opposed to the Lower Ninth Ward, or Mid-City, or New Orleans East, all of which were hard-hit, mostly African American communities.

Mostly, they would say, it was because the people who had organized the trips didn't know anyone from those black spaces, but had connections—be they with church pastors or civic leaders, or even family members—in the whiter locales. Others said that they were honestly afraid to go into the Lower Ninth Ward because of all they had heard about the community in the media (most of it false, of course). Still others didn't really know why they were headed to places like Chalmette: apparently the people through whom they were working had simply matched them up with those communities.

I found the placements in St. Bernard Parish especially interesting. On the one hand, there was no doubt that "da Parish," as it's known by locals, had been devastated by the flooding. Next to the Ninth Ward (literally), Chalmette was probably the hardest hit area in the metropolitan vicinity. But on the other hand, the fact that so many volunteers were being sent there to help rebuild struck me as telling, given the racial dynamics of the area. Whereas the Ninth Ward was 93 percent black before the storm, Chalmette was the exact opposite: 93 percent white. More to the point, it was a community where more than seven in ten whites had voted for neo-Nazi David Duke in the 1991 Governor's race. And it was a place where, in the immediate wake of the flooding, Parish officials had sought to prevent people of color from moving into the community by passing a "blood relative renter law," restricting rental access to persons who were blood relatives of the landlords from whom they'd be renting. The purpose of the law, quite obviously, was to block blacks from returning to the area and settling in St. Bernard, since almost all the property owners in the parish were white.

Did the volunteers know these things? Did they know that they'd be helping people who were actively advocating institutional racism, and who, in many cases, had supported a Nazi for Governor? Especially if the clean-up groups were integrated, did they realize that the volunteers of color would be helping a community where, had it been up to local officials, they couldn't have lived? In almost no instance had they heard anything about this. They were shocked. Local organizers of volunteer efforts had neglected to mention these details to the clean-up teams, mostly because they believed the racial tensions or inequities to be irrelevant: people were in need, they would say, and shouldn't be neglected because of their racial views. But shouldn't that have been left up to the volunteers? Didn't they deserve to know? Apparently not, according to some.

The way in which the racism of St. Bernard whites was glossed over was amazing. At one point, the generally liberal Sierra Club gave a leadership award to Henry "Junior" Rodriguez, the Parish Council president, because of his environmental record; this, despite his history of using racial epithets publicly, and supporting the blood relative renter law right up until it was ultimately blocked by the courts. Even to white liberals, racism was a secondary issue, hardly worth discussing when compared to a politician's record on, in this case, wetlands restoration.

What was most disturbing about the whitewashing of St. Bernard's racial dynamic was how implicated it had been in the tragedy that had transpired in the first place. After all, it was nothing if not ironic that those who had had the luxury of believing themselves superior to black people ended up in the same boat as those they so feared and despised. What did it say that the same elites who hadn't cared much for the lives of blacks in the Lower Ninth also hadn't cared enough of white lives in Chalmette to prioritize proper levee construction that would have protected both? Perhaps if whites there hadn't been so busy scapegoating black and brown folks for their misfortunes, they might have extended their hand to blacks in the Lower Ninth Ward, and together they could have marched on the Corps of Engineers, on Baton Rouge, or on Washington to demand a more people-centered set of budget priorities. But they hadn't, and now they had all ended up with their stuff jacked, so to speak. Skin color had trumped solidarity. And for what?

* * *

WHETHER IN ST. Bernard Parish or New Orleans itself, the rhetoric of white victimhood was ubiquitous within months of Katrina. For a bunch who always seemed exasperated by the very real claims of victimization coming from people of color, white folks sure had learned quickly how to play victim ourselves; this despite the relative lack of power held by the black or brown, with which they could truly oppress whites as whites had oppressed them over the years. In a place like New Orleans, despite thirty years of black political leadership by the time of Katrina, whites still controlled the reins of economic power. Even political power was often in the hands of whites, who had been able to elect Ray Nagin as mayor, despite the majority of African Americans voting for his opponent.

Even when people of color hold positions of power, their ability to oppress or in any way impinge upon the lives of whites is typically negligible. Though I had come to recognize this in New Orleans, it would become even clearer to me the first time I traveled to Bermuda. I visited this crown jewel of the dying but never fully deceased British Empire in the fall of 2005, invited in to discuss race and racism—issues that permeate much of what goes on there.

Of course, to hear many whites there tell it—be they native-born Bermudians or expatriates from the U.K., the U.S., or Canada—race is not an issue in Bermuda. In this island paradise, one is assured, they have conquered the demons that still bedevil we lesser intellects in the states, or in other lands around the globe. Bermuda, they say, is different. Indeed, in some ways it is, but in other ways, Bermuda is all-too similar to the United States, and its history is intertwined with that of the United States, especially as regards the history of white racial supremacy in the hemisphere.

It was, after all, Captain Christopher Newport who sailed the largest of the ships carrying whites (though they weren't called that yet) to what became Jamestown, Virginia, in 1607, and who then shipwrecked on Bermuda with Admiral George Somers in 1609, while returning to the colony with supplies from England. Newport (who I recently discovered is my seventeenth great-grandfather), by virtue of his seamanship, ultimately contributed directly to the initiation of North American genocide and white conquest, beginning at Jamestown. And his hurricane-forced landing on Bermuda began the process by which Great Britain would come to hold the tiny Atlantic island as property of the empire. Newport—who had made his name as a pirate, raiding ships of other nations and delivering their riches to wealthy investors back home—carried with him on the shipwrecked vessel John Rolfe, who would later introduce export tobacco to the Americas, which development would then lead to the enslavement of Africans for the purpose of cultivating the cash crop.

That neither Rolfe nor Newport died in the wreck has proven to be among the lynchpin moments in history. Had they done so—rather than remaining alive, repairing their ship, and sailing on to Jamestown—the colonists would likely have perished, and with them the hopes for permanent colonization of the Americas. Having failed to plant adequate crops, and without the arrival of the supplies expected from England thanks to the shipwreck in Bermuda, the colonists in Jamestown were starving and dying in droves. Only Newport's arrival in 1610, almost a year after he was anticipated, had allowed for colonization to be sustained. And had that initial experiment failed, as it would have without Newport, the Tsenacommacah confederacy, led by Chief Powhatan, would have likely had time to organize against future attempts to penetrate into indigenous lands. Although I suppose I must be grateful for

Newport's having survived, since, as a direct contributor to the genetic line from which I derive, I would literally not exist without him, the fact remains that his survival has been a decidedly mixed bag so far as persons of color are concerned.

As for Bermuda, it is not only divided by race, demographically—about 55 percent of the sixty five thousand persons there are black, roughly a third are white, and the rest are a mix of other groups of color, including a growing number of Asians—it is also divided by a vast gulf of perceptions. Blacks there believe race to be among the island's most vexing issues, while whites generally do not; and as with the United States, it is blacks who have a firmer grasp on reality, to say nothing of the history that has brought them to the place where they find themselves today.

As with the United States, Bermuda was a nation whose early economy was built largely on the backs of slave labor. And although slavery there was abolished in 1834, immediately upon emancipation, blacks were confronted with laws restricting voting to those who didn't own sufficient property. As a result, less than five percent of votes for a century after the end of slavery would be cast by blacks, despite blacks being a majority on the island for this entire period. Among the methods employed to dilute the black vote and reinforce white racist rule was plural voting, whereby rich whites could buy up property in each precinct of the island and then vote in each place where they owned land, as well as syndicate voting, whereby groups of rich whites could buy up property and then get however many votes in a precinct as there were owners on the piece of property. If fifty whites went in together on a piece of land (which none of them alone could have afforded), they would suddenly find themselves possessing fifty votes in the given precinct, whether or not they lived there. So although blacks were the majority of eligible voters in Bermuda, even by the early 1900s these various schemes intended to allow multiple votes by whites meant that the clear majority of votes being cast on the island would remain white votes, well into the late-twentieth century.

As in the United States, hospitals, schools, churches, the civil service, the military officer corps, theatres, restaurants, neighborhoods, hotels, and even graveyards were segregated by race for most of the nation's history. For most of these forms of formal institutional racism, legal change came only in the 1960s. As in the U.S., it was common practice throughout the twentieth century for land to be confiscated from black owners and communities to make way for commercial development benefiting whites, or even so as to develop a country club, or private community, which would then practice racial exclusivity in terms of membership or residency.

Electorally, universal suffrage has only existed in Bermuda since the late '60s, with white Bermuda long having viewed blacks as incapable of self-government. Indeed, the founder of the United Bermuda Party (which ruled the island from the '60s until 1998, when it was defeated by the majority-black Progressive Labour Party) famously argued against universal suffrage by claiming that it would be disastrous for the island until black Bermudians had become sufficiently educated and "disciplined."

Equally troubling for black opportunity in Bermuda has been a long-standing preference for foreign guest workers (who are overwhelmingly white), in housing and employment. Guest workers are given housing subsidies unavailable to locals, and often procure jobs that are all but off-limits to local blacks as well. These preferences not only push black Bermudians out of job opportunities, but also drive up the price of housing and other goods and services by distorting market rates for land, making Bermuda an extremely expensive place to live. Black Bermudians are especially resentful of guest worker preferences, since their purpose has always been seen as a way to whiten the island. Though white elites insist guest workers are needed to fill certain professional positions for which locals are unqualified, the claim fails to withstand even a moment's scrutiny. Most foreigners working on the island do not work in professional positions requiring a particularly intense level of education or skills, and less than two in ten have management level positions. That most foreign workers are found in medium- and semi-skilled jobs calls into question the extent to which worker importation is really about filling skills gaps and economic necessity, as opposed to being for the purpose of achieving a whiter Bermuda.

Interestingly, the largest opportunity gaps on the island appear between natives, either black or white, and not between black natives

and white foreigners. Although black Bermudians with college degrees
are roughly as likely to have management-level jobs as white foreigners in the country, relative to white Bermudians, blacks are not doing
nearly as well. Forty-three percent of white Bermudians with college
degrees have management level jobs, as opposed to only 28 percent
of similarly educated black Bermudians. Black Bermudians are 54
percent of all natives with college degrees, while whites are only 38
percent of similarly educated natives. Yet, 60 percent of natives with
top-level management jobs are white, and slightly less than a third
are black. While 38 percent of white Bermudians with college-level
educations have positions in senior or executive management, only 22
percent of similarly educated black Bermudians do.

But despite the solid evidence of ongoing white hegemony in
Bermuda, many whites there seem mightily anxious about the way that
political power—having been assumed by a black-dominated party—
may tilt the balance against them. Despite the advantages they have
obtained and continue to enjoy, many whites in Bermuda seem convinced that they are the targets of reverse discrimination and that their
victimization, if not in evidence yet, is never too far around the corner.

While I was in Bermuda, a prime example of perceived white victimhood emerged. In the days leading up to my arrival, a controversy had
exploded when the premier at that time, Alex Scott, fired off an angry
e-mail regarding something said to him by a white conservative on the
island, Tony Brannon. Brannon, who has a reputation for berating politicians (especially in the mostly black PLP) for what he perceives as
their incompetence and corruption, had sent an e-mail to the premier,
in effect blaming him for Bermuda's sorry economic state and a decline
in tourism. The premier, thinking he was sending a reply only to his
close associates, apparently hit "reply all" to the message, letting loose
with the impolitic and offensive remark that he was tired of getting flak
from "people who look like Tony Brannon."

Brannon, naturally, went to the press about the premier's remarks,
and it had become something of a scandal by the time I arrived on
the island that October. The premier, chastened by significant public
backlash to his remarks, backpedaled, insisting that he hadn't meant
the comment as a racial remark against Brannon or whites generally.

Virtually no one believed him, because frankly, the claim of innocence was wholly unbelievable. The remark had obviously been about color.

Since I was there at the time, talking about race, the local press sought my opinion on the matter, as did individuals, black and white, during my stay. To me there seemed to be a couple of key issues, both of which spoke to the larger subject of institutional white privilege. On the one hand, I made clear that I thought the premier's comments had been inappropriate and offensive. But that was the easy part. In a larger sense, whites in Bermuda desperately needed to imagine themselves in the position of the premier, and especially as the head of a majority-black party. After all, there has been a long history in Bermuda of whites verbalizing their doubts that blacks were capable of self-government.

So against that background noise, for a white man like Brannon to criticize the premier by calling into question his *competence* would naturally cause alarm bells to go off in the ears of virtually any black person hearing it. Though Brannon may well have meant nothing racial by his critique, for a black premier to have his competence questioned (which is different than a simple disagreement over a particular policy) is to trigger a litany of negative stereotypes and call into question the extent to which the white person issuing the challenge may be offering it from behind the veil of those prejudiced beliefs about blacks as a group.

That whites wouldn't understand this (and largely didn't when I explained it) was due almost entirely to privilege. If a white politician is criticized for being incompetent, or not intelligent enough to run a country, for example (and certainly one heard barbs regularly about George W. Bush's intellect during his presidency), no white person would have to have worried that the critique might have been intended as a group slam against whites. We wouldn't have to wonder whether the individual white politician had somehow triggered, by virtue of his or her actions, a larger group stereotype about white intelligence as a whole, because there is no such negative stereotype when it comes to white intelligence. But stereotypes about black intelligence are common. So when a comment is made that could be perceived as stemming from that stereotypical view, it is understandable that a black person on the receiving end of the critique might react in a way that seems hypersensitive. The larger social context didn't make Scott's comment acceptable, I explained, but it did allow us—provided we as whites are willing to consider it—to understand the way privilege and its opposite work.

But even more significant than putting the comment in historical context, the most important aspect of the incident, to me at least, was Scott's apology and the fact that he had felt compelled to issue it. The very fact that the premier had felt compelled to backpedal after his remarks were made public is testimony to how little power he had, in effective terms. After all, if power truly resided in his hands, or the hands of other blacks such as himself, he (and they) would be able to regularly insult whites, say terrible things about them, and never have to apologize at all. Premier Scott would then have been in a position to say, in effect, "screw Tony Brannon" and everyone like him. But he couldn't, and that was the point. A black man was forced to apologize to white people for a simple comment, while whites have still never had to apologize for the centuries-long crimes of slavery, segregation, and white institutional racism.

Alex Scott, despite holding political power in Bermuda, had essentially no power to effectuate his biases against whites. Even were we to grant that he was a vicious antiwhite bigot (and frankly, as unfortunate and inappropriate as his remarks were, this charge seems extreme), the fact would remain that he would have been utterly impotent to do anything with those biases. He couldn't have expelled whites from Bermuda, taken away their right to vote, or imposed discriminatory laws against them in terms of hiring and education. He couldn't have done any of the things that had been done to blacks in Bermuda over the years, political power notwithstanding. Totally dependent on tourist dollars—most of them spent by white tourists—and white-dominated corporate investments, to say nothing of ultimate British control of the island, black politicians in Bermuda could be as racist as they like, but to no effect, except insofar as they might be able to hurt white feelings. That's about it.

It is also worth noting that the very same whites who were so incensed by Premier Scott's remarks had said nothing when the black premier of the more conservative (and white-dominated) party told blacks in 1989 to "lower their voices" regarding the issue of racism. In other words, telling black people to shut up is fine; telling white folks to do so makes you a racist. And so whites in Bermuda, as with the United States, insist that racism is no longer a barrier for blacks—despite the evidence of widespread disparities that have virtually no alternative explanation but racial discrimination—but has become one for them: a charge that takes white denial to a pinnacle unrivaled in the annals of human irrationality. To avoid dealing with the legacy of white supremacy, we will change the subject, blame the victims, *play* the victim, and generally do anything to avoid confronting the truth that rests just in front of our eyes.

* * *

SPEAKING OF WHITE victimhood, forget New Orleans, forget Bermuda; all you really need to do is take a look at Champaign-Urbana, Illinois.

I went there to speak at the University of Illinois during the spring semester of 2007. While there, I had the occasion to meet with a number of different groups: residence hall advisors, fraternity and sorority members, student life personnel, faculty, staff, and students of all types. The timing of my visit couldn't have been better, or worse I suppose, depending on your perspective. For the previous year, Illinois, like many other schools, had been under intense pressure from the National Collegiate Athletic Association (NCAA) to no longer caricature American Indian peoples, by way of their team mascot: Chief Illiniwek. The chief had been a staple of U of I athletics for over eighty years, at least thirty-five of which had involved protests of the mascot from indigenous students and their supporters. As with Indian mascots around the country, the chief had come under fire for making a mockery of Indian traditions, reducing Indian peoples to a stereotypical image of warriors or "noble savages," and papering over the very real oppression faced by indigenous persons, past and present, in the United States.

In the case of Illiniwek, the chief had always been played by a white man (most recently a very blue-eyed, blonde-haired white man at that), and he wore an outfit that bore no resemblance to what actual Illini Indians would have worn prior to being driven off the land where the college now stood. Furthermore, the dance performed by Illiniwek at halftime shows, though touted as a traditional "fancy dance," was, in truth, a mix of inauthentic Indian dance moves and gymnastics, and had been largely created by remnants of the local Boy Scouts, early in the twentieth century.

The NCAA, in 2005, had announced that schools with Indian mascots would no longer be allowed to host basketball tournament games. Some schools complied and changed their mascot names while others, like Illinois, dug in and tried to challenge the NCAA in court. But by the time I arrived on campus in early 2007, the governing board of the university had decided to give in, realizing that continued legal opposition to the NCAA's move would likely prove fruitless, and concerned about the loss of revenue that would follow from enforcement of the new regulations.

A few weeks prior to my time at the U of I, the chief had done what was billed as his "final dance," during the halftime of the Illinois-Michigan basketball game. A somber, tight-lipped white man, in a regionally inappropriate headdress, covered in buckskin, gesticulated around the gym floor, on national television, while thousands of white Illinois fans (especially the ones with the big Greek letters on their chests, signifying fraternity or sorority membership) wept openly in the stands. The sight was nothing short of amazing; here were white people having an existential meltdown in front of millions of television viewers, all because they weren't going to be allowed to play dress-up anymore. It was as if someone had cut off the limb of a parent, or killed a small puppy in front of their eyes. They were being victimized, to hear them tell it, by political correctness.

There were young women, cute little scrunchies in their hair, tears flowing down their cheeks, standing next to young men with backward baseball caps, wearing looks of icy, future-corporate-executive rage on their faces. These were people who had likely never spent one second of their lives crying over the fact that indigenous peoples had lost some ninety million souls, their traditional cultures, religions, and almost all of their land to make way for folks like themselves, but who couldn't help but sob at the thought of losing a few seconds of entertainment.

Tradition. It was the word on the lips of just about everyone I met at Illinois. For those defending the chief, and who were beside themselves at the thought of losing him, tradition was being ripped apart and discarded, all to make a handful of militant Indian activists happy. What were the feelings of native peoples compared to tradition? Tradition, to these folks, was a noble and worthy thing, in need of being defended and carried on, though for reasons they could rarely articulate. To the opponents of the chief, tradition was also an important word, though one spoken with far less reverie. Tradition, to these folks, was something used to oppress, to vilify, to spread racism, and to further marginalize students of color on the campus.

Yet, what neither group seemed to realize was that tradition is a choice we make. In other words, there are many traditions in our culture, and the ones we choose to venerate are not foregone conclusions but are the result of conscious and volitional acts, for which we have to be responsible. By ignoring this aspect of tradition—which ones we choose to discuss and remember, and which ones we discard—the rhetorical combatants at the University of Illinois fell into a trap from which extrication seems highly unlikely. If defenders of the chief feel as though there is only one tradition to which they can cleave—the tradition of impersonation, or what they like to call "honoring" Indian peoples—and if the opponents feel that that, too, is the only thing meant by the term tradition, then both sides dig in, and the development of constructive resistance to racism becomes less likely. To abandon or preserve tradition becomes an all-or-nothing gambit for both sides in the debate.

But what if students had understood that there was another tradition they could choose to uphold? What if they had been made aware long before, and during their time at the university, of the tradition of resistance—resistance to Indian genocide and racism, not only by people of color, but also whites?

What if they knew about, and had been encouraged to identify with, Europeans like Bartolomé de Las Casas, who wrote eloquently against the crimes of Columbus, having traveled with the "peerless explorer" and having witnessed his depraved treatment of the Taino on Hispaniola? What if they knew of and had been encouraged to identify with whites like Helen Hunt Jackson, Matilda Gage, or Catherine Weldon, all of whom spoke out forcibly against the mistreatment of indigenous persons in the mid-to-late 1800s? What if we were encouraged to follow the example set by Lydia Child, who not only demanded justice for Indian peoples but was also the first white person to write a book calling for the abolition of slavery? What if whites knew of and had been encouraged to emulate the bravery of Jeremiah Evarts, a white man who spearheaded opposition to Andrew Jackson's Indian Removal Act and the forcible expulsion of the Cherokee peoples from the Southeast?

But we haven't been taught these histories. We know nothing, by and large, of these alternative traditions; and so we are left, all of us, but especially white folks, with a pre-fabricated and utterly inaccurate understanding of what our options are. Whites like those at Illinois seem to feel as though the only or best way to "honor" Indian peoples (to the extent they honestly think that's what they're doing) is to portray them, to dress like them, to act as we assume they act, or once did.

Yet if the alternative tradition were the one to which we had been exposed, we might choose resistance, as other whites have done, and commit our schools to something more meaningful than symbolic representation by way of mascots. We might uphold that alternative tradition by pushing for the quadrupling or quintupling of indigenous students on our campuses, or by working towards the establishment of well-funded Native American studies programs. Even better, we could uphold tradition—the tradition of folks like Weldon and Evarts—by partnering with organizations that work with indigenous peoples, so as to improve the economic and educational opportunities available to such folks, on and off campus.

Tradition is, after all, what we make it. The definition of the term is simply this: "a story, belief, custom, or proverb handed down from generation to generation." There is nothing about the word that suggests tradition must be oppressive, or that it must necessarily serve to uphold the status quo. It is simply the narrative we tell ourselves, and as such, could just as easily involve resistance to oppression or injustice, as the perpetuation of the same. But if we aren't clear in articulating the alternative tradition, we can hardly be surprised when persons don't choose the direction in which it points, having never been appraised of its existence.

In the South, for instance, too many white folks cleave to the tradition of the Confederacy, and one of the battle flags most commonly associated with it. But that is not because the Confederacy *is* southern history, or synonymous with the South. Rather, it is because of an ideological choice those white southerners make to align themselves with that tradition as opposed to the other, equally southern traditions with which they could identify. White southerners who wave that flag are choosing to identify with a government whose leaders openly proclaimed that white supremacy was the "cornerstone" of their existence, and who over and over again made clear that the maintenance and extension of slavery into newly stolen territories to the west was the reason for secession from the Union.

But white southerners could choose to identify with and praise the forty-seven thousand whites in Tennessee who voted against secession—almost one-third of eligible voters—or the whites in Georgia whose opposition to leaving the Union was so strong officials there had to commit election fraud in order to bring about secession at all. We could choose to remember and to celebrate abolitionists in the South like Kentuckian John Fee, a Presbyterian minister, who was removed from his position by the Presbyterian Synod for refusing to minister to slaveholders, so unforgivable did he consider their sins. Instead of venerating Jefferson Davis, the Confederate president, we could praise the brave women who marched on Richmond in 1863 to protest his government and the war, shouting, "Our children are starving while the rich roll in wealth," and who Davis then threatened to shoot in the streets if they didn't disperse. Instead of identifying with soldiers who perpetrated atrocities against black Union forces—like Nathan Bedford Forrest (for whom there is a garish statue a few miles from my home, and with whom one of my relatives fought, sadly, at the Battle of Sand Mountain)—we could proudly note the bravery of those one hundred thousand or more white Southern troops who deserted the Confederate forces, many because they had come to see the battle as unjust. Or the thirty thousand troops from Tennessee alone who not only deserted the Confederacy but went and joined the Union army, so changed did their beliefs become over time.

White southerners could choose to venerate the tradition of the civil rights movement, which rose from the South and lasted far longer than the confederacy. We could choose to valorize the tradition of historically black colleges and universities, which grew throughout the South as a form of institutionalized self-help because of the denial of educational opportunity to persons of African descent. We could choose to identify with the tradition of resistance to racism and white supremacy by black southerners to be sure—John Lewis, Ella Baker, Ed King, Amzie Moore, Unita Blackwell, Fannie Lou Hamer, or E. D. Nixon, to name a few—but also by white southerners: persons like Thomas Shreve Bailey, Robert Flournoy, Anne Braden, Bob Zellner, Mab Segrest, and hundreds, if not thousands of others throughout history.

That we are familiar with few of these names, if any, leaves our ability to resist compromised, and limits us to playing the role of oppressor, or at least quiet collaborator with that process. It is always harder to stand up for what's right if you think you're the only one doing it. But if we understood that there is a movement in history of which we might be a part, as allies to people of color, how much easier might it be to begin and sustain that process of resistance? For me, I know that such knowledge has been indispensable. And what I know also is this: the withholding of that knowledge from the American people, and especially white folks, has been nothing if not deliberate.

* * *

AS THE PRESIDENTIAL campaign began to heat up early in 2008, it became obvious that race was going to be in the picture, however much folks did or didn't want to speak of it. Though most voices tried to mute the racial element of the campaign, occasionally the underbelly of racism made itself known.

Dozens of You Tube clips emerged in which white supporters of Republican candidate, John McCain, slung blatantly racist derision at Barack Obama: saying they would never vote for "a black," or that if Obama were elected he was going to "enslave white people," or that he was a "secret Muslim" who "hated whites." They said he wasn't born in the U.S. and was a terrorist. Some said we should "bomb Obama," and paraded with stuffed monkey toys, intended to symbolize the Illinois Senator and Democratic Party candidate.

Others sent around e-mails with pithy questions like, "If Obama wins, will they still call it the White House?" or suggesting that Obama wanted to tax aspirin because "it's white and it works." White racial anxiety, in other words, was on full display for the better part of the presidential campaign season.

At no point did this become more apparent than after the media, led by FOX News, began running with a story concerning certain comments made by Senator Obama's former pastor, the Rev. Jeremiah Wright, of Trinity United Church of Christ on Chicago's south side. Wright had been the minister who had brought Obama to Christianity and the pastor who had married he and Michelle, but in the media narrative that began to spin out of control in March 2008, he was only relevant as a symbolic weapon with which to beat up on Obama. He was a radical, an anti-white bigot, an America-hater. And upon what evidence were such arguments made? In part it was because he had discussed the history of U.S. foreign policy, including the indisputable bombing of innocent civilians in Hiroshima and Nagasaki at the end of World War Two, and the history of racism in the country. In part it was because he had dared suggest that people of color owed no automatic allegiance to a nation that had neglected them for so long. But mostly, it was because he had said that the events of 9/11 had a predicate: they were not simply the acts of crazy people who hated our freedoms (the dominant and inherently narcissistic explanation offered by most whites, and certainly the Bush Administration), but rather, the acts of people who believed, rightly or wrongly, that such attacks would serve as payback for the history of U.S. actions in the Middle East and Arab world. The symbolism of "chickens coming home to roost," which Wright had deployed shortly after the attacks (and which now was being used as a political weapon against candidate Obama), was not meant to justify the horror of that day, but merely to place it in historical context. Whiteness, of course, requires a lack of context; it requires that historical memory play no role in understanding anything. To whiteness, the past is the past and the present is the present, and never the two shall meet: historical amnesia is a virtue, even a pseudo-religious sacrament.

I was traveling during the initial dust-up over the Wright videos that had begun to circulate, often edited and cropped to suggest that far more incendiary things were being said than actually had been at the time of the original sermons. I knew of Trinity, and had communicated with Rev. Wright's daughter, Jeri, a few years before, when she had asked if they could reprint some of my articles within their church newsletter. I had said yes, of course, and felt perfectly comfortable in doing so. The church was a progressive, community-centric place, from which amazing local programs were being directed around AIDS awareness, economic injustice, and any number of other issues. Trinity was solidly within the mainstream of the United Church of Christ, and Rev. Wright had developed an intense following among not only his black parishioners, but his white ones as well, of whom there were far more than commonly believed.

What seemed to bother white America was that Rev. Wright was unapologetically black, and he endorsed what he referred to as a black value system, extending back to Africa, in which community well-being took precedence over individualism and the me-firstism that has long characterized much of white evangelical Christianity. His was the opposite of the prosperity gospel so popular around that time (including among many black preachers), in which ministers insisted Jesus wanted nothing so much as for people to drive a Bentley and wear a Rolex, or at least for their pastors to do so; this, despite nothing in Scripture to suggest such a thing, and much to indicate the opposite.

Whites never minded *that*—no beef with Creflo Dollar, he being perhaps the most venal and cynical of the Christian money-hustlers in the black community—but to tell the truth about America was a no-no. Wright called bullshit on that, and *that* was the problem. He said that the purpose of Christians was to stand in solidarity with the poor, the oppressed, the prisoner, the ill, the despised (which had been, of course, exactly what Jesus had said, no matter the words put in his mouth later by everyone from the Apostle Paul to Billy Graham), and this, as much as anything, is what much of white America couldn't stand. How dare this black man tell us what it means to follow Jesus! Seeing as how whites had long had the luxury of believing Jesus *was* white, the reaction should not have been particularly surprising, I suppose.

Concerned about the lack of historicism that animated so much white reaction, I penned a piece defending not just Rev. Wright, but the larger historical point he had been trying to make: namely, that the United States was not all goodness and light. Yes, we had killed many innocent civilians over the years as a result of our militarism and imperialism;

yes, we were implicated in global suffering. Although I didn't agree with everything Wright said or implied (like the part in which he speculated the government may have created HIV/AIDS deliberately so as to destroy certain "undesirable" populations), I also knew the historical basis for the claim, and was well aware that the U.S. government had indeed released diseases deliberately in poor communities of color before—as documented in Harriet Washington's award-winning book, *Medical Apartheid*, released around that time. So although I didn't think that had happened this time out, it wasn't insane to engage the question, as Wright had, given the history.

When my essay ran, Rev. Wright was with his family on a long-scheduled cruise to celebrate his pending retirement from Trinity after many years of service. They had been on the cruise when the controversy blew up surrounding his comments from seven years earlier, about which no one had cared until they could be used against Barack Obama. After the family vacation ended, I heard from Jeri Wright that it had been a nightmare: others on the ship who were watching the news were shooting her father dirty looks, taking pictures of him, and making him feel like a pariah based on the misinformation they were getting from media. What should have been a celebratory moment, to relish thirty-six years of diligent service on behalf of the people in his community, became an exercise in self-defense, in which the family had to protect their father from the glares and comments of people who knew nothing about the man they were being encouraged to hate, but knew that they hated him nonetheless.

Jeri noted that her father had gotten to see my essay while on the cruise and was eternally grateful; it had been one of the only bright spots, she said, in a larger miasma of hostility. I told her it was the least I could do, and that I was equally grateful to her dad and the entire Trinity family for their work. Allyship required that I come to Rev. Wright's aid in that moment, and I was only too glad to do so.

Sadly, the political reality in America is such that Barack Obama felt he had little choice but to sacrifice his former pastor on the altar of electoral expedience. And so, one week after proclaiming that he would never throw Rev. Wright under the bus, and could no more disavow Wright than his own mother or grandparents, he did just that:

condemning Wright in particularly vicious terms, so as to curry favor with white voters who all but demanded the obeisance as a condition of their vote. Putting aside whether Obama had acted ethically in doing so, the political meaning of the act was clear: white power was still in full effect. As with Alex Scott in Bermuda, Barack Obama had to pander to the feelings of white people in order to secure his political future. When he won in November, his victory (given the racially neutered dance he was forced to perform in order to achieve it) confirmed white privilege, rather than argued for its eradication.

PARENTHOOD

THE WEEK BEFORE the presidential election, the school that both of our girls now attend held a mock vote for the students in which they got to cast their ballots for the candidate of their choice. Barack Obama won handily, and can rest assured that he received the vote of Ashton Wise (and would have secured Rachel's, but she was still in pre-school at the time). We hadn't tried to push either of the girls to support one candidate over the other, but it seemed almost intuitive on their parts that they would support Obama. They appeared to instinctively sense something terribly wrong with Sarah Palin, and something angry and menacing about John McCain. At one point, Rachel asked me what Sarah Palin's "problem" was, entirely unbidden I should add, to which I responded, somewhat tongue-in-cheek, "she doesn't care if the polar bears die and she likes to shoot moose." Both Ashton and Rachel were horrified. When my father-in-law went to dinner with them one night, wearing a button with pictures of McCain and Palin on it, Rachel took one look at the button and said, "There's that crazy lady who hates polar bears!" Some things, as you see, get lost in translation.

I tell this story mostly because it symbolizes, for me at least, how children pick things up; how they are, indeed, *always* picking things up, for good or bad, from their parents, the media, peers, and any number of other sources. By our statements, our actions, or alternately by our silence and *inactions*, we teach lessons constantly, and children are incredibly adept at learning them, even when we think they aren't paying attention at all. This is why, when it comes to race, parents have to be very deliberate and mindful of the lessons we're imparting to our kids.

Sadly, too often parents (and especially white parents) begin by sending the wrong messages to children when it comes to race. Over the years, I've asked several hundred people in workshops, "When was the first time you really noticed someone of a different race or color than yourself, and what happened?" And by far, the most common reply has had something to do with having seen a person of color in a supermarket or mall, while shopping with one's parents. Time after time, whites will describe a similar scene: they noticed the person who looked different, they tugged on their mom or dad's clothes to get their attention, they referenced the person they'd seen while pointing at them, and then they were met by a forceful and immediate, "*Shhhh!*" from the parent.

To the parent, the shush means one thing, but to the child it means quite another. To the adult, the shush is likely intended as a short, sharp way to convey the notion that pointing is rude. But to the child, especially if very young, the shush suggests that something is wrong, specifically with the person being referenced. It says, *don't notice that person*, or even, *that person is bad, or dangerous,* and one should be quiet around them so as not to attract their attention—the kind of thing you might be told were you to happen upon a dangerous wild animal while on a camping trip. When white parents shush their children, when those children have merely pointed out something different for which they have no words or explanation, they send a message of negativity with regard to the difference being noticed.

The other problem with the way parents, and especially white ones, deal with race, is that they *don't* deal with it at all when it comes to their children. They largely ignore it. Over the years, hundreds of white parents have proudly proclaimed to me that they rarely ever discuss racism with their children. "I want my kids to be able to hold on to their innocence," some say. Others insist that "children don't see color until we *make* them see it," as justification for their silence about race. "We're raising our kids to be colorblind," still others maintain, as if such a parenting plan were the ultimate antiracist technique, and as if avoiding the topic of racism could instill such colorblindness in the first place.

But colorblindness doesn't solve the problem of racism. First, it doesn't work. Kids see color, and research suggests they begin to draw conclusions about color-based differences early on. As early as pre-school, children have begun to pick up cues about race and gender from popular culture, from parents and from peers, such that they begin to form hierarchies on the basis of those identities. Kids observe the world around them and draw conclusions about that world, with or without our guidance. When it comes to race, unguided conclusions can prove dangerous.

Children can discern, for instance, that there are vast gaps in resources between the parts of town lived in mostly by whites and the parts of town in which mostly folks of color reside. They can see people of color disproportionately represented on the news in stories about crime or poverty. They can see mostly whites in leadership roles, the president notwithstanding. Having observed disparities, children, like anyone else, will seek to make sense of them, subconsciously if not consciously; and if they're being told—as most everyone is in the United States—that "anyone can make it if they try hard enough," but then they see that some have decidedly *not* made it to the extent others have, why should it surprise us that some (perhaps many) would conclude that there was something wrong with those at the bottom: that they were, in fact, inferior? And if the disparities have a distinct racial cast to them, how surprising can it be that those conclusions would be linked to notions of racial *group* inferiority?

So unless parents are discussing inequity with children, and placing it in its proper sociological and historical context—in other words, unless they are talking about discrimination and racism, past and present—those children will likely develop an internal narrative to explain the inequities they can see, which will lean heavily towards a prejudicial, even racist conclusion.

This is why the old saying that "you have to be taught how to hate," has always seemed overly simplistic to me. Yes, if you're deliberately taught to be a racist it certainly makes it more likely that you'll turn out to be one. But a child can be taught bias—perhaps not hatred, but certainly a form of racism—indirectly too, by combining their recognition of social inequities with the standard message of their society that where we end up on the ladder of life is all about our own effort. As such, only color-consciousness (and especially a consciousness of the way color continues to divide our society) can really prepare children to confront the world around them honestly and effectively.

Perhaps even more importantly, kids pick up on inconsistencies between what we say as parents and what we do, paying far closer attention to the latter than the former. If you tell your kids not to fight, for instance, but then they see or hear you fighting with your spouse or partner, they will have a hard time internalizing the "no fighting" message given the actual behavior they're witnessing. Likewise, we can say we believe in diversity and equity, and value multiculturalism and integration, but if we send our children to monoracial, monocultural schools, live in monoracial, monocultural neighborhoods, and expose them to social settings in which everyone looks like them, they will see the inconsistency, translate it as hypocrisy, and conclude that we, as parents, are lying to them when it comes to that which we value.

What's more, because children tend to be egocentric, they commonly presume that their stuff is the best: their school, their neighborhood, or their circle of friends, for instance. If those schools, communities, and friendship circles are overwhelmingly white, it becomes natural for those children to conclude that the reason black and brown folks are not to be found in them must be because they aren't as good as whites; if they were, after all, surely they'd be around us. Only if a parent is committed to *living* an integrated and multicultural life can they effectively preach the same to their kids. And only if we are committed to challenging the way in which our kids sometimes presume the normalcy of the racial divisions they see, can we hope to imbue them with enough of a sociological imagination to critically assess the world around them and then change it for the better.

* * *

THE GOOD NEWS is, kids are incredibly capable of engaging these matters, and at a much higher level than that for which we normally give them credit.

In the past few years, I've had the opportunity to speak in dozens of middle schools, and even a few elementary schools, to kids between the ages of seven and twelve. In a few cases, I've even discussed issues of race and racism with pre-school children as young as five. Contrary to what many parents seem to believe, not only can they handle the subject matter, they can often lead the conversations, with very little formal facilitation.

I've often asked children where we get our ideas about people who are different than ourselves, especially when it comes to color; inevitably, it takes them no time to begin offering answers. "From the media," is the most common answer, and when I ask them what they mean, they demonstrate a savvy grasp of the way that various sources of racial imagery effect their consciousness, from television to music videos to video games to things they see on the internet. In fact, at several schools when I've engaged kids on these matters, they can talk for a half hour straight, with almost no active facilitation, just pointing out example after example of racial imagery, as well as gender and class imagery in media, and the way those images can sometimes give false and misleading impressions about members of certain groups.

One young woman at a middle school in San Francisco, for instance, told me (and her peers, all gathered in the gym for a discussion) that she had been afraid of homeless people because of the stories she had heard on the news about various crimes committed by the homeless, or how the city had been trying to move the homeless out because of so-called "aggressive panhandling" in commercial and tourist districts. She then mentioned how she had gotten to know a homeless man who often walked up and down the street where she and her family lived, by speaking to him one day after he had asked her a question. Through their conversation she came to realize that most of her assumptions had been wrong. Yes, she understood, there may be some homeless people who fit the stereotype so commonly believed to be true, and so often portrayed in the news, but she also realized that she couldn't and shouldn't be so rigid in her thinking as to assume those things to be true in each and every case, or even most cases.

Other students have been able to discuss, in a very sophisticated manner, the way that media gives negative impressions about poor folks, Arabs, Muslims, immigrants (especially of color), and, of course, young people. In each case, the students often know far more about the problems with the images than we likely give them credit for, but rarely, they note, has anyone ever discussed these kinds of things with them or asked them to really think about the issue.

Almost as soon as Ashton had turned two (and Rachel was coming into the world), I had begun to think about how media images would impact their consciousness around race, gender, and class, and how those dynamics interact. From Disney films to advertisements, I wondered how their image of themselves and others could be misshapen by outside influences, and how Kris and I might best inoculate them against the worst aspects of those influences. Especially given the way in which female body image is influenced by advertisers—and how white women are especially given, according to the research, to heightened concern about weight and body type—these were the kinds of things that I knew we'd need to think about by the time they were in school.

Yet, we didn't want to be the kind of parents who overly policed what they would see, to the point of sheltering them, unrealistically. I wasn't going to be the parent who plopped the "Kill Your Television" sticker on his car, or who self-righteously preened about how there was no pop culture in our home, or how Mickey Mouse was evil and so there would be no Disney either. Fully aware of the problems with pop culture, and more than a little aware of how troubling much of the Disney brand has been over the years, I nonetheless would prefer that my child be conversant with the dominant culture and develop a way to eventually critique it—to see its good and bad elements—than to be kept from it, only to covet it more than ever. One thing that had always bothered me about many of my compatriots on the left was that their ability to relate to average, everyday folks seemed compromised by their desire to view, with contempt, all aspects of the dominant material culture— to look down on the cultural diversions of working class folks, even as they claimed to be fighting for the interests of those same people. I've been guilty of it too, frankly, taking more than a few sideways glances at NASCAR, for instance, but the truth is this: if progressives can't figure out a way to speak to the people I see walking down Main Street U.S.A. in Disney's Magic Kingdom—and that doesn't mean telling them how the Disney-fication of the culture reinforces racism, classism, and patriarchy—then all hope is lost for a better society.

*   *   *

EVERY NOW AND then, Disney even manages to provide a moment of opportunity for deeper discussion about important issues, though that might not have been their intent. For instance, of all the problematic Disney films out there, the only one that I really didn't want my kids to see was Pocahontas. Something about the way that Hollywood (or in this case, Burbank) had managed to characterize Matoaka (Pocahontas's real name)—as an intensely spiritual stereotype whose ability to commune with nature allowed her to converse at length with an old lady in the form of a tree—struck me as deeply troubling. Not to mention, Matoaka's story is quite a bit less romantic than the Disney version, involving as it does her forced abduction by Englishmen, from which abduction she was only able to obtain release if she agreed to marry John Rolfe, whose lust for her overrode concerns like her young age at the time of their first sexual encounter. Not only does Disney ignore the coerced relationship with Rolfe, they fabricate a love interest between she and the mercenary captain, John Smith, which historians agree never existed. When descendants of Matoaka offered to help Disney tell a more accurate version of her story, Roy Disney, nephew of Walt, refused.

But as much as I had hoped not to bring the film into our home, I ultimately capitulated when Ashton, at the age of 4, pleaded for me to purchase it while visiting Disney World in 2005. I agreed to do it, but knew in my own mind that we'd have to process it together and discuss some of the elements of the film, if not the first time we watched it, at some definite point in the future. I'd be watching it, pen and pad in hand, taking notes for later conversation.

The film was dreadful. Disney's Pocahontas is drawn as a thin, angular, somewhat Asian-looking beauty, while her father, Chief Powhatan, is portrayed as a large, threatening Indian leader, and her native suitor, Kocoum, as an overly war-like brat. The white characters are often drawn in less-than-flattering ways too, although in the end the message seems to be that even we can get in touch with nature and live peacefully, if subjected to the wisdom of Grandmother Willow—the tree to which Pocahontas introduces Smith. That in the wake of Matoaka's capture the English would come to decimate the Powhatan people calls into question such a sanguine account, but to Disney, historical details such as this can't be allowed to intrude upon the telling of a good princess story.

Frankly, Ashton wasn't really crazy about the movie. It didn't really hold her interest, but nonetheless, I knew I'd want to speak with her about some of the details. Fortunately for me, that task was made easier after watching a few of the "extras" on the DVD. After the movie ended we watched some of the special features and one in particular stood out: it was a few minutes during which the chief illustrator on the film was describing his artwork to an auditorium filled with people, either at an illustrator's convention, or perhaps a Disney function of some sort. As he stood on the stage, an overhead projector displayed an image of his Pocahontas, and then contrasted it with the actual image of Matoaka, drawn during the time she was in England, after being taken there by Rolfe. Needless to say, she looked nothing like the image he had created—a fact about which he proceeded to joke, noting sarcastically something to the effect that "as you can see, we remained very true to the original." Laughs all around. Hilarity reigns. My what a cut-up!

I saw it as my opportunity.

"Hey Ashton," I said.

"Yeah?" she replied.

"Why do you think they decided to make her look different like that?" I inquired.

"What do you mean?" she responded

"Well, you saw that picture right?" I continued. "The one of the real Pocahontas? And how different she looked from the way the movie made her look? Why do you think they did that?"

She looked puzzled for a minute, like she was trying hard to come up with a good answer. "I dunno," she said. "Maybe they thought she was prettier that way."

"Yeah," I replied, "I bet your right. In fact, it sorta seemed like he was making fun of the way she actually looked, huh?"

"Yeah," Ashton responded.

"Hmmm," I noted. "So, how do you think you'd feel if someone wanted to make a movie about your life and decided they didn't like your red hair, or the color of your skin, or something like that, and decided to change it?"

"I think that would hurt my feelings," she replied.

"Yeah, I bet it would," I said. "So how do you think Native Americans might feel, seeing him joke like that about how much prettier his version of Pocahontas is, compared to the actual Pocahontas?"

"I think they might feel bad about that," she responded, clearly taking in the point I was hoping for her to see. "I think it would hurt their feelings. I don't see why they couldn't just make her look the way she really looked."

"Yeah, that's a good point," I replied. "I guess sometimes the people who make the decisions don't always take everyone's feelings very seriously, huh?"

"Yeah," she said, disturbed by the implications of what she'd come to see.

Lesson learned, I was glad we'd watched Pocahontas.

* * *

DON'T MISUNDERSTAND THOUGH: my kids are no less susceptible to internalized biases than anyone else's children. I'd love to tell you that wasn't the case—that growing up in the Wise/Cason home was the perfect inoculation for such a thing—but if I told you that, I'd be lying.

It was early 2008, on a rainy Sunday afternoon at the beginning of the summer, when I fully came to appreciate just how deep the roots of racism can be planted in children, even when you think you've done everything you can to protect them from the poison.

We were sitting at home, unable to do anything outdoors because of the weather, the kids—at that point six and four—growing bored and restless, and looking for anything to occupy their time. Not up for playing any games, they requested to watch a movie on cable, to which we quickly agreed. If it would keep them from whining about how bored they were, and could bring us up to dinner time, we were all for it.

I queued up the On Demand cable satellite movie thing, looking for any films that might be good for kids and families, and preferably something they hadn't seen already. Within a few seconds the trailer for *Evan Almighty* popped up. The comedy, which stars Steve Carell as a newly-elected Congressman and Morgan Freeman as God—the latter of whom has apparently chosen the former to build an ark and recreate the Biblical story of Noah—is a cute flick, which, as it turns out, my kids and wife had already seen when it was still playing at the local theatre. As such, they didn't really want to see it again; but because they recognized the dialogue and the actors in the trailer, it got their attention.

Rachel looked up, saw Morgan Freeman in the role of God, in the flowing white robes, and said exactly what any four-year-old would say. "Daddy, is that God?"

Realizing that she knew nothing of the Screen Actor's Guild or casting directors at that age, I laughed, thinking her innocent query to be among the cutest things she had said in a while.

"No sweetie, that's not God," I explained. "That's an actor named Morgan Freeman. He just plays God. Often. But he's just an actor playing a part."

I really assumed that would be the end of the discussion, but sadly, I was mistaken. By now, Ashton was curious as to what we were talking about, and had looked up from the book she was reading. She too saw Morgan Freeman in the role of God. It took her no time at all to chime in, dismissively to her sister.

"Rachel, that *can't* be God," Ashton said defiantly, as if to suggest that claiming otherwise would have been the most preposterous thing ever spoken into the universe.

In that moment I hoped that her doubt as to Morgan Freeman's divinity was going to turn on a technical point—for instance, that God would be far too busy to bother making a feature film, or that if he did so bother he'd surely make one capable of getting better than a 23 percent approval rating on the Rotten Tomatoes website—but somehow I knew it wouldn't be that simple, or innocent. I felt certain I knew why she had been so sure that Freeman couldn't be God, and though I hardly wanted to have my suspicions confirmed, I knew I'd have to ask.

"Why not Ashton? Why can't that be God?" I inquired, hesitantly.

In the split second before she answered I had this fantasy, in which she replied with an answer quite different from the one I anticipated. I hoped that perhaps she would say that Freeman couldn't be God because God was a woman. Better still, I wished for some existentialist answer like, "Oh Father, what *is* God, anyway?" A proclamation of transcendentalist skepticism would have been a welcome relief in that moment. But I got nothing of this kind; rather, she responded as I knew she would, without any sense of irony or misgiving.

"That can't be God because God isn't black. God is white."

Now it probably won't surprise anyone reading this book to learn that in our home, there are no racialized images of a deity; there are no pictures that would have given my child the impression at such an age that God had any racial identity, let alone that the said identity matched her own. We hadn't allowed those pernicious Bible Story picture books for kids, in which Adam and Eve are drawn in such a way as to give the reader the impression that they had resided in the Garden of Sweden. But still, at some point Ashton had seen those images—perhaps in the church she attends with her mom and sister; perhaps in bookstores or libraries; or perhaps on the Christmas cards sent to our home every year with pictures of Jesus on the front that would give one the impression he had been born in a manger somewhere in Bethlehem, Pennsylvania. No matter our own efforts, she had internalized the notion that divinity was white like her, not black like Morgan Freeman, or for that matter, like several of her friends and classmates, or her kindergarten teacher that very year.

At first, I asked why she had said that, and of course she offered the stand-by six-year-old answer, given for pretty much every question, no matter the subject: "I dunno."

I thought a while about how to process the event, and a little later decided to revisit the subject.

"So Ashton, let me ask you about that whole color of God thing," I said.

"What about it?" she replied.

"Well, let's think about it for a second. So, tell me something. What did God do, so far as the story goes?" I inquired.

"Um, God created everything I guess," she said.

"Okay," I replied. "So, God created people?"

"Yeah," came the answer.

"Okay," I continued. "So where were the first people?" I asked this knowing that she knew the answer. The previous year, there had actually been a bulletin board in her pre-school class that showed, visually, how humans had arisen in Africa and branched out from there, so I figured she would remember what she'd learned.

"Um, Africa, right?" she replied, concentrating hard, wanting to get the right answers.

"Right, okay," I said. "So, God created people and the first people were in Africa. Now, what color are people in Africa?"

"Black," she shot back, not having to think long about that one.

"Okay," I replied. "So God created people, the first people were in Africa, and Africans are black. Now, in whose image were people created?"

This one stumped her a bit. After all, she was no Biblical scholar. Although she and her sister are being raised Episcopalian and attend church with their mom, she hadn't really committed to memory little scriptural details such as this.

"Um, I don't know," she said. "What do you mean?"

"Well," I replied. "According to the story, God created people in the image of someone or something. In whose image do you think that might have been?"

"Uh, in the image of God, I guess?" she answered.

"Exactly," I replied. "So, let's think about it. God created people, the first people are in Africa, Africans are black, and they were made in the image of God. So, final question: What color is God?"

Her eyes got wide as the implications began to sink in.

"I guess God could be black?" she exclaimed.

End of lesson.

Now of course, one could say that the lesson was meaningless, and perhaps it was. Obviously these kinds of matters will have to be revisited many times over the years, and frankly, I no more want Ashton to believe in a racialized *black* God than a racialized white one. But simply to get her to challenge her own assumptions of white divinity was sufficient for that particular moment. We'll deal with the rest later. Seeing as how I'm a militant agnostic myself (I know, a contradiction in terms, but still), the odds are pretty good that she'll end up somewhat skeptical of any supernatural being. Indeed, she already seems to be headed in that direction (unlike Rachel, who comes across as a prime candidate for the Episcopal priesthood). But what the incident and conversation suggested to me was that kids are capable of thinking things through if we believe in them enough to engage the difficult issues, and if we do so in a way that leads them to the conclusions we hope they'll reach, rather than just hit them over the head with those conclusions.

Interestingly, the lesson seemed to have stuck. Several months later, during which time we had never revisited the matter, Ashton came up to me one morning before school and with a puzzled look on her face asked if I really believed God could be black.

"I don't know, what do you think?" I replied.

"I don't know, I guess so," came the answer.

"Very good then," I said. "Have some cereal."

Little victories are nice.

*   *   *

PERHAPS THE MOST important thing I've learned about kids when it comes to racism is how important it is for them to learn of role models from whom they can take direction. In our home, obviously, it's a bit easier than for most. Ashton and Rachel know what their dad does, and what both their parents' beliefs are when it comes to these matters. And because I'm very careful not to berate them about these subjects, they don't feel the need to backlash against my views just to get back at dad when they're angry at me. It's a lesson I learned in my own home growing up. My mom and dad never tried to indoctrinate me into any particular way of thinking. They just made clear what their values were, exhibited a consistency between what they said and what they did, and encouraged me to always think critically—this last trait being one that almost by definition tends to mitigate against the adoption of right-wing or consciously racist viewpoints.

I've met plenty of parents who worry, however, about how to teach these lessons without scaring their children about oppression (especially children of color), or instilling guilt in their white children once the latter become aware of the history of racial subordination and white privilege. The concerns are understandable. Learning about injustice can be frightening, especially if the injustice has been directed at people like yourself. And learning about unearned advantage can cause kids to feel guilty if the subject is not handled carefully.

A year or so ago, I was having a conversation with a teacher whom I'd met at a workshop session I was facilitating. She taught kindergarten, and around Martin Luther King Jr. day had discussed with her class who Dr. King was, what he had done, and ultimately what had happened to him in the end. She didn't want to pull punches or soft-pedal the matter, she said, and so she had been brutally honest and straightforward about the subject.

A few days later, she noted, she got calls from both white *and* black parents, complaining about the lesson. The white parents expressed concern that she had made their children feel bad. One of the white students had apparently said something at dinner about white people being mean because a white person had killed Dr. King. The black parents expressed concern that she had scared their child to death and made him wonder if his white classmates were going to hurt him because he was black, or if some other white person would at some point in his life. Both the white and black parents asked the teacher to refrain from discussing these matters any further in the class, and both said something about wanting their kids to retain their innocence around the matter of race for as long as possible.

"What should I have done differently?" was the question she put to me.

On the one hand, I told her, she had done the right thing by broaching the subject with the students. Whatever "innocence" parents may believe their children possess around these kinds of issues often doesn't exist—as they are already beginning to think about matters of race and color whether they mention it to us or not—or is going to be stolen soon enough. The only question is whether we can burst that bubble in a deliberately controlled way, not whether it's going to be popped at all. And frankly, I'd rather teachers speak honestly about what Dr. King and the movement were about, rather than water it down the way so many do nowadays. Too often I've met kids who seem to think King's fundamental message were he alive today would be "don't hit back if someone hits you," or "don't join a gang." While there is little doubt that the good Reverend would agree with both of those points, to suggest that the fulfillment of such banal platitudes were the purpose of his life's work cheapens that work and the larger movement of which he was a part.

But, I noted, one of the things that might help in the future would be to teach about King and the issue of racism and discrimination through a lens of resistance and allyship, rather than a lens of oppression and victimization. Imagine, I explained, how different it might sound to a student of color to hear about the oppression meted out to members of his or her group, but beginning with a narrative of rebellion and resistance: in other words, discussing slave rebellion at the outset of a discussion on slavery, discussing the sit-in movement and freedom rides well before discussing the murder of King or other civil rights martyrs. Likewise, imagine how different it would feel to a white student in the class if the lesson spent time on white allies who stood in solidarity with people of color and opposed racism, rather than merely mentioning the white folks who clubbed protesters, shot civil rights leaders, or blocked schoolhouse doors.

By beginning with resistance and allyship, both the students of color and the white students get a message that they have choices to make. The students of color do not have to be passive recipients of other people's mistreatment; they are not inevitable victims to whom things are simply done and who have no agency to exercise in the matter. And the white students are more likely to see that they needn't be either active oppressors of others or passive observers, standing on the sidelines while people of color have to go it alone; they too have agency to exercise, and they can exercise it in an anti-oppressive way. By focusing on resistance and allyship, both the fear and the guilt that comes with the victimization and oppression lens can be largely avoided. So too with discussions about sexism, heterosexism, classism, or any other form of oppression.

I knew as I described this method to the teacher that it could work. I'd seen it in children as young as five, in fact. Back when Ashton had been in pre-school, her teachers had asked me to come in and discuss racism with the class. Honestly, I was petrified. The night before the event I had been speaking at the University of North Carolina, and as with all of my presentations to "big" people, I had no hesitation, no fears, no trepidation whatsoever. With my own kids, I didn't worry too much either, because I knew that even if I screwed up, or tried to teach a lesson that flopped, I'd have plenty more chances to get it right. But with other folks' kids—especially kids in my own daughter's class—I was utterly terrified. I stayed up all night, caught the early flight home, and went to the pre-school bright and early.

As it turned out, there had been no reason to worry. Although Ashton didn't say much—she was so excited and proud that I had come to speak to her class that she just sorta sat there smiling—the other kids were amazingly engaged. I spent just a few minutes talking about why it's so important to speak out against discrimination and racism, and then asked them, point blank, what they would do if they saw someone being mistreated because of the color of their skin. Hands shot up in the air immediately, as the children all but fell over one another to get a chance to answer. Their answers, though basic of course (they were only five, after all), nonetheless betrayed a seriousness of commitment. I had no idea if they would likely maintain that commitment over time, but it was clear to me in that moment that if the spirit of resistance is nurtured and cultivated, children can become teens who become adults who become and remain allies in the struggle against injustice. Their sense of fair play at that age and their almost instinctive resistance to unjust treatment of anyone makes allyship and solidarity natural and normative behaviors. But unless we are encouraging them to think about injustice, and empowering them to speak out and do something about it, that natural tendency for resistance can become muted over time, to the detriment of us all.

REDEMPTION

"Life is tragic simply because the earth turns and the sun inexorably rises and sets, and one day, for each of us, the sun will go down for the last, last time. Perhaps the whole root of our trouble, the human trouble is that we will sacrifice all the beauty of our lives, will imprison ourselves in totems, taboos, crosses, blood sacrifices, steeples, mosques, races, armies, flags, nations, in order to deny the fact of death, which is the only fact we have. It seems to me that one ought to rejoice in the fact of death—ought to decide, indeed, to earn one's death by confronting with passion the conundrum of life. One is responsible to life: It is the small beacon in that terrifying darkness from which we come and to which we shall return. One must negotiate this passage as nobly as possible, for the sake of those who are coming after us."

—JAMES BALDWIN,
THE FIRE NEXT TIME, 1963

AS I WAS writing this book the first time, I stopped to read a few of the stories to Kristy, some of which she had heard me speak of before, but several of which she had not. Once I finished reading a few of the more disturbing vignettes to her, it was apparent that she was upset. "Sometimes it seems so big, so awful," she lamented. "It makes me wonder if things are ever going to really change."

Though I'm sure some might be alarmed by such a thought—the notion that perhaps racism isn't ever going to be finally vanquished—I must say that as horrible as such a truth may be, if indeed it's true, it doesn't make me feel the least bit defeated. The fact is, I would have liked to be able to tell her not to worry, to remind her that good people have done great things and have changed the world before, that committed movements of committed people can shift mountains, and that the evidence for this kind of transformation was all around us. But I didn't say that, not because it wasn't true, but because it wasn't the point.

Several years back, when legal scholar Derrick Bell wrote *Faces at the Bottom of the Well*, in which he suggested that racism may be a permanent feature of American life, never to be fully and finally undone, I remember the uproar it caused in many a white liberal circle, and among white liberal students who were often assigned to read it in class. White liberals, and radicals for that matter, place a huge amount of faith in the inevitability of justice being done, of right winning in the end, of the triumph of all that is good and true. And they take even the smallest victories—which are sometimes what we have to settle for—as evidence that in just a few more years, and with a little more work, we'll arrive at that place of peace and goodwill. Bell was challenging that faith, at least as it applied to race, and white folks didn't like what they were hearing.

When you're a member of the privileged group, you don't take kindly to someone telling you that you can't do something, whether that something is making a lot of money or ending racism. What do you mean racism is permanent? What do you mean we'll never have justice? How dare anyone imply that there might be some problems too large for the determined will, or perhaps I should say the determined *white* will, since clearly the determined wills of black and brown folks haven't been sufficient.

But Bell's assessment, at least for me, was a liberating tract—no cause for pessimism but rather cause for recommitment to the purpose and mission at hand. This may seem counterintuitive, since for some, committing to fighting a battle you may never win seems futile. But fighting that battle is what people of color have always done and will continue to do, no matter the outcome. Is it appropriate then for me to say that if the fight wouldn't end in victory there was no purpose? What would that kind of attitude say to black and brown folks who have always fought injustice as if ending it were possible, but who always knew they might well never see change come about?

What whites have rarely had to think about—because as the dominant group we are so used to having our will be done, with a little effort at least—is that maybe the point is not victory, however much we all wish to see justice attained and injustice routed. Maybe our redemption comes from the struggle itself. Maybe it is in the effort, the striving for equality and freedom, that we become human.

Kristy's pessimism—which was nothing if not understandable, given the magnitude of the challenge—took me back to a letter I had received many years ago from Archbishop Tutu, during the divestment battle at Tulane. It was almost as if he were reading our minds, or at least mine, knowing that I was doubting the relevance of our efforts. After all, it wasn't looking as though we were going to be able to force the board to capitulate to our ultimate demand, and even if we (and every other college) did obtain divestment, would things really change in South Africa as a result?

His letter was brief, but in its brevity offered an obvious yet profound rationale for the work of any freedom fighter: "You do not do the things you do because others will necessarily join you in the doing of them," he explained, "nor because they will ultimately prove successful. You do the things you do because the things you are doing are right."

There's much to be said for such simplicity, as it's usually a lack of complication that allows people to feel, to remain in touch with their humanity—a humanity that can sometimes be distorted by too many layers of analysis and theory. There is redemption in struggle.

If you ask those who believe in God—any God, any creative force from which we come and to whom (or to which) they think we are accountable—whether they can prove the existence of that God, they will likely say no. Most will tell you that such matters are matters of faith, and that they live their lives, or try to, on the basis of that faith. Believers do this, even though they could be wrong. Although I'm agnostic on matters of God, I've always found that aspect of faith somewhat beautiful. And frankly, we all take something on faith: whether the existence of a higher power or the possibility of justice, because none of us have seen either of those things before. All I am suggesting here is that we should live our lives as if justice were possible too, but whether or not it is, treat it no differently than one treats one's perceived obligations before God. Indeed, if there were such a being, such a force, surely struggling to do justice would be one of those obligations, would it not? And surely one wouldn't be relieved from this obligation merely because justice was not finally obtainable.

Let's be honest: there is no such place called "justice," if by that we envision a finish line, or a point at which the battle is won and the need to continue the struggle is over. After all, even when you succeed in obtaining a measure of justice, you're always forced to mobilize to defend that which you've won. There is no looming vacation. But there is redemption in struggle.

Of course, that there is redemption in struggle, and that victory is only one reason for fighting, only seems to come as a surprise, or rather, as a source of discomfort to white folks. Invariably, it seems it is we in the white community who obsess over our own efficacy and fail to recognize the value of commitment, irrespective of outcome. People of color, on the other hand, never having been burdened with the illusion that anything they touched would turn to gold, usually take a more reserved, and I would say healthier view of the world and the prospects for change. They know (as they must) that the thing being fought for, at least if it's worth having, will require more than a part-time effort, and will not likely come in the lifetimes of those presently fighting for it. And it is that knowledge that allows a strength and a resolve that few members of the dominant majority will ever know.

This is not to sentimentalize suffering or the strength often born from it. In fact, this last statement should be taken less as a comment about the strength of persons of color than as an observation about the weakness of those without it. For it is true, at least in my experience, that whites, having been largely convinced of our ability, indeed entitlement, to affect the world around us and mold it to our liking, are very much like children when we discover that at least for some things—like fundamentally altering the system of privilege and domination that first vested us with such optimism—it will take more than good intentions, determined will, and that old stand-by to which we euphemistically refer as "elbow grease."

Regardless, there is something to be said for confronting the inevitable choice one must make in this life between collaborating with or resisting injustice, and choosing the latter. Indeed, it is among the most important choices we will ever be asked to make as humans, and it is a burden uniquely ours.

I have no idea when (or if) racism will be eradicated. I have no idea whether anything I say, do, or write will make the least bit of difference in the world. But I say it, do it, and write it anyway, because as uncertain as the outcome of our resistance may be, the outcome of our silence and inaction is anything but. We know exactly what will happen if we don't do the work: nothing. And given that choice, between certainty and promise, in which territory one finds the measure of our resolve and humanity, I will opt for hope. Letting go of the obsession with outcome, even while one fervently fights for victory, can in the end only make us more effective and stronger in our resistance—healthier even. After all, if one is constantly looking for the payoff, but the payoff is slow in coming (as is pretty much always the case), burnout is never too far around the corner. But if we are committed to the struggle because we know that our very humanity depends on it, that the fight for human liberation is among the things that give life meaning, then burnout is far less of a threat. We do the work to save our lives morally and ethically, if not physically.

Many years ago, the first time I spoke at the University of Oregon, I gave a workshop in the Ben Linder room of the student center—a room named for a man who, in April 1987, in Nicaragua, was murdered by contra forces armed and trained by my government and his, killed for the crime of helping bring running water to rural villagers. And as I sat there, inspired by a painting of the village where Ben died, and the tribute to his work that greets visitors to this room, I reflected on how I'd felt as a college freshman upon hearing of his assassination. I remembered why both he and the revolution of which he was a part ultimately had to be crushed. They both posed, as we used to say, the threat of a good example. That's when I realized that Ben Linder's life and death sum up, as well as anything I could say, why I do what I do, and what I have come to believe is required of us. And what is required is that we be prepared to die for our principles if need be, but even more so, to be unafraid to live for them.

So let us begin.